GLORY AND HONOUR

GLORY AND HONOUR

The Renaissance in Scotland

Andrea Thomas

BIRLINN

In memory of Raymond Thomas

First published in Great Britain in 2013 by
Birlinn Ltd
West Newington House
10 Newington Road
Edinburgh EH9 1QS

www.birlinn.co.uk

ISBN: 978 1 84158 872 8

The publishers gratefully acknowledge the support of

Creative Scotland
the Russell Trust
the Scotland Inheritance Fund
and the Strathmartine Trust
towards the publication of this book

British Library Cataloguing-in-Publication Data
A catalogue record for this book is available on request from the British Library

Typeset by Mark Blackadder

ENDPAPER ILLUSTRATIONS.
Sketches of two of the finest ships of James V's navy. At the front, the *Great Unicorn*, built in Scotland
in 1539; at the back, the *Salamander*, built in France in 1536–7. *Salamander* was a present from King
Francis I to the king of Scots, and inspired James to build his own ships. Both vessels were captured by
the English in 1544 and these pictures were made by one of Henry VIII's ordnance officials, Anthony
Anthony, in 1546. The sketches show the Scottish ships flying English colours. (See pages 116–18.)

PICTURES ON PP. II AND 226.
A ceiling from Crathes Castle, Aberdeenshire, painted for Katherine Gordon c.1599. The ceiling depicts
the nine Muses and seven Virtues all represented by female figures with symbolic attributes. (See Chapter 4.)

Printed and bound in Britain by Gutenberg Press, Malta

CONTENTS

ACKNOWLEDGEMENTS

I owe thanks to many people who have assisted and advised me whilst writing this book. At Birlinn, Hugh Andrew had the original idea to commission the work, and Mairi Sutherland has gently and patiently guided me as I gradually put it together. Alison Rae also worked very hard on the illustrations, which were funded by generous grants from Creative Scotland, the Russell Trust, the Scotland Inheritance Fund and the Strathmartine Trust. Professor Michael Lynch was kind enough to read through all the main chapters for me and made extremely useful suggestions, whilst Professor Alasdair MacDonald, Dr Jamie Reid-Baxter, Dr Julian Goodare and James Ross have read selected chapters and offered extremely good advice. I have also been very glad to receive additional assistance from Dr Amy Juhala and Dr Steven Reid. I am enormously grateful to them all for being so helpful, generous and supportive, even when I contacted them at inconvenient times. Their enthusiasm and encouragement spurred me on when I was flagging. Naturally, any remaining errors are entirely my own responsibility. My husband, David, has done all the proof-reading for me, cheerfully fixed computer glitches, and kept me sane during the writing process. I owe him more than words can express.

The writing of this book was seriously delayed by two episodes of severe ill health. Without the expertise, compassion and dedication of whole teams of doctors, nurses and other medical professionals, it would not have been completed at all, and I would not be here to tell the tale. This book is dedicated to them all, with my respect, admiration and deepest gratitude.

ANDREA THOMAS
Reigate

OPPOSITE. The Morton Valances, tapestries woven for the earl of Morton in Scotland or France c.1580. The valances were later stitched together to form a larger wall hanging. They depict figures in French courtly fashions, thought to represent scenes from classical myths or Bible stories. (See Chapter 3.)

Prima virum que tano a
Troye qui primus ab c

ABBREVIATIONS

BL	British Library	*PSAS*	*Proceedings of the Society of Antiquaries of Scotland* (1851–)
EUL	Edinburgh University Library		
HS	Historic Scotland	RCAHMS	Royal Commission on the Ancient and Historical Monuments of Scotland
IR	*Innes Review* (1950–)		
NG	National Gallery, London	*ROSC*	*Review of Scottish Culture* (1985–)
NGS	National Galleries of Scotland		
NLS	National Library of Scotland	*SHR*	*Scottish Historical Review* (1903–28, 1947–)
NMS	National Museums of Scotland		
NPG	National Portrait Gallery, London	SNPG	Scottish National Portrait Gallery
NRS	National Records of Scotland (formerly the National Archives of Scotland)	*TA*	*Accounts of the Lord High Treasurer of Scotland* (13 vols., Edinburgh, 1877–1978)
NT	National Trust	*TSES*	*Transactions of the Scottish Ecclesiological Society* (1903–)
NTS	National Trust for Scotland	V&A	Victoria and Albert Museum

OPPOSITE. An exquisite illumination from a manuscript of Virgil's *Aeneid*, painted in Paris c.1460 by an Italian artist for a Scottish patron. The scenes show Dido's reception of Aeneas at Carthage, whilst the border includes the Scottish royal arms inside a heraldic collar and the mysterious initials P and L. (See pages 80–1.)

I

INTRODUCTION

Scotland and the Northern Renaissance

The Renaissance is one of the most fascinating episodes in history. For many people, the word conjures up images of colourful characters, artistic geniuses and an explosion of confident, expansive creativity: Leonardo, Michelangelo, warrior popes and Medici palaces naturally spring to mind. Indeed, the associations with Italy are so strong that the very idea of a Renaissance in Scotland has sometimes seemed absurd. However, a Scottish Renaissance not only occurred, but flourished, as this book seeks to demonstrate.[1]

A search for the term 'Scottish Renaissance' on the internet, or in many standard reference books, will yield several articles on the literary revival of the early twentieth century, but scarcely any information about Scotland's connections with the European Renaissance of the fifteenth and sixteenth centuries. One might well be forgiven for imagining that late medieval and early modern Scotland did not participate in the Renaissance, since the term is absent from many historical studies of the period. Indeed, this impression has been reinforced by the customary organisation of many Scottish history books, which designate the period before 1560 as 'medieval', and the period afterwards as 'the Reformation', leaving little or no space for the Renaissance.[2] From 1560, the Protestant Kirk also promoted a narrative of national 'progress' from idolatry and superstition to enlightenment and godliness, which sought to denigrate, and in many cases eradicate, the cultural heritage of the Catholic era. Many religious paintings, carvings and books were deliberately destroyed in a furious iconoclasm, whilst many ecclesiastical buildings were 'cleansed' and reordered. A second phase of image-breaking in the Covenanting period of the 1630s and 1640s disposed of many of the remnants of Scotland's Catholic cultural heritage. The powerful combination of these factors has therefore obscured the very existence of the Renaissance in Scotland.

The Renaissance was the pre-eminent intellec-

OPPOSITE. The crown steeple of the chapel of King's College, Aberdeen, built by about 1520 to demonstrate the university's close connection to the 'imperial' monarchy of the Stewarts. (See page 10.)

tual and cultural movement of western Europe in the fifteenth and sixteenth centuries. It straddled the notional boundaries between the late medieval and early modern eras, and has long been regarded as an episode of intense creativity, in which the foundations of the modern age were laid. The term 'renaissance' means 'rebirth', and the movement is so called because it involved a revival and reapplication of the cultural achievements of classical Greece and Rome, which were regarded as having reached the pinnacle of civilisation. We conventionally use a French term for the concept because the idea of describing an entire historical period as a time of rebirth was first popularised by the French historian Jules Michelet in the 1860s. At the same time, a Swiss historian, Jacob Burckhardt, identified the Italian peninsula as the birthplace of the European Renaissance and outlined the movement's key characteristics.[3]

In Italy, the early stirrings of the Renaissance can be detected in the mid-fourteenth century when the Tuscan poet Petrarch, first described the centuries which separated his own time from the glories of ancient Rome as a 'dark age'. He is often identified as the first Renaissance humanist (humanism is explained below), who promoted a revival of Latin literature in an attempt to resuscitate Italian culture, and he particularly revered the literary style of the ancient Roman writer, Cicero.[4] Petrarch's ideas became very influential in the fifteenth and sixteenth centuries, when many Italians regarded themselves as living in a new 'golden age' inspired by the classical world. For Burckhardt, this idea of historical self-awareness was crucial to his understanding of the Italian Renaissance. He saw the princes, popes and merchant elites of the age as self-consciously fashioning themselves and their regimes, following ancient

models, in order to project an image of patriotic fame and glory that would endure for generations. This notion of historical self-awareness as a form of new individualism could also be applied to the writers, scholars, artists and architects of Renaissance Italy, who were the foremost practitioners of the revival of antique styles. The same impulse towards historical self-consciousness could also be detected in the humanist agenda of active engagement with public life and the rational, scientific investigation of the natural world.[5]

Burckhardt's explanation of the Italian Renaissance was powerful and hugely influential but also attracted some criticism. Neat and rigid classifications seldom reflect messy reality. Medieval historians in particular challenged the view that the Middle Ages were culturally or intellectually 'dark', in contrast with the enlightened, 'modern' Renaissance.[6] An interest in the classical past, and a thriving intellectual culture, have been identified at many points in medieval Europe, so that the Renaissance now looks much more like a distinct development of late medieval culture rather than a sharp reaction against it. Yet the concepts of a conscious break with the past and a revival of the antique were not invented by Burckhardt, but were current in Italy at the time. For example, in the 1550s and 1560s the Florentine artist and historian, Giorgio Vasari, used the Italian term for rebirth, *rinascita*, to describe the cultural achievements of his era.[7] However, the critique of Burckhardt's work has ensured that there is now much greater acceptance of the view that, especially in northern Europe but also in parts of Italy, the late medieval styles and ideas of International Gothic culture overlapped and mingled with Renaissance impulses in the late fifteenth and early sixteenth centuries. It was a very creative and inventive

blend.[8] This hybrid, transitional style is a notable feature of the Renaissance in Scotland, and will be illustrated at many points in the following chapters.

There are also some hazy boundaries at the end of the Renaissance era. For Vasari, the Renaissance ended with the death of Michelangelo in 1564. In the English tradition, the death of Shakespeare in 1616 usually marks the end of the period, and in northern Europe in general, the Renaissance is seen as gradually mutating into the Baroque, c.1600–c.1620. The Baroque was a cultural movement noted for emotional flamboyance and florid embellishment, but which also utilised and adapted (or distorted, as the name suggests) the Renaissance attachment to classical models. The Baroque style came to dominate European culture in the seventeenth and early eighteenth centuries. There was also a transitional movement called Mannerism which, in its witty and sophisticated style, eased the evolution of the Renaissance into the Baroque at the turn of the seventeenth century. The Baroque has strong associations with the militant Catholicism of the Counter-Reformation (also called the Catholic Reformation), and this has made the use of the term problematic in Protestant states. In Scottish cultural studies, the term 'Mannerist' appears rarely, and the term 'Baroque' hardly ever,[9] which throws the analysis of the arts in seventeenth-century Scotland into some disarray. It is common for the euphemism 'late Renaissance' to be used to describe Scottish cultural life up to 1707, a tendency which, perhaps unwittingly, avoids acknowledging the existence of the Scottish Baroque. Recent research has focused very sharply on challenging the myth that there was no Renaissance in Scotland, but the myth that there was no Baroque has yet to be confronted. A similar problem has also been identified in the study of the Renaissance in Denmark, a country which might reasonably provide a good comparison with Scotland.[10]

The artists of Renaissance Italy pioneered the imitation of Greek and Roman forms. The rules of harmony and proportion devised by the Roman writer Vitruvius in his *Ten Books on Architecture* influenced many buildings, whilst painters and sculptors focused on realism and naturalism, and developed new genres such as portraiture and landscape. The invention of artificial perspective, the use of classical proportion, the manipulation of light and shade to create the illusion of solidity, and anatomical precision in representing the human form were also key features of Italian Renaissance art. In the early decades of the sixteenth century, artists such as Raphael rediscovered Roman styles of decorative painting in the ruins of ancient palaces and villas. Because many of these ruins were underground, the twining, mutating Renaissance style they inspired came to be called 'grotesque' (i.e. found in grottoes). The flowing, floral and foliate style called 'arabesque' (because it derived ultimately from Islamic art) was also popularised in Italy at this time. Many of these Italian ideas were adopted by the northern Renaissance, particularly the realistic representation of the human form and the natural world. However, in the north there was also a strong and persistent attachment to the magnificent decoration of the late-medieval International Gothic style, so classical motifs often featured as one element amongst others in an architectural, sculptural, or painted scheme. This was certainly the case in Scotland, where classical motifs were introduced alongside a revival of the native Romanesque (originally a pre-Gothic style) in the fifteenth century,

and where classicism was often modelled on the French court style in the sixteenth century.

The traditional view of the spread of the Renaissance throughout Europe sees the movement starting in Italy and spreading northwards, where it arrived rather late in the British Isles and Scandinavia. Certainly, the Renaissance spirit entered northern European states at different times and with varying degrees of Italian influence, but the Italians were not invariably the pioneers of every innovation. The use of oil paints and the technology of printing with moveable type were developed in the Low Countries and Germany respectively and later spread south to Italy, for instance. In many cultural areas there was considerable interplay and cross-fertilisation. For example, some of the finest composers and manuscript illuminators of the age came from the Low Countries, and were in great demand in Italy. For many years it was customary to assess the northern Renaissance according to the extent to which it imitated Italian models, which undervalues the distinct ways in which northern Europeans adopted and adapted the Renaissance to their own purposes. The Renaissance was a very international and cosmopolitan cultural movement. There were national and regional variants of the Renaissance impulse across the Continent, and the diversity of styles and practices is now more commonly seen as a strength rather than a weakness. Thus the scarcity of direct Italian influences in Scotland and the hybrid nature of the Scottish Renaissance are no longer thought to indicate a wholly inferior experience. Indeed, it is hoped that this book will demonstrate the remarkable diversity and quality of the Renaissance in Scotland, despite the patchy survival of the historical evidence.

Scotland in the fifteenth and sixteenth centuries was certainly a much more cosmopolitan and outward-looking society than is often imagined.[11] Scots were closely connected to the ecclesiastical, academic, diplomatic, dynastic, military and trading networks of the period. From 1225, the Scottish Church had been designated a 'Special Daughter' of Rome, which meant that it was under the direct jurisdiction of the papacy and had no primate of its own. The bishopric of St Andrews was elevated to an archbishopric in 1472 and to the Scottish primacy in 1487, but by then the routine of traffic between Scotland and Rome was ingrained. Before 1560, Scottish clerics maintained regular correspondence with Rome and other ecclesiastical centres, with many travelling regularly to Italy and France on administrative and legal business. Both clergy and laity undertook pilgrimages to Rome, Compostella, Amiens, Cologne and elsewhere. Italians, amongst others, also travelled to Scotland as emissaries of popes, cardinals and monastic orders, and a few foreign prelates held posts in the Scottish Church *in commendam* (in 'care') and usually *in absentia*. The Church was also at the heart of the academic networks. Four Scottish universities were founded in the fifteenth and sixteenth centuries, three by bishops under papal bulls (St Andrews in 1411 by Henry Wardlaw, Glasgow in 1451 by William Turnbull, and King's College, Aberdeen, in 1495 by William Elphinstone), and the fourth (the

OPPOSITE. A portrait of James IV copied for Charles I by Daniel Mytens from an anonymous sixteenth-century original, which has since been lost. James IV (1488–1513) is often presented as the archetypal Renaissance prince.

'Tounis College' of Edinburgh which started in 1583) was founded by a royal charter but partly funded from the legacy of Robert Reid, bishop of Orkney (see Chapter 7). These universities had a very international outlook and Scottish students and teachers often spent time in Continental universities: Paris, Orléans, and Louvain were popular destinations before the Reformation, Leiden became more favoured afterwards, but Bologna, Padua and Pavia were also possibilities.

The Stewart monarchs of the period all took foreign consorts, so diplomatic traffic between Scotland and the European courts was enhanced by bonds of kinship. James V, Mary, queen of Scots, and James VI all travelled abroad in person in pursuit of their respective marriages, and their Scottish courts provided a warm welcome for Continental knights, artists, poets, and musicians. Scots were noted abroad as fierce warriors and many fought in the Italian wars (1494–1559) and later conflicts, whilst specialist German and Dutch armourers and gunsmiths were employed by Scottish monarchs. International trade was largely channelled through the Scottish 'staple' (a port with special privileges), which was based successively at Bruges, Middelburg and Veere. Trade also led to Scottish merchant communities settling in the ports and market towns of Scandinavia, the Baltic, northern France and the Low Countries, whilst a few Danish, Dutch and French merchants also established offices in Edinburgh, Dundee and Aberdeen (although residence could be brief). Even after the Reformation, when the ties to Rome were considerably reduced, many Scotsmen still travelled abroad to study, fight and trade.

Although it is difficult to be precise about exactly when the first traces of the Renaissance impulse were felt in Scotland, this book will begin in 1424 with the return of King James I from a long captivity in England. His period of exile from 1406 covered his formative years, from the age of 12 to the age of 30, exposed him to the culture of the English, French and Burgundian courts, and gave him a strongly international outlook. James returned to Scotland with a well-developed sense of royal dignity, and a steely determination to restore and extend royal authority. He has famously been described as 'a king unleashed'.[12] His political programme aimed to make the Stewart monarchy the source of all justice and the guarantor of peace and prosperity for the whole nation. This agenda included removing threats to his power from the great magnates, developing the role of the nobles as servants of the Crown, and increasing the regularity and stability of royal income. He also sought to promote the prestige and dignity of his dynasty in Europe. James I thus set the agenda for the adult reigns of his immediate successors (interrupted by regular minorities), all of whom pursued some, and occasionally all, of his ambitions, although not without setbacks.[13] Thus noble challenges were removed by forfeiture: of the Albany Stewarts in the 1420s, the Black Douglases in the 1450s and the Lords of the Isles in the 1490s. New noble houses, more dependent on Crown patronage, were promoted: amongst other creations, the Gordons were earls of Huntly from 1445, the Campbells earls of Argyll from 1458, and the Hepburns earls of Bothwell from 1488. James I also set the cultural agenda for his successors, since he was careful to surround himself with the trappings of a newly exalted monarchy. He built palaces, founded a monastery, purchased ships and artillery, was a practising poet and musician, and a noted patron of the arts. The culture of the Renaissance court was intended

to support the Stewart political programme by binding the nobles to the kings through ties of chivalric honour and spectacle (see Chapter 8).

The rising European profile of the Stewart dynasty stemmed from the marriage of James I's eldest daughter Margaret to the dauphin (heir to the French throne) in 1436. Through her French royal connections, three of her sisters also married into grand Continental houses, whilst her brother, James II, married a niece of the duke of Burgundy, Mary of Gueldres, in 1449.[14] Both James III and James IV subsequently made significant foreign marriages: James III wed Margaret of Denmark in 1469, and her dowry brought the Orkney and Shetland Islands to the Scottish Crown; James IV married Margaret Tudor in 1503 (the marriage of 'the thistle and the rose'), in an alliance which was supposed to secure 'perpetual peace' between England and Scotland. In the short-term this failed, but Margaret's legacy was the Union of the Crowns in 1603. The arrival in Scotland of both Mary of Gueldres and Margaret Tudor prompted a notable expansion of the exuberance and confidence of Renaissance court culture. The grandest European marriages were made by James V, who married Princess Madeleine, the eldest daughter of Francis I of France, in 1537, and Queen Mary, who married the dauphin (later King Francis II) in 1558. James V's second wife (and the mother of Mary, queen of Scots) was Mary of Guise, whom he married in 1538. She was also French (from a ducal rather than a royal family), so the French influence on Scottish Renaissance culture was particularly powerful in the mid-sixteenth century, and was reinforced by a military alliance in response to the 'Rough Wooing' (a sustained assault from England between 1544 and 1550, see Chapter 5). Through such prestigious dynastic connec-

tions, the Stewarts were clearly asserting their parity with other princes and injecting Continental influences into Scottish Renaissance culture.[15] Even during royal minorities, when the cultural influence of the Crown was relatively weak, European impulses could still operate: Mary of Gueldres ruled for her son, James III, between 1460 and 1463 and naturally had a very Burgundian outlook; Jehan Stuart, duc d'Albanie (Regent Albany), who ruled for James V between 1515 and 1524, was thoroughly French; as was Mary of Guise, who was Regent for her daughter between 1554 and 1560. The French influence was broken only by the deposition of Mary, queen of Scots, in 1567. Her son, James VI, had great ambitions to succeed the childless Queen Elizabeth of England (which he did in 1603), so the culture of his court was directed to supporting this aim, and took much inspiration from England as well as from the Continent.

The royal court was thus at the centre of many Scottish cultural developments, and certainly had the most prestigious international connections, and opportunities for innovative patronage. Cultural patronage was also exerted by the Church, the universities, the nobility and the burgh communities. Yet it is also fair to say that the most influential clerics, academics, lords and burgesses of the period also had strong ties to the royal court. From the time of James III, Edinburgh was acknowledged as the nation's capital, and was therefore also the most important place where the court interacted with the wider community, but other royal sites such as Stirling, or the ecclesiastical centre of St Andrews, were also important locations of cultural exchange and innovation. The loss of artistic patronage by the Church after the Reformation of 1560, and by the court after the Union of the Crowns of 1603, were thus major obstacles to the development of

ABOVE. John Slezer's engraving of Stirling Castle, published in the second edition of *Theatrum Scotiae*, 1729. The picture shows the forework towers at their full height and the western part of the palace block, which has been lost. Stirling Castle was a major centre of Renaissance patronage.

OPPOSITE. James VI (1567–1625) by Adrian Vanson, 1595. This was the last major portrait of James as king of Scots before the Union of the Crowns in 1603.

the later Scottish Renaissance and the early Baroque. The impact on music was particularly severe (see Chapter 6). In the early seventeenth century, a 'country-house' culture was emerging for the educated elites, a group which encompassed the wealthy burgesses. The earlier interest in civic humanism, which stressed public service, was gradually giving way to a greater emphasis on the private contemplation and retreat from the world advocated by the philosophical movement called Neostoicism (see Chapter 4), as promoted, for example, by the Flemish writer Justus Lipsius in *De Constancia* (On Constancy), 1584.

The Renaissance in Scotland was thus developed from a mixture of influences, both foreign and domestic. There was some Italian influence, but, more frequently, cultural inspiration can be traced to northern Europe, especially France and the Low Countries, occasionally England, Germany and Scandinavia. The Italian notion of historical self-awareness and self-fashioning in pursuit of individual fame and glory resonated strongly in Scotland. In northern Europe, this idea was adopted enthusiastically by Renaissance monarchs, including the Stewarts, who used Roman imperial models to validate their authority, sought to present their kingship as a unifying national force, and promoted the magnificence of courtly spectacles as evidence of their virtue and greatness. The imperial theme became a very important feature of the Scottish

Renaissance. Figures of Roman emperors such as Julius Caesar and stories from Roman history and mythology were prominent features of the cultural landscape. The imperial theme was also important in political life. This idea was based on the Roman law principle that 'the king is emperor in his own kingdom' and therefore has sovereign power, acknowledging no superior authority under God. The most famous expression of this notion was Henry VIII's Act in Restraint of Appeals of 1533, which stated unequivocally 'this realm of England is an empire'. Here the king of England was asserting his independence from the jurisdiction of the pope, but it was also possible to claim imperial authority and remain within the Catholic communion. An early example was in 1469, when the Scottish Parliament declared that James III possessed 'full jurisdiction and free empire within his realm'. This imperial sovereignty was symbolised by a 'closed', arched crown, as worn by the Holy Roman Emperors, rather than the 'open' circlet worn by medieval kings. The image of an arched, imperial crown first appeared on the coins of James III in the 1480s and was soon used extensively in heraldry and on seals, sculptures, manuscripts, paintings and even the steeples of churches with royal connections such as St Giles', Edinburgh, St Michael's, Linlithgow, and the chapel of King's College, Aberdeen. The first Scottish king to actually wear an arched crown was James V in 1532 and his crown (as it was refashioned in 1540) is today part of the Honours of Scotland (see Chapter 8).[16]

Alongside the imperial theme, humanism was also an important feature of the Renaissance in Scotland. Humanism at this time meant the academic disciplines of the *studia humanitatis*: poetry, grammar, history, moral philosophy and rhetoric in Latin or Greek. Humanists believed that their studies could identify deep universal truths of great moral force, so they promoted an active engagement in public life by intellectuals. In the rather idealistic theories of the time, humanist scholarship was considered to be practical and useful: providing a civilising influence in society, encouraging a peaceable, law-abiding citizenry to use reason rather than violence to settle disputes, and promoting the importance of the public good (the *res publica* or 'commonweal') over private benefit. The humanists stressed the dignity and rationality of mankind, the value of learning from the wisdom and eloquence of the ancients, the importance of promoting literacy and education for the laity as well as the clergy, and the scientific method of exploring the natural world by observation, deduction and experimentation. They laid great stress on reading ancient texts in the original languages, and were keen to spread knowledge widely through the use of accurate vernacular translations and the new technology of printing with moveable type (see Chapter 7). In addition, they took an interest in the more arcane subjects of alchemy, numerology, the occult, and the symbolism of emblematics: disciplines which, at the time, also seemed to be part of rational science. The symbolism and imagery developed by the Renaissance humanists to represent their high ideals were often used in painted or sculpted schemes, architectural designs and public spectacles to demonstrate the cultivated tastes of the wealthy and powerful elites. The idea of imitating classical harmony and proportion also shaped the development of Renaissance music. The humanist programme was adopted enthusiastically in Scotland and adapted to local needs by intellectuals with a high public profile such as William Elphinstone, Hector Boece and George Buchanan.[17]

To the cultural strands of the imperial theme and humanism was added an obsession with chivalry and heraldry that provided continuity with the medieval past. The Scottish monarchs, nobles and lairds shared a deeply rooted interest in pedigree and ancestry, which had traditionally validated their status and could be embodied in the display of shields of arms, heraldic badges and mottoes. Indeed, the first Scottish armorial registers appear at this period, and the Stewart monarchs were keen to stress their descent from Robert Bruce, which supported their claims to be the guardians of Scottish independence and freedom. Virtue could also be demonstrated by adherence to the knightly code of chivalric honour, which demanded reverence for the clergy, courtesy towards adversaries, the care of widows and orphans, and a concern for justice, even whilst engaging in the violence of warfare.[18] Medieval chivalry was developed around the military needs of an elite class of mounted warriors, but over time it evolved into the more honorific and ceremonial concerns of Renaissance courtiers. As late as 1559 it was still possible for King Henry II of France to be killed in a jousting accident, but the shock of his demise led to an adjustment in the nature of jousts, tilts and mock battles: they became less warlike and more theatrical, whilst still being designed to bring glory to the participants (see Chapter 8). It is likely that this enduring fascination with heraldry and chivalry contributed to a persistent attachment to medieval defensive features, such as battlements, turrets and gunloops, as decorative elements in Scottish Renaissance buildings, and to the hybrid, transitional artistic style which combined aspects of Gothic and Renaissance art in the sixteenth century (see Chapters 2, 3 and 4).

Having started a survey of the Renaissance in Scotland with the return of King James I in 1424, this book will examine cultural developments until the death of James VI in 1625, by which time the Baroque style was beginning to emerge. In the two centuries under consideration, the imperial, humanist and chivalric themes were expressed in different and creative ways, many of which are explored here. For practical reasons, it has not been possible to investigate absolutely every aspect of the subject: developments in law, philosophy, science and mathematics receive very little attention. Nor has the Gaelic culture of the Highlands and Islands been discussed here, because it had a distinct, insular identity, culturally very important in its own right, but which was not a part of the wider European Renaissance. Such exclusions hopefully allow for a clearer and sharper examination of the main cultural developments in the visual arts, military technology, music, education and literature, and chivalry and pageantry. Even within these categories, it has been necessary to be selective over the specific examples under consideration. This study attempts a broad overview of the major elements of the Renaissance in Scotland, and the author hopes that the reader will forgive her if a particular favourite artefact has not been included in the discussion. The buildings, decorative pieces, paintings, guns, musical compositions, books and ceremonies which are examined here, provide evidence of a notable cultural achievement, which has been ignored, under-rated or obscured for too long. Scotland was smaller, less populous and poorer than the great European powers of the period, and its artistic output cannot in any way be compared to that of Italy or France. Yet it did participate fully in the European Renaissance and it fostered a cultural flowering of considerable range, diversity, innovation and creativity, easily commensurate with its size and status.

2

PALACES OF HONOUR

Renaissance Architecture

From the evidence of the surviving buildings, it appears that the architecture of medieval Scotland largely followed the European pattern of building in the Romanesque style in the eleventh and twelfth centuries, with Gothic designs introduced from the thirteenth century and dominating the scene by the early fifteenth century. The Romanesque and the Gothic styles are still clearly visible in the medieval churches of Scotland, with both styles seen side by side at ecclesiastical sites which were constructed over several centuries, such as St Andrews Cathedral or Jedburgh Abbey. The Romanesque style has a heavy simplicity and is characterised by the use of rounded arches, barrel vaults, massive cylindrical piers, chevron decoration and small, round-headed windows, whereas the Gothic is more embellished, with a soaring airiness, and uses pointed arches, ribbed vaults, shafted columns, and large windows formed by multiple lancets or elaborate tracery. The Scottish Romanesque was heavily influenced by English fashions, whilst the Gothic took more inspiration from France and the Low Countries, but both styles were adapted to suit local tastes.

Because the boundaries between medieval and Renaissance culture were very indistinct, Gothic architecture was constructed alongside the new Renaissance style at the end of the fifteenth and beginning of the sixteenth century in Scotland, as in other countries.

At the same time, and again following wider European trends, the castles and towers which provided the main residences of the medieval land-holding classes were characterised by architectural features designed for defence: crenellations, machicolations, massive gateways, projecting turrets, tiny external windows and arrowloops and gunloops. The Scots seem to have become peculiarly attached to the castellated style of architecture and, long after the defensive needs had waned, many of these features continued to be used as decorative elements on houses built for gracious living.[1] The Scottish baronial style originated in medieval fortifications, but was also influenced by the architecture of France and Flanders, and saw continuous, if uneven, application from the sixteenth to the twentieth century. The castellated style was also used for some of the major tolbooths: the Leith

tolbooth of 1564 had crenellations and water-spouts in the form of cannons, the Canongate tolbooth of 1591 has a corbelled parapet which mimics machicolations and conical bartizans (overhanging turrets) on its tower, and the Glasgow tolbooth was built in 1626–7 with a spectacular crown steeple, which is the only part of the building to survive. The use of the baronial style in these instances could be used to stress the idea that the burghs were (like the nobles) 'chief vassals' of the Crown.[2] This thread of continuity with the chivalric and heraldic past is a characteristic of Scottish Renaissance architecture and weaves its way through the fabric of the new style, which began to develop during the fifteenth century.

Some of the earliest traces of the new Renaissance spirit in Scotland may be detected at a few religious sites. One of the most significant ecclesiastical developments of the fifteenth century was the increasing popularity of the collegiate church. This was a community not of monks but of secular priests, who were charged with maintaining a daily round of devotions. The foundations were housed in their own churches or chapels and endowed with lands (often appropriated parishes) to support their staff. The prayers and masses were intended to hasten the passage through purgatory of the souls of the founders and their families in perpetuity. Although there had been earlier examples, such as St Mary of the Rock at St Andrews, which probably dates from the thirteenth century, about 40 new collegiate churches were founded in Scotland between the mid-fifteenth century and the Reformation.[3] This enthusiasm probably reflected a growing sense of personal responsibility for their own salvation felt by the patrons, who may have been influenced by the brand of popular piety which flourished in the

Low Countries at this time, known as the *devotio moderna* (modern devotion). Almost all of the new collegiate churches were built in the Gothic style, echoing two centuries of medieval architectural design, but there were a few which adopted a more innovative approach.

At Rosslyn, in 1446, William Sinclair, earl of Orkney and later of Caithness, founded the collegiate chapel of St Matthew, which was built in a style rather different from the usual Scottish Gothic. The grandiose plan was intended to be much bigger than the surviving structure, but only the east end was actually built. The chapel incorporates many Gothic features, such as pointed arches, tracery windows, and flying buttresses, but it is also much more heavily embellished with carved decoration than any other Scottish church of the period. There is hardly an inch of the surface which is not encrusted with incised details in a flamboyant scheme, which pushes the late-Gothic style to extremes. This idiosyncratic exuberance might be taken as an early indication of the Renaissance spirit of individualism at work, and the segmented, chequered choir vault is somewhat reminiscent of ancient Roman coffering and has been described as having 'classical overtones'.[4]

Another oddity was the collegiate chapel of the Trinity and St Mary at Restalrig, more commonly known as St Triduana's Aisle, built for King James III in the 1470s and 1480s. Again, there are indications that a larger scheme was originally intended but not fully realised. Today only the lower chapel survives of what was once a hexagonal structure of two storeys, unique in Scotland. The design has been attributed to Anselm Adornes of Bruges, who became a trusted confidant of the king and whose family had a long tradition of making pilgrimages to the Holy Land.[5] James III

A sculpted corbel from James IV's triple chimneypiece
in the great hall of Linlithgow Palace, built in the
French style. The corbel depicts a lady playing a lute
with some angelic companions and would originally
have supported a statue, now lost.

had a restless piety and repeatedly expressed the unfulfilled desire to go on pilgrimage to the shrine of St John at Amiens (which had been established by crusaders, who brought the relic of the Baptist's head from Constantinople) or to Jerusalem. The demands of kingship prevented James from travelling, so in 1470 Adornes was instead commissioned to make a pilgrimage to the Holy Land on his behalf. A Latin account of the journey was written by Adornes's son, and a copy presented to the king. A hexagonal plan, such as that used at Restalrig, was popularly associated with the church of the Holy Sepulchre at Jerusalem and a hexagonal lantern had been placed atop an octagonal tower at the Adornes family chapel in Bruges, the *Jeruzalemkerk*. It was also common at this time for reliquaries and containers holding consecrated wafers, known as pyxes, to be hexagonal in form, so James III's remarkable chapel may have had multiple connotations of crusade, pilgrimage, and veneration of the body of Christ, as well as displaying strong Flemish influences.[6] Whilst the concepts of crusade and pilgrimage have deep medieval roots, like the persistent attachments to heraldry and chivalry, they endured well into the Renaissance and helped to shape the culture of the age.

Apart from these unusual examples, the ecclesiastical architecture of the period was largely traditional and Gothic in style, although it is impossible to know what form might have been taken by churches and chapels now lost. For instance, it would be fascinating to discover the appearance of the chapel of the Virgin of Loretto near Musselburgh. This pilgrimage centre was established in about 1533 by Thomas Doughtie, a hermit who brought to Scotland relics from the shrine of Loreto in Italy, whither the house of the Virgin Mary was said to have been transported by

angels. Doughtie's chapel was built at a time when the architecture of the royal court was imitating the French Renaissance court style and the new shrine was visited by James V and Mary of Guise. James V also gave offerings to the Virgin of Loretto whilst he was in France in April 1537 and when he was on board ship on his return journey in May, which seems to imply that Doughtie was in the king's entourage for the French visit. Might the chapel of Loretto have been built in a Franco-Italian Renaissance style? It was torn down at the Reformation and its fabric used to rebuild the Musselburgh tolbooth, so we shall probably never know.[7] Before 1560, there was, of course, considerable embellishment of the interiors of Scottish churches (see Chapters 3 and 4) much of which was done in a very modern Renaissance style influenced strongly by France and the Low Countries. There was also the construction of crown steeples at sites such as St Giles', Edinburgh, St Michael's, Linlithgow, and King's College Chapel, Aberdeen, which stressed the links of these churches to the 'imperial' monarchy of the Renaissance.

King James I had been an ecclesiastical patron of some note, who established the only Scottish house of Carthusians at Perth in the 1420s. The Perth Charterhouse was destroyed at the Reformation, and nothing remains to indicate its architectural style or the form of James's favoured residence at the Blackfriars, also in Perth. However, the king also rebuilt a royal residence at Linlithgow after a fire in 1424 and here we have much more evidence of early Renaissance impulses arriving in Scotland. His work at Linlithgow was a significant new departure: the first royal residence described as a palace, and clearly built for domestic comfort and courtly display rather than defence. The east range, containing the spacious great hall, some royal lodgings and with some striking exterior sculpture, was largely built for him and it is also likely that the quadrangular plan of the palace dates from this period. Certainly, it had taken on this shape by the time of James III, when Anselm Adornes was briefly keeper of the palace, and stylistically it has been regarded as innovative, combining a revival of the Scottish Romanesque, with classical overtones, within the form of an Italian princely castellated palace.[8] The later phases of work at Linlithgow also display Flemish, English and French influences, so it was an impressively cosmopolitan creation.

The revival of Romanesque motifs can be seen in the rounded arches used in and around the great hall, which was one of the largest secular spaces of its period. The rounded windows on the courtyard side and the barrel vault at the dais end of the great hall (where there was a raised platform for the high table) might also be seen as part of the same impulse, but they date from the reign of James IV rather than the time of James I. This unusual use of antiquated features might indicate an awareness of the classical interests of Italian architects, or it might owe something to Flemish influence, but it has also been explained as a patriotic rejection of the English Perpendicular Gothic style, with which James I would have become very familiar during his captivity.[9] The theory that Linlithgow imitates an Italian princely fashion for quadrangular palaces with square towers at the corners and crenellated decoration is an intriguing possibility but is difficult to establish with any certainty, since such features were also common elements of baronial residences in England and northern Europe at the time, and in any case the final form of the palace seems to have evolved gradually during the reigns of James III, James IV

and James V rather than following a coherent master plan.

The sculpture which decorates both the external and internal portals of the east range is markedly Flemish and Gothic in tone: the outer wall shows the royal arms supported by angels flanked by two, now empty, canopied niches, whilst angels hover above three canopied niches on the inner wall. All of the niches would once have contained statues: the three on the courtyard side are known to have depicted the pope, a knight, and a labouring man, which Historic Scotland suggests might represent the three estates of the Scottish Parliament and realm (clergy, nobility, burgesses).[10] We do not know what the statues on the outer face depicted, but images of the royal patrons, Saints James and Andrew, would be likely candidates. All the carvings would have been painted and gilded. From all this, it is clear that James I established at Linlithgow a modern residence appropriate to his new vision of Scottish kingship and the site was further embellished by his successors.

The Linlithgow works undertaken for James IV, James V and James VI show the same desire to keep up with the latest fashions of other realms to support the prestige and dignity of the Scottish Crown. In the 1490s and 1500s, amongst other things, James IV built an imposing, triple-towered bulwark outside the east entrance, probably in the traditional castellated style, a magnificent, finely carved, triple chimneypiece in the great hall, which would not have been out of place in a French Renaissance château, and the elegant three-storied gallery across the courtyard side of the south range, which has such an English appearance that it must have made Queen Margaret Tudor (whose dower house Linlithgow became) feel quite at home. In the 1530s, James V's works included the creation of a new entrance to the south with castellated outer and inner gates and sculpture above the portals in a similar arrangement to James I's east entrance. The statues over the outer face of the inner gate displayed the Stewart heraldic beasts (a lion and two unicorns), whilst the inner face represented an Annunciation scene of the Virgin Mary hailed by the angel Gabriel. The outer gateway displayed the arms of the orders of chivalry to which James V belonged. Although the carvings on the outer gate are Victorian restorations of the earlier work, the bright colours and gilding are true to the original (see Chapter 8). James V also commissioned the beautiful, tiered fountain in the centre of the Linlithgow courtyard. This combines Gothic and Renaissance motifs in one elegant composition: the quatrefoil (four-petalled flowers) and cusped decoration and the arcs which mimic flying buttresses are typical late-Gothic details, whilst the naturalistic statuary, portrait roundels and arched, imperial crown are thoroughly Renaissance in character. Sadly, we do not know who designed the fountain, but it clearly suited the king's tastes, since similar features also appear elsewhere in the royal works of the time. Perhaps it was influenced by Sir James Hamilton of Finnart, a prominent and cultured courtier who had visited France in his youth and who was master of works at Linlithgow and Blackness in the 1530s. He also had a major impact on

OPPOSITE. The fountain in the courtyard at Linlithgow Palace, built for James V c.1540. There is a Victorian copy of this fountain in the forecourt at the Palace of Holyroodhouse.

the works at Stirling Castle, discussed below, and the development of fortifications, discussed in Chapter 5.[11]

The roof of the north range of Linlithgow Palace, which had clearly been unstable for some years, collapsed in 1607. Luckily, the palace was not in regular use because King James VI had been in England since 1603, but he returned to Scotland in 1617 and ordered the entire wing to be rebuilt. The works were accomplished swiftly in 1618–20 under the command of Sir James Murray of Kilbaberton as master of works and William Wallace, master mason.[12] More than a century after James IV's eclectic works, James VI's range is a much more coherent Renaissance design in its balanced symmetry and restrained use of classical motifs in the window pediments. The scheme perhaps took some inspiration from the courtyard of the Danish royal castle of Kronborg, newly finished in 1585, just before James VI's visit of 1589–90.[13] At Kronborg, the courtyard façades also have symmetrically positioned windows topped with classical pediments arranged around a central, projecting stair-turret. The Linlithgow design was sympathetic to the existing fabric of the palace, since the crenellated parapet at the roofline integrates the new building into the old courtyard very neatly.

By the end of the fifteenth century, similar quadrangular royal palaces for elegant, courtly living were also being developed at Holyrood, Falkland, Edinburgh and Stirling. At Holyrood there was one principal courtyard to the west of the abbey church with adjoining service quadrangles to the south. At Falkland there was just the one courtyard as at Linlithgow, whilst within the fortresses of Edinburgh Castle and Stirling Castle the quadrangles were formed of free-standing buildings arranged around a square. All of these palaces were impos-

ing structures built with traditional castellated features and assertive heraldic decoration, combined with varying degrees of the new Renaissance style. They were clearly intended to provide the theatrical backdrop for the dramatic display of the Renaissance court.

At Edinburgh Castle, the royal lodgings were ranged around the quadrangular space known today as Crown Square. The principal medieval royal apartments were contained within David's Tower, the remnants of which have been swallowed up by the half-moon battery of the 1570s. James I began to extend the royal lodgings onto the site of the current palace block when he built a new great chamber there in the 1430s and James IV built more extensively on this, the eastern side of the square in the 1490s. In the early 1500s, he also built a new great hall on the southern side of the courtyard. On the northern side was the fourteenth-century church of St Mary and the western side held the royal arsenal.[14] The great hall, completed in 1511–12, is a largely traditional building, with a fine hammerbeam roof in the English style. However, the roof is supported by a sequence of carved stone corbels sculpted by an Italian mason called Cressent. They are in the form of scrolled consoles and each carries a heraldic or decorative image, painted and gilded. There are thistles, roses, *fleurs-de-lys*, an image of Venus and a Green Man (an ancient pagan fertility symbol), all of which would have been appropriate to celebrate the marriage of the king to Margaret Tudor in 1503, which perhaps indicates the starting date of the construction. These are probably the earliest sculptures in the British Isles in the classically inspired, Italian Renaissance style and are a remarkable survival.[15]

The palace block at the time of James IV had

three elegant oriel windows (projecting on corbels) looking out over the burgh, of which only the stumps now remain, and it probably provided reasonably comfortable and certainly prestigious accommodation. However, for most of the sixteenth century, the main royal residence was at Holyrood and the castle had primarily military usage. It was thus for reasons of security that in 1566 Mary, queen of Scots, chose to give birth to her son and heir in the small chamber within the castle, which was later (1617) decorated as a kind of shrine to the event. The palace block sustained some damage at the end of the Lang Siege in 1573, when men loyal to King James VI (with English help) finally overpowered the remaining supporters of Queen Mary, who held the castle. In 1615–16, the palace block was therefore repaired and refashioned in preparation for the king's 'homecoming' in 1617.[16] The remodelled exterior is an elegant Renaissance composition, similar to the north range at Linlithgow and built by the same team of Murray and Wallace. The structure aims at a balanced regularity in the arrangement of the windows around projecting stair turrets, uses classical pediments over the windows on the east face and is topped by a crenellated parapet. There is also lavish use of heraldic decoration, which stresses the Union of the Crowns in its combination of Scottish and English badges.

However, the Edinburgh palace block also exhibits some stylistic elements which herald the Baroque style of the seventeenth century: the segmented rustication (a pock-marked finish) of one of the doorways and the ogee-capped turrets (onion-shaped domes) are indicative of the next new style seeping into Scottish architecture at this time. The interiors also included plaster ceilings decorated in ornate strapwork patterns (now lost), a

feature typical of Baroque ornament and which may be seen at, for example, Winton House or the House of the Binns, dating from the 1620s and 1630s. The northern Baroque style involved a rather playful variation (or distortion) of the classical details of Renaissance architecture. Classical pediments were curved into half-moon shapes, or broken open at the top; obelisks, caryatids, strapwork, cartouches, buckle quoins and ogee domes were used in decorative profusion. The northern Baroque style was developed more fully at other Edinburgh sites: Heriot's Hospital of 1628, Moray House of c.1628 and the Parliament House of 1633–9. Heriot's Hospital was started by William Wallace and completed by William Ayton, whilst the Parliament House was built by Sir James Murray, so the styles of these architects demonstrably evolved over time. The northern Baroque style can also be seen in the Nithsdale wing of Caerlaverock Castle of 1634 and the Skelmorlie Aisle at Largs of 1636–9, amongst other places.[17] All of these buildings are usually described as part of the Scottish Renaissance, with the term 'Mannerist' occasionally deployed, but it seems clear to this writer that Scotland was following Continental fashions and adopting the Baroque.

At the other end of the Royal Mile from Edinburgh Castle, the Palace of Holyroodhouse was the principal seat of the court for much of the period. The Augustinian abbey of Holyrood was a royal foundation by David I in 1128 and the monastic guest house was customarily used as regal accommodation during the Middle Ages. As Edinburgh developed as the nation's capital during the fifteenth century, Holyrood became increasingly important as a royal centre, and James II built some lodgings there in the 1440s. The royal Palace of Holyroodhouse was built by James IV from

The royal palace at Edinburgh Castle, refashioned in 1615–6 for James VI's
'homecoming' of 1617, which celebrated his Golden Jubilee as king of Scots.

1501 in preparation for his marriage (some work continued after 1503). Almost all of the works by James II and James IV have disappeared in subsequent redevelopments of the site and are known only from the surviving financial records.[18] The original palace occupied the ground to the west of the monastic cloister on which the modern palace now stands and seems to have taken the quadrangular plan which still persists. It contained spacious accommodation, including suites of apartments for the king and queen and a private chapel, but all that now survives is one wall of the

outer gateway, incorporated into later work. James IV's new palace was built quickly and was sufficiently advanced to receive the new queen, Margaret Tudor, whom he married in the abbey kirk in August 1503. An English herald, John Young, wrote an account of the marriage festivities for the Tudor court, which is glowing in its appreciation of the splendours of the halls and chambers and their rich furnishings but gives little indication of the architectural style, other than noting the use of heraldic designs in the stained glass windows.[19]

Holyroodhouse was then largely rebuilt for James V between 1528 and 1536 and, although it was looted and partially burned in an English assault of 1544 and neglected after 1603, the palace built at this time remained in use as the principal royal seat until it was reconstructed for Charles II in the 1670s. The first structure built for James V was the north-west tower, which was retained in Charles II's redevelopment and survives today. This was a tower lodging, providing private chambers for the king on the first floor and the queen on the floor above, and was constructed in the traditional medieval castellated style with small barred windows (which were later enlarged and the iron grilles removed), projecting corner turrets, gunloops and battlements. It was originally free-standing and the main entrance was across a drawbridge. It was also decorated in traditional style, with heraldic designs used in the stained glass windows, carved and painted armorial panels, and gilt weather vanes.[20] It clearly provided the young king with a secure and private retreat and was largely complete by 1532. The fact that James embarked on such a project at this time suggests that the tower was very important to his status and dignity. After a long minority, the 16-year-old James V commenced his adult

The north-west tower of the Palace of Holyroodhouse, built for James V, 1528–32.

reign in the summer of 1528 and had to pursue military campaigns against his own stepfather and uncle (respectively the earl of Angus and Henry VIII of England, who supported Angus) in order to assert his authority. By 1534, James had succeeded in making himself the undisputed master of his realm, but had failed to enforce a sentence of treason upon Angus, who was given asylum in England. The Holyrood tower was built whilst these crucial conflicts were played out and was clearly a statement of intent by the young king, who employed all the imposing, exuberant features of chivalric display to embody his new authority in stone. The resemblance to many of his father's works was surely deliberate.[21]

The second phase of James V's Holyrood works

James Gordon of Rothiemay's view of the west front of
the Palace of Holyroodhouse in the 1640s.

took place in 1535–6, when he was preparing for his marriage to a French princess, and again, the new buildings were clearly intended to project an image of modern regal dignity, but with more stress on comfort and display than defence. The west range of his father's palace was demolished and replaced with a new 'forework', or west range, which adjoined the new tower; whilst the northern and southern ranges were extensively remodelled. All of these works were demolished in turn when the palace was rebuilt for Charles II and are known only from documentary sources.[22] The forework contained a sequence of spacious, well-lit state reception rooms, which were linked to the private apartments in the tower, the chapel in the south range and further reception and council chambers in the north range. The whole sequence of rooms was approached by an imposing scale staircase (in a straight flight) from the courtyard, which was an innovative feature at a time when most Scottish stairs were spiral. The layout of the rooms is known from a survey of 1663 when plans were being made for the redevelopment of the palace. The survey also shows that James V intended to build another tower at the south-west corner of the complex to match the one completed in 1532. The scheme was not carried out at the time, but was eventually realised in the building of the modern palace in the 1670s. However, the west range running between the James V tower and the Charles II tower was completely rebuilt in the Baroque splendour of the Restoration period, as were the other three sides of the main quadrangle.

The architectural style of James V's palace of the late 1530s can be imagined from only two seventeenth-century prints. James Gordon of Rothiemay made an engraving of the palace in the 1640s. This shows the surviving tower of 1532 and the western façade of the west range of 1536 standing alongside it. It is clear that an arched entrance to the palace courtyard ran through the centre of the ground-floor rooms, which were probably used for storage and service, whilst the state rooms on the first floor were lit by a symmetrical sequence of large mullioned windows with several projecting bays. A crenellated parapet marked the line of the pitched roof, which was capped by turrets, spires and heraldic weather vanes. The second picture is the large-scale view of Edinburgh by Wenceslaus Hollar, which is usually dated 1670, but was possibly made in the 1640s. This shows a panoramic view of Holyrood: the north-west tower and the west range are clearly visible, as is the quadrangular plan of the complex and the formal gardens. The turrets flanking the main entrance are shown rather taller than in Rothiemay's print, but the array of gables, spires, cupolas and crenellations is similar in both pictures.[23] As at Linlithgow, the whole effect is reminiscent of contemporary buildings in England, France and the Low Countries and is very much in keeping with the architectural taste of the northern Renaissance, with its attachment to late-Gothic and chivalric embellishment. The rounded turrets with conical caps on the great tower have a very French flavour, whilst the prominent bay windows of the west range recall Henry VIII's Hampton Court.

There are no surviving fragments of the interior decoration of James V's west range, but the accounts of the masters of works and the surviving interiors of the tower chambers give some indi-cation of the scheme. The rooms in the Holyrood tower have flat timber ceilings formed of panels and ribbed mouldings, which were probably built for James V, although carved and painted heraldic decoration was clearly added later for Mary, James VI and Charles I. The ceilings in the west range seem to have been similar but with the additional adornment of many pendant bosses ('great hanging knobs'), perhaps similar to those in the great watching chamber at Hampton Court. Carved armorial panels were also prominent in the interior and exterior decoration and all the sculpture, timber mouldings, window frames and weather vanes were painted and gilded, so that the cumulative effect would have been very colourful, even gaudy. To further enhance the dazzling brilliance, some of the stained glass from James IV's palace was salvaged and reset in the new windows, and new stained or painted glass panels were added to the scheme. The accounts describe the new glass as 'Flanders rounds and square antique pieces' and 'borders and antique faces'.[24] Flemish influence is explicitly acknowledged here and the use of the term 'antique' is a clear indication that the latest Italian Renaissance fashions were being adopted. In the English accounts of the period, 'antique' usually signified the grotesque style, which originated in Rome in the 1490s and was popularised by Raphael. It was so called because the paintings within Roman ruins, on which it was based, were excavated from sites buried in what seemed like caves or grottoes. Sadly, only one example of pre-Reformation Scottish stained glass survives, in the Magdalen Chapel, Edinburgh, completed in 1541. Here, four glass roundels depict the royal arms of James V, his queen Mary of Guise, and the founders of the chapel, Michael MacQuhane and his spouse, Janet

ABOVE. The courtyard frontage of the south range of Falkland Palace, remodelled
in the 1530s for James V by French masons in the French Renaissance style.

OPPOSITE. Stained glass roundels of 1541 from the Magdalen Chapel, Edinburgh. The arms
depicted are those of James V (top left), Mary of Guise (top right), Michael MacQuhane (bottom left)
and Janet Rynd (bottom right). The top two panels were originally swapped in position.

Rynd. In the now incomplete border surrounding
the arms of Janet Rynd is an Italianate arabesque
pattern (of curled tendrils), which may hint at the
type of glass that was installed at Holyrood on a
much grander scale. Certainly, the basic design of
coats of arms within foliage wreaths (chaplets) is
known to have been installed at Holyrood in the
1530s.[25]

The Edinburgh Castle corbels and the Holyrood
glass clearly indicate that Italian fashions were
gradually seeping into the chivalric style of Scottish Renaissance architecture, and at Falkland
Palace there was a more thorough example of the
adoption of Continental designs. The early castle
at Falkland had been a property of the Albany
Stewarts, was confiscated by James I upon their

forfeiture in 1425, and was later granted to Queen Mary of Gueldres. A quadrangular palace to the south of the old castle was built for James IV between 1501 and 1513 with a great hall on the north side, the chapel to the south, and royal lodgings to the east. It is not clear what stood to the west at this time, perhaps only a wall, but in 1539 there were offices there.[26] Both the north and west ranges have been lost, with no surviving visual record, but the south and east ranges were extensively remodelled for James V between 1537 and 1541 and have survived, although the east range is mainly ruined.

James V began to plan the rebuilding at Falkland whilst he was in France for his first marriage, and the palace was granted to both of his queens in turn as part of their marriage settlements. The new works were thus closely connected to the renewal of the French alliance and the palace was expected to house discerning French ladies.[27] The most remarkable feature of James V's Falkland works is the contrast in styles between the external and the internal façades, which were built at roughly the same time. This may have occurred simply because different masons were given responsibility for different parts of the scheme, but it is more likely that there was deliberate intent. The external frontage of the south range was remodelled and embellished with statues (now lost or defaced) carved by Peter Flemishman, from the Low Countries, and a new entrance tower was built alongside it, all in the imposing castellated style with turrets, battlements, gunports and gargoyles. Indeed, the new gatehouse tower bears a strong resemblance to the Holyrood tower and

was built by the same master mason, John Brownhill. Meanwhile, James IV's east range was given a new internal courtyard frontage in the most elegant and modern French Renaissance style by a French mason, Moses Martin. After his death in 1538, another French mason, Nicholas Roy, was sent to Falkland by Mary of Guise's mother and created an accomplished, matching façade for the courtyard side of the south range, to which a gallery had been added. To the world outside, James V's Falkland turned the traditional face of assertive Scottish kingship, but those who entered the palace were presented with the sophisticated French courtly style: 'a display of early-Renaissance architecture without parallel in the British Isles'.[28]

The Falkland courtyard design divides the buildings into regular bays marked by Corinthian columns, inverted consoles, and statuary. The large main windows are arranged symmetrically, and flanked by a sequence of medallion heads within foliage wreaths, carved in a mature classical style. Each head is individual and strongly characterised: there is a beautiful young lady, a soldier in Roman garb, a bearded man and a laughing woman. A marked French flavour is imparted by the conical-capped stair turrets, pedimented dormer windows and tall, slender chimneys. Today the buildings are partly ruined and heavily weathered, but the former splendour was captured in an engraving published by John Slezer in the 1690s. James V clearly took inspiration for his Falkland scheme from the palaces and châteaux he had seen in the Loire and Paris regions during his visit to the court of Francis I in 1536–7, and Moses Martin had been with him on the journey. Several châteaux

OPPOSITE. The laughing lady: one of the lively
Renaissance roundels from Falkland Palace.

John Slezer's view of the courtyard at Falkland Palace, from *Theatrum Scotiae*, 1693. Slezer used some artistic licence here: the proportion of the figures is far too small and the east range is shown intact, although it was already badly damaged by this time.

have been cited as sources for the Falkland court-yard façades including Villers-Cotterêts, Fontaine-bleau, Amboise and Bury, the first two of which employ similar decorative features to the Falkland scheme, whilst the last two have the same contrast between a traditional military exterior and a modern courtly interior.[29] In addition, Château de la Verrerie in the Loire is one of several places where carved heads within medallions were employed in a Renaissance decorative scheme in the 1520s. It is particularly tempting to think that this may have influenced the Falkland design,

since it was owned by the Stuarts of Aubigny, French noblemen of Scottish descent. The Falkland courtyard façades, designed and built by Martin and Roy, represent the earliest wholly Renaissance architectural scheme in the British Isles. Here classical motifs are an integral part of the design rather than decorative details applied to a traditional form as happened, for example, with the terracotta roundels made by a Florentine sculptor for Cardinal Wolsey at Hampton Court Palace in about 1520.

Another impressive Renaissance quadrangu-

lar palace was created at the same period around the inner close of Stirling Castle. There had been a royal fortress on the Castle Rock of Stirling from at least the twelfth century, and probably much earlier, but the surviving buildings are all from the 1490s or later. At the end of the fifteenth century, James IV focused strongly on Stirling Castle as a royal centre and improved the grandeur and dignity of the structures there. His parents were buried nearby at Cambuskenneth Abbey and he was accustomed to spend Holy Week in a spiritual retreat at the Stirling house (which he had founded) of a strict monastic order, the Observant Franciscans, to atone for his part in the rebellion of 1488 in which his father, James III, was overthrown and killed. The first head of the house advised the king to wear an iron belt in perpetual penance, which he famously did for the rest of his life. James would emerge after Easter for a season of celebrations and rejoicing leading up to May Day, which required a modern, regal setting at the castle.[30] The two oldest buildings around the inner close, for which we have only archaeological evidence, were the chapel royal and the 'auld kirk'. The chapel royal, which was possibly built by James III and established as a collegiate foundation in 1501 by James IV, stood on the north side of the square on an east–west alignment, which related awkwardly to later buildings. This possibly explains why it was demolished in 1594 and replaced by a building with a more convenient orientation for the baptism of Prince Henry. The 'auld kirk' probably stood on a similar alignment at the south-west corner of the square and although it was rebuilt for James IV in 1504–5, it was subsequently absorbed into a kitchen building.[31] We have no surviving visual record of the architectural styles of either the old chapel royal or the 'auld

kirk', but they were probably Gothic structures.

In about 1495–7, James IV built a new lodging on the west side of the square, the core of which lies within the modern King's Old Building. It originally held some spacious chambers approached from a spiral staircase topped by a polygonal turret and with a timber gallery running alongside. It was much altered in the eighteenth and nineteenth centuries and it has taken considerable detective work to establish its initial form.[32] Between about 1500 and 1508, James IV also rebuilt many of the castle's defences, constructing an impressive approach from the south, known as the forework. This had an imposing central gateway flanked by four circular turrets with conical caps and with walls stretching either side to square towers at either end of the range: the Prince's Tower to the west and the Elphinstone Tower to the east. The whole arrangement of walls and towers was topped with battlements. Again, it has been much altered: the central gateway was once much higher and has lost its conical caps and outer flanking turrets, whilst the Elphinstone Tower is now reduced to a stump. The gateway at its full height was recorded in a Slezer engraving at the end of the seventeenth century, although the Elphinstone Tower had already been cut down by the time the picture was made (see Chapter 1). It has been suggested that because the main gateway has three portals (one large central carriageway with a smaller pedestrian entry on either side) it was intended as a Roman-style triumphal arch, but the resemblance is not very close, whereas triple portals were common in late-medieval churches and halls.[33] The gateway in its original form had a very French aspect and may well have provided the inspiration for James V's later towers at Holyrood and Falkland, which adopted a similar style.

OPPOSITE. The beautifully restored great hall of Stirling Castle,
built for James IV in 1501.

ABOVE. The French-inspired Renaissance decoration of the
palace block at Stirling Castle, built for James V c.1540.

It may also give some indication of the form of the now-lost bulwark at Linlithgow. The forework was clearly as much an impressive chivalric display as a means of defence.[34]

The most imposing of James IV's works at Stirling Castle is the free-standing great hall on the east side of the inner close, which was completed in about 1501, and has been recently restored to its former splendour after many years' service as barracks. Much larger than the great hall at Edinburgh Castle, it follows an English arrangement of high windows in the body of the hall and large bay windows at the dais end, all under a monumental hammerbeam roof, whilst decorative elements such as the curved window tracery, corbelled parapet and conical turrets again have a French

flavour. Meanwhile, the waterspouts, battlements, carved angels and heraldic badges are in the familiar Scottish castellated style. The limewashed plaster finish is authentic and allows the hall to be seen for miles around, glowing in shafts of sunlight. It certainly provided a glorious setting for courtly ceremonies and entertainments such as the baptisms of the heirs to the throne of 1566 and 1594 (see Chapter 8).[35]

James V's contribution to Stirling Castle was just as impressive as his father's. Between 1538 and 1541, on the southern side of the square, he constructed a new set of royal lodgings, known as the palace block, which is itself quadrangular in form, enclosing a small inner courtyard traditionally known as the Lion's Den. James probably did not own a lion: an attempt was made to buy one for him in Flanders in 1537 but Henry VIII's agent secured the beast for his master instead. It was suggested to Henry that he might present the lion to James, and in 1539 Henry wrote to James indicating that he intended to send him the animal, but it is not clear if he actually did so. However, James VI had a lion at Stirling in 1594, so perhaps the name was coined at that time.[36]

The remarkable palace block, which has also just undergone a major restoration, held matching suites of chambers for the king and queen at first-floor level, consisting of an outer hall, presence chamber and bedchamber each, with small private rooms, or closets, off the bedchambers. The Italians of the time called this arrangement the *piano nobile* (the principal, or noble, floor) and it was becoming fashionable in both France (e.g. Fontainebleau) and England (e.g. Hampton Court). Following the courtly protocols established by the dukes of Burgundy in the fifteenth century, the graduated sequence of apartments gave princes increasing levels of privacy, since only the closest servants and companions would have been admitted to the closets, whilst a more general throng would have had access to the outer halls.[37] The doorways and window openings of the royal apartments have finely carved edge-roll mouldings, which later became fashionable throughout Scotland, whilst the fireplaces have particularly ornate surrounds, carved by French masons in the French Renaissance style and originally colourfully painted.[38] The king's apartments were in the north range, the queen's in the south range and their bedchambers and closets met in the east range. The west range now holds just an access gallery, but part of this range collapsed at the end of the sixteenth century and we do not know what was originally there. An indication of the proportions of the west range can be seen on the same Slezer engraving which depicts the forework.

The design of the palace block was possibly devised by Sir James Hamilton of Finnart, who took charge of the works before he fell from favour and was executed in 1540, but French masons also contributed. The decorative scheme on the outer walls of the three complete ranges is astonishing. The crenellations and the pitched roof with crow-stepped gables capped by heraldic lions are familiar elements of the traditional Scottish castellated style (regrettably, second-storey windows were punched through the battlements in about 1700), but below this level the French Renaissance has been transplanted into Scotland. More flamboyant and whimsical than the comparatively restrained classicism of Falkland, the scheme makes a powerful impact. Large rectangular windows are evenly spaced along the exterior walls and interspersed with cusped, arched recesses. Each recess carries a distinctly characterised statue atop

a candelabrum-style baluster or column. The parapet is decorated by more statues on spiral columns and every corbel is also figuratively carved. Many of these stylistic elements have classical Roman connotations and the spiral column was associated with the biblical temple of Solomon. Some of the sculptures are derived from a series of engravings of planetary deities by the German artist Hans Burgkmair, including Sol, Venus, Saturn and Jupiter. The scholars of the Renaissance were fascinated by astrology, which they viewed as an integral part of natural science, and the scheme has been interpreted as invoking planetary protection for the king's house.[39] Other figures wear contemporary dress and may represent real people of the royal court. The male statue at the north-east corner is thought to represent the king himself, and other figures include a crossbowman, cupholder, pursebearer, cook and gunman, all of whom can be found in the records of the royal household. The most recent research suggests that these external statues represent classical deities and allegorical figures, which portray the court of James V as a recreation of the antique 'golden age'.[40] Finally, a statue of the devil sits in the middle of the south façade to threaten enemies; St Michael, the patron of the chapel royal, stands at the south-east corner, probably also on protective duties; and above him his traditional companions, all the angels, fly in a sequence of carved cherubs running the entire length of the cornice. The scheme has been compared to the architecture of many French châteaux including Blois, Châteaudun and Nancy, all of which would have been familiar to Mary of Guise. James V clearly wished to recreate in his homeland the courtly sophistication he had seen in France.[41]

At the north side of the inner close stands the chapel royal, which was rebuilt in 1594 for the bap-

A detail of the sculpture on the palace block at Stirling Castle, c.1540. This figure is one of the 'garitours', armed watchmen on the south parapet. He carries a crossbow.

The entrance to the chapel royal at Stirling Castle, built by William Schaw
for James VI in 1594, for the baptism of Prince Henry Frederick.

tism of James VI's heir, Prince Henry Frederick. This was placed on a more convenient alignment to the earlier building (which was demolished) and, like James VI's works at Linlithgow and Edinburgh, is more closely related to Italian styles than the buildings of his predecessors. In form it is a simple, single-storey rectangle with the main door in the centre of the southern wall, a plain window at the east end and a dais (raised platform) at the west end. The rounded double-windows are Florentine in style and once had decorative roundels at their heads, whilst the main doorway follows a classical arrangement of paired columns supporting an entablature (a superstructure consist-

ing of an architrave, frieze and cornice), probably based on a design published by the Italian architect Sebastian Serlio in 1540.[42] The arched entrance is certainly Roman in style and the columns are often described as Corinthian, but their shafts are not fluted and their capitals are not as heavily carved with foliage as most Corinthian columns. Perhaps the variation in the column design was intended to invoke antiquity at the time of the biblical King Solomon? There is something of an ancient Egyptian flavour to them, and a reference to a pyramid ('pirament') once having been at the chapel door reinforces this impression. James VI was fond of comparing himself to Solomon and

A Renaissance ruin: Mar's Wark, Stirling, built in 1570–2 for the
earl of Mar in the most fashionable courtly style.

the architect of the chapel royal, William Schaw, was one of the founders of modern freemasonry in Scotland, which claimed descent from the builders of Solomon's temple. Indeed, the Stirling chapel royal used the same proportions as those recorded in the Bible for the temple of Solomon, and placed the king's seat within an area corresponding to the Holy of Holies. The possible interpretations of the symbolism of this building and the idea of monarchy projected by James VI are quite breathtaking.[43]

William Schaw was also the architect of another Renaissance palace, that belonging to Anna of Denmark at Dunfermline. The Benedictine abbey

of Dunfermline had been founded by St Margaret and the monastic guest-house frequently provided royal accommodation throughout the Middle Ages, as at Holyrood. Gradually, a quadrangular residence evolved to the west of the cloister, incorporating medieval monastic buildings. The monastery was formally annexed by the Crown in 1587 and granted to Queen Anna on her marriage to James VI in 1589. From 1590 to his death in 1602, Schaw remodelled many of the existing buildings and built a new house for the queen. Sadly, much of the complex was ruined during the seventeenth and eighteenth centuries and the queen's house was demolished in 1797, leaving a

sparse documentary record. A few drawings and engravings indicate that the palace had battlements and projecting stairwells with conical caps, features familiar from other royal works. All that now remains is the shell of the south-west quarter, which housed the great hall, kitchen and withdrawing rooms on the first floor, with further chambers above. The core of the building is medieval, but in the 1590s (with possibly some earlier work) it was given fine rectangular and oriel windows and decorated corbels. Dunfermline became Queen Anna's favourite residence, so it must have compared well with Falkland and Linlithgow (both of which were also part of her marriage settlement) for comfort and style, but since so much has been lost, we can only imagine its former glories.[44]

The Franco-Italian styles favoured by the royal court were adopted to an extent by the Scottish nobles of the sixteenth century. In the 1550s, Archbishop John Hamilton remodelled his castle at St Andrews to provide more palatial accommodation. It is now ruined, but the large, regularly spaced windows, arched entrance and elegant mouldings of his new wing demonstrate the cultivated tastes of a man who had lived in France in the 1540s. The range probably included a sequence of oriel windows at the upper level and the decoration combines Hamilton cinquefoils (five-petalled heraldic flowers) with classical columns.[45] An outstanding example of imitation of the court style is Mar's Wark at the head of Broad Street in Stirling. Built for John Erskine, earl of Mar, in 1570–2 as a stately town house convenient for Stirling Castle, it originally followed a U-plan but was probably unfinished at the earl's death and may have been intended to form a full courtyard. It is now a shell, with only the ruined street front surviving. Investigations have shown that the central gatehouse was once much taller and it must have been very imposing when new. The regular arrangement of large, rectangular windows framed within finely moulded string-courses is reminiscent of the Falkland courtyard, whilst the profusion of carved decorative pillars, corbels, pediments and statues (now mostly lost or mutilated) clearly owes much to James V's Stirling palace.[46] At Crichton Castle in the 1580s, Francis Stewart, earl of Bothwell, built a new north wing in a thoroughly Italian style. He had returned from finishing his education on the Continent in 1581, and he had possibly visited Rome, so he might have drawn direct Italian inspiration for his new lodgings, which are unique in Scotland. There is a classical loggia (an open arcade of arches) at ground level, with the main chambers on the first floor (the *piano nobile*) and further chambers above. The windows are placed symmetrically within a remarkable diamond-faceted façade (perhaps inspired by the Palazzo dei Diamanti at Ferrara) and accessed from a scale-and-platt staircase (straight flights turned at landings), which was now becoming more common in Scotland. The Scottish nobles also started to adopt the more horizontal designs of quadrangular palace building pioneered by the royal court, but most of the examples are now demolished, ruined or redeveloped.[47]

More popular with the Scottish nobility than the Italianate, classical styles were the Franco-Burgundian chivalric, castellated architectural forms, which had also been prominent in the works of the

OPPOSITE. The Italian-inspired range at Crichton Castle, built for the earl of Bothwell in the 1580s.

The flamboyant oriel windows and frieze added
to Huntly Castle by the marquess of Huntly c.1602

royal court. Since these impulses had evolved from medieval fortifications, it was natural for ancestral towers and castles to be adapted and incorporated within the more refined, stately homes of the Scottish Renaissance. However, the martial details of this period were not of any practical defensive use; rather they were decorative and symbolic of noble pedigree. Charles McKean argues that the mid-century fashion for round towers and asymmetrical plans was a direct imitation of the style of French châteaux under the influence of Mary of Guise and her court.[48] There are dozens of examples of the Scottish baronial style in the sixteenth century, with many of the most impressive to be found in the north-east. The characteristic medieval elements of battlements, crow-stepped gables, machicolations, projecting towers, bartizans, conical turrets and gunholes were used in decorative profusion, and combined with heraldic imagery. More obviously Renaissance motifs were introduced in the form of large, symmetrically arranged windows, especially bays, dormers, or oriels; along with pediments, columns, pilasters and friezes. One of the finest collections of bay and oriel windows of the age is to be found at the, now ruined, palace in Kirkwall built for the notorious earl of Orkney, Patrick Stewart, in about 1607. (He was traditionally known as Black Patie because of his cruelty and avarice.) The windows are variously rounded or angled, with corbels decorated with chequer patterns or rippled mouldings, and were once under lofty turrets in a very elegant arrangement.[49] Even more grandeur was achieved by George Gordon, 1st marquess of Huntly (who was also educated in France), at Huntly Castle, where in about 1602 he combined a sequence of lofty oriel and dormer windows with a declamatory frieze in giant Roman letters celebrating his

marriage (of 1588) to the king's French-born kinswoman Henrietta Stewart. He may also have built a loggia at the castle, now lost. At the same time he also added a splendid heraldic frontispiece (ceremonial entrance) which presented in an ascending sequence the combined arms of himself and his marchioness, the combined arms of James VI and Anna of Denmark, a representation of the Passion and Resurrection of Christ, and a depiction of St Michael subduing the devil. The sequence of panels was topped by a statue of St Michael, and the religious imagery clearly emphasised his defiant (if not entirely consistent) Catholicism. The religious images were later defaced by Covenanters and the castle is now ruined.[50]

One of the greatest builders of the period was Alexander Seton, 1st earl of Dunfermline and chancellor of Scotland. He had been educated in Italy and France, and was described by Sir Richard Maitland of Lethington as 'a great humanist in prose and poetry, Greek and Latin; well versed in mathematics and with great skill in architecture and heraldry'.[51] His family home, Seton Palace, was one of the finest houses of Renaissance Scotland and was capable of hosting visits from the royal court, but was demolished in 1789. Alexander Seton was sensitive to Scottish architectural traditions and blended his advanced Continental tastes with local customs in the manner of the Scottish Renaissance. In about 1598, he employed William Schaw to remodel his castle at Fyvie, and they produced one of the finest examples of the Scottish baronial style. The show-front to the south is a balanced, symmetrical arrangement of towers and windows, drawing the eye upwards to the roofline, which is a riot of battlements, dormers, decorated corbels and conical-capped turrets. At the centre, the entrance has a relatively modest classical portal sur-

mounted by an ascending sequence of heraldic panels and windows, climbing to a lofty rounded arch, which connects the flanking towers at the roofline to form an imposing frontispiece.[52] Fyvie is a masterpiece of the genre, but Seton was capable of building in another style too. In about 1613, he remodelled Pinkie House, Musselburgh, to fashion a Neostoic suburban villa as a retreat from the cares of state in Edinburgh. Its exteriors were much more restrained than Fyvie's, with regular ranks of rather plain windows and chimney stacks along the east façade, although the house has now lost its original decorative chimney caps and dormers. The painted interiors were also very impressive (see Chapter 4). The main role of Pinkie House was to provide rest and contemplation and so the gardens, with their fountains, pools and woods were a particularly important part of the scheme, as a carved inscription (originally in Latin) states:

[Seton] has laid out and ornamented this villa and gardens near the city, for his own pleasure and the pleasure of his noble descendents, and of everyone of culture and urbanity. This is no place of warfare, designed to repel enemies. Instead, there is a welcoming and kindly fountain of pure water, a grove, pools, and other amenities: everything that could afford decent pleasures of heart and spirit.[53]

This stress on peace and privacy was particularly poignant at a site which had witnessed the humiliation of the Scottish forces in the Battle of Pinkie 66 years earlier. The Doric fountain at the entrance to Pinkie House is a graceful successor to the one in the Linlithgow courtyard, with strict classical arches, columns and entablatures; it is capped by

The King's Knot at Stirling Castle: the relic of a Renaissance pleasance.

a slightly distorted imperial crown, indicating Seton's role as a minister of the king.[54]

At Pinkie, the house and gardens were designed together to provide a restful retreat, whereas the gardens and parks attached to all the other palaces and castles in this survey often evolved over generations, with considerable space devoted to the practical production of fruit, vegetables, fish and game for the table. The accounts of the royal masters of works include frequent references to building and maintaining garden walls, dykes, gates, banks and benches; and gardeners are recorded tending orchards, kitchen gardens, and ornamental flower beds or knots. The parks and gardens also had recreational uses. They often housed tennis courts (walled courts for real or royal tennis rather than modern lawns), bowling greens, archery butts, and lists for jousting. Very few gardens (or pleasances) of the period have survived in a state even approximating to their original forms, but we know from other countries that the practice of the period was to create very formal designs marked out in symmetrical patterns, called knots or parterres, within walled or fenced enclosures. The relic of such a design can be seen in the King's Knot below the castle walls at Stirling. This is now a geometric pattern of unplanted earthworks, but it is likely that it once held beds defined by low box

hedges with specimen shrubs at key points.[55] The current design was probably marked out for Charles I in 1628–9, but a persistent tradition associates the King's Knot with an Arthurian round table created for James IV, and given the king's fascination with chivalric romance, this is not unlikely. Intriguingly, Sir David Lindsay of the Mount mentions a 'tabyll rounde' at Stirling in his poem *The Testament of the Papyngo* (1530).[56]

The finest surviving garden of the period is at Edzell Castle, which was created for another David Lindsay in about 1604. The formal beds were replanted in the 1930s in a suitably authentic manner, but the glory of the Edzell pleasance is in the enclosing walls. The garden is a walled quadrangle, with a turreted summer house and a bath house (the latter now just foundations) at the corners furthest from the castle. The walls are divided into bays articulated by columns (now lost) and capped by canopied niches protruding above the coping. Whatever sculptures, perhaps busts or urns, were intended to sit in the niches are also lost, but the Lindsay heraldry is incorporated into the stonework of the walls. There is also a sequence of panels carved with personifications of the Liberal Arts, the Cardinal Virtues and the Planetary Deities, the designs taken from German and Flemish engravings, much like the planetary images on the Stirling palace block. The panels of the Planetary Deities were copied from engravings of 1529 by Iorg Bentz of Nuremberg, a pupil of Albrecht Dürer, and the panels of the Liberal Arts and the Virtues were copied from engravings by Maarten de Vos of Antwerp.[57] Michael Lynch has recently identified some oddities in the ordering of the Virtues, which he explains in relation to aspects of Lindsay's personal life. Conventionally, Faith is placed first in the sequence, but at Edzell she is

fourth, perhaps because Lindsay claimed he did not find true faith until he was an adult. Likewise, Justice is normally at the end of the sequence, but at Edzell Temperance comes last, perhaps suggesting the importance of this quality in a family where violence was not unusual.[58]

It is possible that the lost columns at Edzell were once capped by obelisks or slender caryatids (female figures formed into columns or finials), in which case Edzell might have provided another example (along with the palace block at Edinburgh Castle and other sites discussed above) of the Baroque style creeping into Scottish use.[59] However, Edzell lacks a feature which became characteristic of later Scottish Baroque gardens: the multi-faced sundial. These elaborately decorated sundials were often mounted on columns and every face was carefully calibrated to show the same time. The earliest example of such a sundial was probably the one created at Holyrood in 1633 to celebrate the Scottish coronation of Charles I (although there was a simpler 'lectern' sundial erected at Dundas Castle in 1623), so the Edzell garden was just a little too early for this development.[60] Nevertheless, the garden at Edzell proclaims that its owner was an educated and cultured gentleman with sophisticated tastes and is one of the most important historic gardens in Europe.

Although much has been ruined, remodelled or destroyed, enough survives of Scottish architecture from the early fifteenth to the early seventeenth century to let us trace the development of the northern Renaissance style within the realm. The early experiments at Linlithgow, which drew on influences from a range of foreign sources, were probably repeated at many other sites now lost to us, and were later developed into the assertive, chivalric style of the last decade of the

reign of James IV. In the 1530s, 1540s and 1550s, the French Renaissance style was adopted with enthusiasm and discrimination at Falkland, Stirling, St Andrews, and elsewhere, giving Scottish architecture of the period a very distinctive, confident and flamboyant flavour, which flowed into the exuberant designs of the later castellated style at places such as Huntly and Fyvie. At the turn of the seventeenth century a slightly more restrained approach, with an emphasis on symmetry and classical detailing, was developed at Linlithgow, Edinburgh Castle, Pinkie House, and elsewhere. The works of this later period also began to exhibit elements of the new Baroque style, which was by then very fashionable on the Continent and would be more thoroughly adopted in Scotland after the restoration of the monarchy in 1660. Much of the impetus for Renaissance architectural innovation seems to have come from the royal court, although this impression might be conditioned by the greater chance of royal buildings surviving. The departure of the court for England in 1603 also meant that relatively little further development was undertaken at the royal sites after this date (the Holyrood of Charles II is the exception), thus preserving the evidence of earlier work, albeit in a state of neglect. Yet it is also apparent that the royal court was not the only source of architectural patronage. From the surviving evidence, it seems that the contribution of the Church was limited. There was some innovation at Rosslyn and Restalrig, but most ecclesiastical architecture remained very traditional until 1560 and, in some cases,

beyond.[61] Immediately after the Reformation there was hardly any new building, although quite a lot of rather destructive 're-ordering' was undertaken. However, nobles such as Hamilton of Finnart, Mar, Bothwell and Dunfermline, did make significant contributions and again, one imagines that there was once much more Renaissance work commissioned for Scottish nobles that has subsequently vanished beneath eighteenth- or nineteenth-century redevelopments. What now remains is a tantalising glimpse of a lost world.

OPPOSITE. The walled garden at Edzell Castle built for David Lindsay c.1604 and restored in the 1930s. This is a very rare surviving example of a Renaissance pleasance.

ABOVE. A carved panel of Venus from the garden walls at Edzell Castle, built for David Lindsay c.1604.

3

COURTLY MANNER

Renaissance Decorative and Applied Arts

All the buildings mentioned in the last chapter would have been furnished and decorated in a similar opulent style to the architecture. As with the buildings, some of the interior decoration was carried out in the enduring late-Gothic style which overlapped with the development of the Renaissance and exhibited strong Flemish and Burgundian influences, but as time went on Franco-Italian classical styles became more common. A lost masterpiece of the finest Renaissance workmanship was the tomb of William Elphinstone, bishop of Aberdeen and chancellor of Scotland, which was erected in the chapel of King's College, Aberdeen, c.1530 and survived for little more than a century. Only fragments remain and the design is difficult to reconstruct from the documentary record. However, it seems likely to have been a 'table' tomb with bronze figures of the Virtues supporting the upper slab (of stone from Tournai) on which reclined a bronze effigy of the dead bishop. The Virtues and the effigy were probably cast in Flanders and imported, perhaps from the workshop of Conrad Meit at Mechelen, and the whole design was probably devised by Alexander Galloway, rector of Kinkell and a rector

of the university of Aberdeen.[1] The tomb seems to have been made in the most magnificent and up-to-date style of the period. We know that Bishop Gavin Dunbar also had a bronze effigy on his tomb at St Machar's Cathedral, and that Bishop George Crichton of Dunkeld imported his tomb of black marble with a brass plate decorated with 'painting and images' from Antwerp. The latter also imported a fine brass lectern from the Low Countries (NMS), which was later looted by English troops from Holyrood Abbey. Other rare survivals include two wooden statues of the Virgin and Child. One, from late-fifteenth-century Aberdeen, was taken to Brussels in the early seventeenth century, where it is preserved in the Church of Our Lady of Finistère and displays the same graceful style as the Flemish statues of the period. The other, said to have come from Holyrood, is in the international style of the early sixteenth century and is now in the Church of the Sacred Heart, Edinburgh.[2] These few examples give some indication of what other stylish Renaissance monuments and church furnishings might once have existed elsewhere in Scotland.

Perhaps more typical of the surviving Renaissance decorative arts than the lost effigies and statues are the carved wooden furnishings, which exist in some numbers. Timber was scarce and expensive in Scotland at this period and was often imported from Germany and the Baltic. Thus carved wooden panelling used to line the walls and ceilings of grand houses and churches demonstrated status, power and wealth, as well as providing some insulating warmth and comfort. Several examples of fine decorative panelling survive from this time, but most have been removed from their original locations, many pieces have been cut, remodelled, or resited and much has been lost. However, inventories of the time record household goods and two examples may suggest how well furnished the homes of clerics and courtiers could be. The inventory of Master Adam Colquhoun, parson of Stobo (near Peebles), who was a canon of Glasgow Cathedral and lived in Glasgow, was taken at his death in 1542, and the inventory of Sir William Hamilton of Sanquhar and McNairston was made in pursuit of a legal action in 1559. The furnishings and contents of the canon's house in Glasgow and Sir William's seat of Newton Castle, Ayr, are recorded in some detail and the inventories note extensive use of carved wooden panels and furniture. The parson had carved oak chests, settles, chairs and carved pine cupboards, whilst his four-poster bed was both carved and gilded. Sir William had three rooms with panels and mouldings of Baltic pine, two of Norwegian fir, and his oratory had panels with 'pictures of raised work' (carvings in high relief). He also had chairs, beds and chests carved in the most 'comely' or 'courtly' manner. Intriguingly, he also had in store (perhaps awaiting installation) 'eight complete doors of Baltic pine with fine

raised and carved work of the most recent and curious fashion used within the realm', with smart metal fittings.[3] These sound like particularly impressive and up-to-date furnishings. Whilst it is difficult to judge how typical these men were of their class, neither was from the very highest rank, so we could reasonably expect the homes of earls and bishops to have been even more lavishly provided.

The Beaton Panels of c.1530 (NMS) give an indication of the enduring attachment to the late-Gothic, chivalric style that has already been noted as particularly powerful in Scotland. They were carved for David Beaton who at the time was abbot of Arbroath and coadjutor of St Andrews (having a shared responsibility with his uncle, James Beaton). He later became archbishop of St Andrews in his own right, bishop of Mirepoix in France, and a cardinal, so he was one of the most elevated prelates of the time. He was also a noted Francophile, politically devoted to the 'auld alliance' and so sophisticated in his tastes that it was said that he could pass as a native during his many lengthy visits to France. He was eventually murdered by vengeful reformers in 1546.[4] The traditional style of the panels he commissioned therefore gives some indication of the international context of late-Gothic art in Scotland, since features such as intricate tracery, vine-leaf borders and stiff, stylised figures were common on the Continent too. Indeed, some elements of the design were probably derived from a French book of Hours of the 1520s. However, there is also an element of Renaissance realism and naturalism creeping into the style, particularly in the curling foliage tendrils, showing that this is a transitional artefact. The panels were probably used to decorate Beaton's chambers in St Andrews Castle, but were later removed to Balfour House in Fife, and

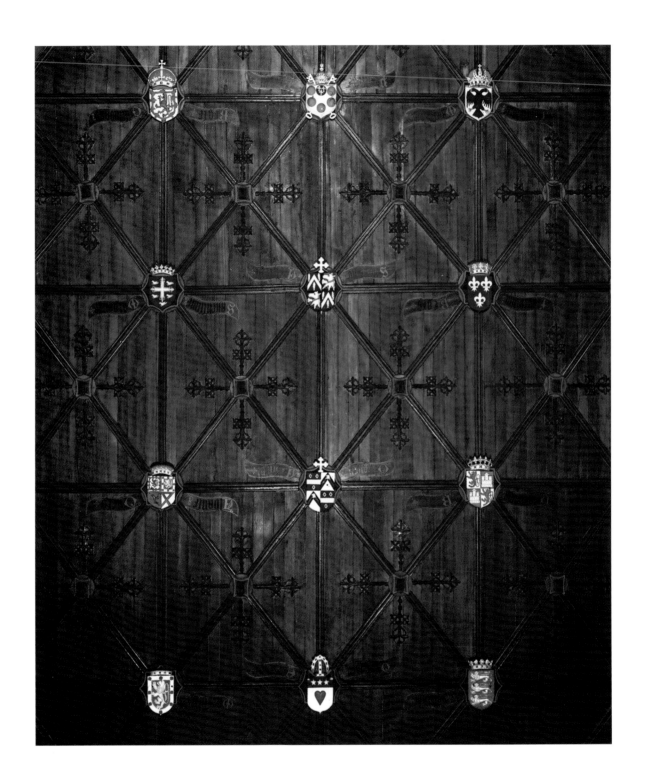

are now in the National Museum. The surviving scenes depict the Annunciation (the Virgin Mary hailed by the angel Gabriel), the Tree of Jesse (a depiction of Christ's human ancestry), the 'Arma Christi' (a coat of arms invented for Christ in the Middle Ages), the royal arms, the arms of the Beatons and other heraldic and chivalric emblems. These themes suggest a fascination with pedigree, inheritance and dynastic honour.[5]

Almost all pre-Reformation Scottish ecclesiastical wooden carvings have been destroyed. However, the high quality of the few scattered remnants suggests that a rich heritage has been lost. St Machar's Cathedral, Aberdeen, has a carved and painted heraldic ceiling dating from about 1520, which has three ranks of shields of arms representing the Scottish Church, the Scottish nobility and the royal houses of Europe, all arranged in a strict hierarchy. The arms of the burghs and university of Aberdeen are included in the scheme, placing the local community in a national and international context. The interconnected nature of chivalric and religious culture at this period is clearly visible in this remarkable ceiling, which was designed and built by locals: probably Alexander Galloway, a canon of the cathedral (who also designed Elphinstone's tomb in King's College Chapel), and James Winter of Angus respectively. The wooden panels form a flat, compartmented, ceiling in the Renaissance manner, which contrasts with the vaulted ceilings of the Gothic style, and the painted heraldry makes a colourful display.[6]

Six choir stalls built after 1486 for Bishop James Chisholm at Dunblane Cathedral, and later resited beside the west door, have also survived. They are carved in a beautiful profusion of tracery, foliage and cusped decoration typical of the late-Gothic style of northern Europe but with some hints of the more naturalistic Renaissance style creeping into the design. A more complete example, still in the original location, are the carved oak choir stalls, canopies and screen of King's College Chapel, Aberdeen, commissioned by Bishop William Elphinstone, which date from 1506–9. Their exuberant tracery, twining tendrils and linenfold decoration indicate a strong Flemish influence, although they are thought to have been carved by a team led by a local craftsman John Fendour. Also in King's College Chapel is the only surviving pre-Reformation Scottish pulpit: Bishop Stewart's pulpit, which had originally been made for St Machar's in the late 1530s. The wooden structure is richly carved with a sequence of profile heads in medallions, a feature already seen in the carved stone decoration at Falkland Palace. The pulpit was probably carved by local craftsmen, rather than the French masons who were at work at Falkland. The heads have a very secular appearance and are not obviously identifiable as saints or biblical characters. The pulpit and the palace date from roughly the same time and indicate that this decorative element, which was so characteristic of Renaissance design, was widespread in Scotland.[7]

OPPOSITE. The heraldic ceiling of St Machar's Cathedral, Aberdeen, c.1520. The left column shows the arms of the Scottish nobility headed by King James V, the middle column shows the arms of the Scottish bishops headed by Pope Leo X, and the right column shows the arms of the European monarchs headed by Emperor Charles V.

ABOVE. One of the original Stirling Heads, c.1540. The winged cherub on
her breast might indicate that the lady is deceased. The sequence of 'os' and 'is'
in the border is thought to be a form of early musical notation.

OPPOSITE. A modern replica of the same Stirling Head, carved by John Donaldson.
This and other replica roundels are now set into the ceiling of the king's presence
chamber (or inner hall) in the restored palace block at Stirling Castle.

The most celebrated example of carved medallion heads of the Scottish Renaissance are the famous Stirling Heads of c.1540. Once set into the compartmented ceiling of the king's presence chamber in James V's palace at Stirling Castle, the carved oak roundels were taken down and dispersed after 1777 when the ceiling became unstable. Consequently, only 34 out of an original set which possibly numbered 56 have survived, with drawings of two others. As part of a major restoration of the palace block, in 2011 Historic Scotland opened a new gallery at Stirling to display the surviving roundels. The presence chamber ceiling was also reconstructed with newly commissioned replicas which have been brightly painted and gilded in an authentic manner (traces of paint were found on the originals). The Stirling Heads are a lively and complex collection of carved panels, which would have created a magnificent impression on the king's guests. The majority of the roundels depict a head-and-shoulders view of male or female figures, many in profile, dressed in elaborate costumes and headwear; whilst some show whole figures such as cherubs (*putti* in Italian), Hercules, or a court jester. Each of the figures appears within a circular frame of foliage or decorative patterns, much like the medallions at Falkland and Aberdeen, and one of these borders is now thought to include a very early type of musical notation, appropriate for a music-loving king and court. We do not know who carved the roundels, but the hands of more than one craftsman are evident. Two Scotsmen, Robert Robertson and John Drummond of Mylnab, are possibilities, as is a French carver called Andrew Mansioun or André Manson.[8]

Historic Scotland has suggested possible identifications for the figures including portraits of real people from the royal family and court, a selection of Roman emperors, several depictions of Hercules and some of the Nine Worthies (*neuf preux* in French, the language of chivalry) with some female Worthies (*neuf preuses*). The mythical figure of Hercules was greatly respected in chivalric lore and was particularly associated with the Emperor Charles V, who used the Pillars of Hercules as a heraldic badge. There was also the legend of the Gallic Hercules, which was especially popular in France: that after completing his twelve labours, Hercules had become king of ancient Gaul and an embodiment of eloquence as well as of strength and courage. James V had cordial diplomatic relations with Charles V and was admitted to his chivalric Order of the Golden Fleece in 1532. He also visited the French court of Francis I in 1536–7 to marry the king's daughter Madeleine, and was admitted to the French chivalric Order of St Michael. Both Charles V and Queen Madeleine are thought to be depicted in the Stirling Heads and perhaps Francis I might have been on one of the lost roundels.

The Nine Worthies were heroes from three phases of history: the pagan classical period, the Old Testament Jewish era, and medieval Christendom. They first emerged as a symbolic group in the thirteenth century and continued as popular subjects in art and literature well into the Renaissance.[9] Like Hercules, they were also regarded as precursors of the chivalric ideal and were lauded as models of knightly decorum; indeed, they were often depicted wearing the most fashionable contemporary armour and heraldic shields of arms were devised for them. There were variations, but the list usually consisted of Hector of Troy, Alexander the Great, Julius Caesar, Joshua, King David, Judas Maccabeus, King Arthur, Charlemagne and

the crusader Godfrey of Bouillon. They also had female counterparts, who embodied womanly chastity and virtue. This group was more fluid than the males, but for the German Renaissance engraver Hans Burgkmair it consisted of three Romans (Lucretia, Virginia and Veturia), three Jews (Esther, Judith and Jael), and three medieval Christians (St Helena, St Bridget of Sweden and St Elizabeth of Hungary), all of whom were considered to be heroines in their own way. It is impossible to say precisely which head might represent which Worthy, but the general identification is a very plausible one.

The reconstructed ceiling of the presence chamber at Stirling is similar to other wooden ceilings of the period in that it is flat, rather than vaulted, and divided into panels by timber mouldings. Similar ceilings (but without the exuberant medallions) can be found at the palaces of Holyrood and Falkland and at St Machars, as we have already seen. Coffered ceilings had been a characteristic feature of Roman design and were widely used in many Italian Renaissance buildings. The fashion for flat, coffered or compartmented ceilings with medallion decoration or carved heads can be found far and wide in Renaissance Europe: from the Casa de los Tiros in Granada, to the Loire chateau of Azay-le-Rideau, Wawel Castle, Krakow, and many other sites. At Granada the 'golden chamber' (*Cuadra Dorada*) was built in the 1520s and 1530s and includes carved medallion heads on the wooden doors and shutters as well as sculpted and painted heads (not in roundels) on the ceiling. At Azay-le-Rideau, which was built after 1518 for a minister of Francis I, the ceiling of the main staircase consists of roundel heads within compartments but carved in stone rather than wood. A particularly striking example is the collection of

carved wooden heads on the reconstructed, flat, coffered ceiling of the Deputy's Hall at Wawel Castle, Krakow, first built in the late 1530s for King Sigismund I and his Italian queen, Bona Sforza. Only 30 heads survive from an original set thought to have numbered nearly 200, but they are as vigorous and characterful as the Stirling Heads and were also brightly painted. They are now set in rectangular compartments, although circular, octagonal and cruciform panels were specified in the 1535 contract of works with the sculptor Sebastian Tauerbach.[10] It is interesting to note that analysis of the oak panels used in the Stirling Heads shows that the timber had been imported from Poland.

The fact that such similar decorative motifs were used at so many widely scattered sites, including Stirling, says much about the diffusion of Renaissance style and taste by the early sixteenth century. Indeed, four carved roundels also on display in the new Stirling Castle gallery were once believed to be part of the Stirling Heads collection and are now thought to have come from wall panels or cabinet doors. There are a further 20 medallion panels said to have come from Stirling Castle, which suggests an extensive scheme of coordinating interior decoration. The same taste may also be seen operating in other surviving examples of Scottish Renaissance woodcarving, on doors, wall panels and furniture. Motifs that appear repeatedly are profile heads in roundels (often in fanciful dress), heraldic beasts and emblems, foliage wreaths and borders, and twining tendrils and arabesques, often in the fashionable 'grotesque' style. Examples include a heraldic panel and ceiling boss from Linlithgow Palace (NMS). The panel combines Renaissance medallion heads with late-Gothic pilasters in the border,

OPPOSITE. A recreation of the king's presence chamber in the royal palace at Stirling Castle,
originally built for James V c.1540. The replica Stirling Heads can be seen in the ceiling.

ABOVE. A carved ceiling boss from Linlithgow Palace, 1617.
The royal unicorn carries an early version of the Union flag.

whilst the unicorn on the ceiling roundel of 1617 holds a prototype of the Union flag, which greatly appealed to James VI's pride in ruling multiple kingdoms after 1603. There are also several panels of the mid-sixteenth century associated with Mary of Guise's residences and a few other sites.[11] This was almost certainly the 'courtly' style of the carved items in Sir William Hamilton's inventory.

Another prominent element of the decoration of important buildings of the period was the use of tapestries and hangings. The Stirling Palace restoration project has not only reinstated the carved and painted interior decoration of the royal chambers, but has also tried to recreate all aspects of the décor and furnishings, including the fabrics. Scarcely any textiles of the Scottish Renaissance have survived into the modern age, with none from the royal collections, so the work has focused on recreating the style of the period from the documentary records and surviving examples from other countries. Many fabrics have been used to furnish the restored palace, but a particularly exciting initiative has been the manufacture of a set of replica tapestries depicting the 'Hunt of the Unicorn'. These are copied from originals held by the Metropolitan Museum of Art in New York, which were woven in Flanders in about 1500. The tapestry workshops of northern France and the Low

A mid-sixteenth-century carved oak door from Mary of Guise's house, Blyth's Close, Edinburgh. An example of medallion heads used as Renaissance decoration.

Countries produced the finest work of the age and their hangings were sold to wealthy patrons all over Europe, including Scotland. The legend of the unicorn was a very popular subject: the mythical creature, which could be tamed only by the purity of a maiden, was often understood as an allegory of love or of religious salvation. Unicorns were also Scottish heraldic beasts, which stood either side of the royal arms as supporters, so the replica tapestries are an eminently suitable choice for the location. In fact, royal wardrobe inventories show that James V owned a set of tapestries telling the story of the unicorn in six panels; whilst Mary of Guise owned two sets, one of which, in four panels, was kept at Stirling.[12]

The surviving financial records of the time show that James IV, James V, Mary and James VI owned extensive collections of tapestries, cloths of estate (fixed behind and above ceremonial chairs), bed hangings and other textiles, all richly worked in fine threads and bright colours.[13] Indeed, James VI had inherited such a large collection from his mother that he made very few new purchases.[14] The monarchs also employed a small staff of French and Scottish tapissers and embroiderers who would have cleaned, repaired and maintained the precious cloths and supervised their carriage and installation as the court moved from one residence to another. Many of the non-figurative soft furnishings were made by these skilled craftsmen, but the fine woven tapestries were imported. All of the fabrics contributed to the image of splendour and magnificence surrounding the sovereign: for instance, the state beds which stood in the inner chambers of the king and queen and were particularly richly decorated, were used purely for display; the monarchs would have slept in smaller, more practical beds in their private closets.

Similarly, the stories depicted on the tapestries focused on themes which enhanced the honour, virtue and power of the prince. Among the subjects known to have featured in the royal tapestry collection in the middle of the sixteenth century were many classical myths and legends of heroic warriors and princes, such as the stories of Aeneas, Perseus, the Judgement of Paris, the Trojan wars, Jason and the Golden Fleece, Hercules, Romulus, and various classical deities. Biblical subjects such as the Creation, Solomon, Rehoboam and Tobit also appeared, as did more chivalric themes such as scenes of hunting, hawking, the 'City of Ladies', and the story of Gaston de Foix and the Battle of Ravenna. The 'City of Ladies' (*Le Livre de la Cité des Dames*, 1405) was the most famous work by the remarkable Franco-Italian female writer Christine de Pizan. The book celebrates the lives of virtuous, capable, heroic women from history and legend and became a popular theme in late-medieval and Renaissance art: tapestries on the subject were also owned by Anne of Brittany, Margaret of Austria, and Elizabeth I of England.[15] Gaston de Foix was a French commander in the Italian wars, who secured victory over the Spanish at the Battle of Ravenna in 1512 but was killed in the process and thus became a chivalric hero. The classical subjects of many of the tapestries suggest that they would have been made in the latest Renaissance style, in imitation of ancient art: indeed, some are specifically described as 'antique work'. However, the chivalric themes might have been presented in more traditional styles. The royal collection also included hangings known as 'verdures' and these were almost certainly designs of plants and flowers in the late-Gothic *mille fleurs* (thousand flowers) style, which was very popular in France.

The fabrics used to furnish the royal chambers included the finest silk, satin, damask, velvet, cloth of gold and of silver. These were often decorated with heavy braids, tassels, fringes and embroidered patterns or borders also worked in silks or gold and silver thread. The houses of great nobles and prelates would also have been furnished in a similarly luxurious style, whilst the lairds, gentlemen and burgesses used hangings of linen and wool. The inventories of both the parson of Stobo and Sir William Hamilton, mentioned above, include wall and bed hangings, table covers and cushions, mainly of linen and wool but with some silk and gold decoration. Of the few surviving Scottish pieces of the period, the set that comes closest to the quality of the royal collection is the Morton Valances (NMS), once owned by the earls of Morton, which were made c.1580 in France or Scotland. They show many characters dressed in French courtly fashions and are finely worked in linen, wool and silk. They are thought to depict scenes from classical myths or Bible stories, but the precise interpretation is obscure (see page vi). Valances are short curtains or pelmets used as decorative borders for wall hangings, canopies or beds and the Morton examples were at some point stitched together to form a rectangular wall hanging. Being narrower and sturdier than the larger draperies, valances have sometimes survived when their matching curtains have perished.

The earliest set of Scottish valances is the Campbell Valances (Burrell Collection), made c.1550 for Sir Colin Campbell of Glenorchy and his wife, Katherine Ruthven. These are typical of the more naïve embroidered hangings used in lairdly homes. They are worked in coloured wool and silks on linen from designs probably taken from contemporary woodcut illustrations. They show the story

OPPOSITE. A recreation of the queen's bedchamber
in the royal palace at Stirling Castle, originally built
for Mary of Guise c.1540.

ABOVE. One of the Campbell Valances worked
for Sir Colin Campbell of Glenorchy and his wife,
Katherine Ruthven, c.1550.

of Adam and Eve, heraldic and mythical subjects like mermaids and unicorns, and shield of arms. The rather stiff, stylised figures are more in the persistent Gothic tradition than the new Renaissance style, but the valances include some Renaissance motifs, such as *putti*. Another rare survival is the Lochleven Hangings (NMS and Burrell Collection) which were made in Edinburgh c.1600, perhaps drawing on French inspiration. They have a red woollen ground with applied floral, fruit and foliage panels and borders in a mature Renaissance style, worked in black velvet embroidered with coloured silks. They are thought to have been produced by professional embroiderers, probably also for the earls of Morton at the New House of Lochleven (rather than the castle). Three very similar panels also survive, known as the Linlithgow Hangings (NMS and St Leonard's School) since

they were traditionally associated with the palace, but their provenance cannot be verified.[16] When complete, the hangings would have made a very warm, colourful and fashionable display.

Both the Lochleven and Linlithgow Hangings were once said to have been worked by Mary, queen of Scots. Mary was certainly an accomplished and prolific needlewoman, but she could not possibly have produced all the embroideries ascribed to her and no work from her years in Scotland can be confidently identified. The embroideries known to be from her hands carry her cipher (initials) and were worked during her English exile. They are predominantly small panels, which could be combined to form larger pieces such as the Oxburgh Hangings (V&A, Oxburgh Hall, and Royal Collection). Like the ladies of the English and European courts, she took her designs from

the illustrations published in Continental emblem books, such as Claude Paradin's *Devises Heroïques* (Lyon, 1557) or Conrad Gesner's *Icones Animalium* (Zurich, 1553). Typically, a picture of an animal, plant or heraldic device would be accompanied by a motto, which would indicate a deeper, personal meaning. This application of personal symbolism constituted a Renaissance emblem or *impresa* (plural, *imprese*) and Mary enthusiastically adopted and adapted many *imprese* for her own use. Amongst her favourites were the sunflower turning to the sun (*Sa vertu m'attire*: its power attracts me), a tortoise climbing a crowned palm tree (*Dat gloria vires*: glory gives strength) and a vine being pruned (*Virescit vulnere virtus*: virtue flourishes from its wounds), but she used many others too. One of the most famous examples of her embroidery is the panel of a ginger cat looming over a mouse (Royal Collection), which is thought to represent red-headed Queen Elizabeth's treatment of her captive cousin. Even more politically charged were the embroideries Mary and her ladies worked for the elaborate hangings on her great bed of state, which were documented in 1586–7. The emblems all centred on Mary's hopes for escape from Elizabeth's power and restoration to sovereignty. The bed and its hangings were sent to Scotland after Mary's execution but disappeared sometime after 1617.[17] Similar panels, with different messages, were undoubtedly worked by her and her ladies during her years in Scotland and the fashion for colourful emblematic embroidery was clearly widespread in the period, even though so little has survived.

Two other rare surviving pieces are worth mentioning at this point because they hint at the rich profusion of embroidered decoration of the period, which has since been lost. The financial and inventory records tell us that before the Reformation, churches and chapels were often sumptuously provided with altar cloths, banners, hangings, palls, book covers and vestments such as copes and chasubles.[18] These are often described as worked in silks, gold and silver threads, with heavy braids and fringes, and with pearls and gems incorporated into the designs. Almost all fell victim to the fury of the iconoclasts after 1560, but one major piece has survived (and some fragments of other cloths), perhaps because it was put away

OPPOSITE. One of the Lochleven Hangings, made in Edinburgh c.1600 for the earl of Morton.

ABOVE. Embroidered panel of a cat, worked by Mary, queen of Scots, during her English captivity.

OPPOSITE. The Fetternear Banner, made in Edinburgh c.1520. This is
a very rare surviving piece of pre-Reformation ecclesiastical embroidery.

ABOVE. An embroidered hawking pouch made for James VI c.1610.
The clasp was probably made by George Heriot of Edinburgh.

unfinished in about 1520. This is known as the Fetternear Banner (NMS) and was worked in coloured silks on linen. It was intended to be used in processions by the Confraternity of the Holy Blood at St Giles' Collegiate Kirk, Edinburgh.[19] Religious confraternities or guilds were very popular organisations in the late-medieval and Renaissance period. They allowed burgesses, tradesmen and craftsmen to club together to undertake the veneration of a particular saint or cult and to make spiritual provision for their own souls after death. Noble and royal members were sometimes admitted too and King James IV was an active member of the prestigious St Giles' confraternity. The veneration of the Holy Blood in Scotland was copied from the more famous cult of Bruges, which still operates today. The Fetternear Banner depicts the Passion of Christ in graphic and gory realism, within a border formed of knotted cords (*cordeliere*), acorns, flowers, shields of arms, and a Rosary: a devotional aid which was also newly popular at the time, having been devised in mid-fifteenth-century Flanders. The main features of the design are traditional, but an awareness of Renaissance style is apparent in the Roman arch decorated with grotesques and festoons, which surmounts the central panel. There is a blank panel just above this, which perhaps was intended to contain more Renaissance imagery or an inscription.

The final intriguing survival of embroidered decoration is a hawking or falconry set which once belonged to James VI (Burrell Collection). It dates from about 1610 and was used by the king whilst in England but it might have been made in France

and the beautiful enamelled clasp of the pouch is probably the work of the Edinburgh jeweller, George Heriot. It passed out of the king's hands in 1619, so it might have come to Scotland with him during his visit of 1617. The set includes simple leather hoods, lures and suchlike items, but the pouch and glove are of fine leather delicately embroidered in coloured silks, with gold and silver threads. The elaborate, twining pattern includes blackberry and mistletoe, which were believed to have protective powers. This is a very special piece because of its quality and royal provenance, but it also indicates the extensive use of embroidered decoration on a surprisingly wide range of artefacts of the period: books, shoes, gloves and even saddles were routinely encrusted in stitched embellishment.[20] Much of this needlework would have involved Renaissance motifs and styles such as the fanciful, twining, foliate grotesque designs, and the use of mottoes.

Scottish patrons clearly displayed their riches and status in the furnishings of their homes and churches, but they also wore their wealth on their backs. For special occasions and everyday wear, garments could make a significant statement. As in other countries, sumptuary laws restricted the quality of clothing permitted to be worn according to social rank, so the ability to purchase and wear fine silks, satins, velvets, furs, feathers, lace, embroidery and jewellery carried special meaning.[21] The fashions in clothing naturally changed over time, but there is nothing specifically 'Renaissance' about the sixteenth-century transitions from skirts gathered at the waist to the 'farthingale' (which fell from a rigid framework at the hips),

OPPOSITE. Gold and enamel locket with a French cameo of Mary, queen of Scots, 1560s.

ABOVE. The Penicuik Jewels, thought to have belonged to Mary, queen of Scots, late sixteenth century.

OPPOSITE. James VI's gold filigree watch case, early seventeenth century.

from soft caps or bonnets to more rigid brimmed hats, or the introduction of neck ruffs and stiffened, upright collars. None of these developments can be linked to classical, humanist, or chivalric inspiration, yet they can all be traced (with some regional variations) across the Continent at roughly the same time. No Scottish garments of the period survive (and very few elsewhere), but the developing fashion for different cuts and styles can be traced in the extant portraiture, whilst the extravagance of the royal wardrobes is documented in the inventories and financial accounts, just as for the tapestries and furnishings.[22] Kings and queens naturally dressed in the finest fabrics imported from Italy, France and Flanders and favoured the most expensive colours of black, white, crimson and purple, whilst people of lesser status made

use of wool and linen dyed with more subdued hues.[23] However, embroidered decoration from the simple to the lavish, including Renaissance motifs, was ubiquitous.

It is slightly easier to trace the use of Renaissance designs in Scottish jewellery than in clothing simply because a few examples have survived. Also, the financial accounts and inventories document many lost pieces and give more details of the decoration than in the descriptions of needlework. The records show that brooches, pendants, bracelets, cap badges, and buttons were often embellished with ciphers (initials), portrait miniatures, heraldic badges such as lions, unicorns, lilies, thistles and roses, or religious images such as the Virgin Mary or St James, all picked out in precious stones or enamel. Mythical creatures, such as mer-

maids, are also listed, along with more obviously classical motifs such as pillars, 'antiques', and heads. James V's collection even included a cap badge depicting the Three Graces, and a pair of bracelets decorated with 'little white heads', which were probably cameos.[24] Cameos were very desirable jewels, since they imitated closely the classical manner of depicting gods and emperors on antique gemstones, and they had to be imported from Italy or France. As with the embroidery, emblematic designs incorporating personal badges and mottoes were popular in the reigns of James V and Mary, but by the end of the sixteenth century Queen Anna's taste was for jewels with portrait miniatures, ciphers and naturalistic designs such as flowers and birds. Anna was probably the most extravagant (and indebted) customer of the Edinburgh goldsmiths such as George Heriot, but she seems to have largely avoided the mythological and allegorical fashions of her predecessors. However, her fondness for jewels incorporating portrait miniatures fostered the manufacture of what became a particular speciality of Scottish goldsmiths.[25]

Describing the return of Mary, queen of Scots, to Scotland in 1561, John Leslie, bishop of Ross, noted:

> Besides the queen's highness' furniture, hangings and apparel, was also in her own company, transported with her majesty into Scotland, many costly jewels and gold work, precious stones, orient pearls, most excellent of any that was in Europe, and many

costly garments for her body with great silver work of costly cupboards, cups and plate.[26]

The National Museum of Scotland holds several items of jewellery associated with Mary, queen of Scots. There are two gold lockets, one in the shape of a heart and the other oval, both with enamelled scrollwork decoration. The heart is the finer of the two, has an elegant Renaissance vase and floral pattern on the reverse, contains an onyx cameo of Mary on the front and is set with diamonds and a ruby; whilst the oval contains portrait miniatures of Mary and James VI and is set with pearls. Both lockets were clearly intended as mementos and the heart locket is thought to have been commissioned by Mary herself from a Scottish goldsmith (using a French cameo) as a gift to a friend. She is known to have distributed such trinkets in large numbers, and all the Scottish monarchs observed the custom of making gifts of jewellery and plate to courtiers at New Year. A third item is the Penicuik Jewels, thought to have been owned by Mary. This set includes a gold and pearl oval locket with portrait miniatures, similar to the other oval locket, a gold and pearl pendant, which was probably once attached to the locket, and a necklace of gold beads, which was probably made from a pair of Mary's bracelets. The larger beads are of fine filigree and could possibly have held little balls of musk for perfume, as was done with Mary's gold pomander (Royal Collection).[27] Another very

fine piece of gold filigree is the watch case of James VI (NMS) from the early seventeenth century. Filigree work was a highly prized jeweller's equivalent of the curling foliage tendrils and arabesques, which were so popular in Renaissance design. The watch case also includes highly stylised images of fruit and seeds, perhaps intended to be pomegranates, which were symbols of fertility.

Three other jewels serve to emphasise the interest in allegory and emblematics, already identified in the embroidery of the period, and again, they are associated with Mary, queen of Scots. The Aberdeen Jewel (Marquess of Aberdeen) is a gold and enamel openwork pendant set with pearls and gemstones and containing a lock of hair, supposed to be Mary's. The design consists of a hand descending (perhaps from heaven) and holding a laurel wreath which encloses the hair in a crystal capsule and is surrounded by scrollwork with a pair of dragons' or serpents' heads.[28] The precise interpretation of the imagery is unclear, and there are no mottoes or inscriptions to enlighten us, but it was obviously a sympathetic memento of Mary. The image of a hand descending from heaven was used by Mary herself in her *impresa* or emblem, *Virescit vulnere virtus* (Virtue flourishes from its wounds), where it holds a pruning knife rather than a laurel wreath. The laurel wreath was used to crown great poets or generals in ancient Rome, so if the jewel had been made after Mary's death it might indicate that she had transcended her earthly tribulations and obtained eternal glory.

Another gold and enamel openwork pendant set with diamonds, emeralds, rubies, opals and pearls is reputed to have been owned by Mary

and is now in the Royal Collection. The central image is of the tree of knowledge from the Old Testament Book of Genesis. A serpent with a woman's upper torso (representing temptation and sin) is twined around the tree and offers fruit to one of two onyx cameos depicting skulls, presumably representing Adam and Eve, who brought sin and death to humankind through their disobedience. The image is surrounded by decorative scroll-work and the French inscription *vie et mort* (life and death) is on the back. The pendant was altered at some point when, amongst other things, two tiny panels with lettering were added to the front, but they have been cut down and do not make any sense.[29] The message of the jewel seems to be a rather morbid reminder that 'the wages of sin is death' and perhaps it might once have been accompanied by another, more optimistic, piece depicting the salvation offered by Christ to the faithful. The design was perhaps influenced by Henry II's engraver and medallist, Etienne Delaune, who in 1570 published a print of the temptation of Adam and Eve which includes two skulls either side of the tree of knowledge. It is notable that the 1570 print was intended as a pattern for goldsmiths.[30]

The third example was probably made for Lady Margaret Douglas, countess of Lennox, who was Mary's aunt and mother-in-law in her second marriage to Henry Stuart, Lord Darnley. It is known as the Lennox or Darnley Jewel (Royal Collection), was probably made in the 1570s, and contains the most elaborate and multi-layered symbolism. It is a gold and enamel heart-shaped locket, set with rubies, an emerald and blue glass. The front of the locket has two small hinged panels

OPPOSITE. The Lennox or Darnley Jewel, probably made in Edinburgh in the 1570s, contains many symbolic images.

which open to reveal images within, whilst the whole locket opens to show further pictures and mottoes, with more decoration on the back. It carries 28 emblems and six inscriptions in total. Amongst the images are female figures representing Faith, Hope, Victory and Truth, winged or pierced hearts, the sun and moon, a crown, a lily, a salamander, a phoenix, a pelican, an hour-glass, a skull, a laurel wreath, an enthroned queen, and figures of warriors in classical armour. The mottoes include *Qvha hopis stil constantly vith patience sal obteain victorie in yair pretence* (Who hopes constantly with patience shall obtain victory in their claim); *Quat we resolv deathe sal desolve* (What we decide death shall undo); and *Tym gars al leir* (Time causes all to learn).[31] Again, the messages are not entirely clear but they seem to allude to the murder of Darnley, the captivity of Mary, the successful marriage of the earl and countess of Lennox, the death of the earl, and James VI's claim to the English throne. Partly because the mottoes are in Scots rather than English, French or Latin, the locket is thought to have been made by an Edinburgh goldsmith: George Heriot, Michael Gilbert and James Gray have all been suggested as possibilities.

If remaining examples of Scottish Renaissance textiles and jewels are extremely rare, so are items of plate. These were often melted down, sometimes in moments of crisis to pay emergency expenses, sometimes simply to be remodelled to keep up with changing fashions, so very few have survived. Almost all the pre-Reformation church plate was dispersed and destroyed, a very rare survival is a pair of bronze candlesticks made in the Low Countries in the early sixteenth century for St Magnus Cathedral, Kirkwall (NMS), which have elegant baluster stems and octagonal bases. Perhaps

the most famous loss was the heavy gold font sent by Elizabeth of England for the baptism of the future James VI in 1566, which was melted down within the year. Yet the inventories of the period are full of lists of silver vessels, vessels of silver gilt, cups, goblets, jugs, basins, spoons, and the like: the parson of Stobo had 40 pieces in his hall, besides the items in his bedchamber and oratory, whilst Sir William Hamilton had a similar collection worth over £900. Sadly, there is seldom any indication of the decoration or style of the pieces, although some are described as having heraldic motifs such as lions, unicorns, thistles, roses and lilies. The finest examples were often set out for display on cloth-covered counters, buffets, or cupboards at prominent positions in halls when feasts or banquets were held, where they would have sparkled in the candlelight and impressed the guests. The intricate silver-gilt mace of St Salvator's College was made for Bishop James Kennedy by Jean Mayelle in Paris in 1461 and is a wholly Gothic design with pointed arches, tracery and crenellations framing figures of the risen Christ, angels, clerics and lions (Museum of the University of St Andrews). Another early, and most unusual, example is a fifteenth-century French silver casket given to Mary, queen of Scots, by her first husband, King Francis II of France (Lennoxlove House). Its design is transitional, with late-Gothic features in the gilt bands with stylised flower decoration and the shallowly engraved birds on the sides, and Renaissance touches in the curling foliate decoration on the lid. The engraved Hamilton shield of arms is a later addition. The casket is reputed to have contained letters (probably forgeries, now lost) which implicated Mary in the murder of her second husband, Lord Darnley.

One of the finest examples of Renaissance plate is the splendid gold cup said to have been given

A fifteenth-century French silver casket given to Mary, queen of Scots,
by her first husband, King Francis II of France. It is beautifully decorated
in a mixture of Gothic and Renaissance styles.

by Mary to St John's Church, Perth (Perth Museums), although it might have come to the church somewhat later. It was made by Christopher Lindenberger of Nuremberg c.1555 and the lid was remodelled by a Dundee goldsmith in about 1640. The original design was a very accomplished and mature piece of Renaissance workmanship, with an elegant candelabrum stem and layers of banded decoration incorporating medallion heads, classical pilasters, festoons, and arabesques. It was probably first intended for secular use and again demonstrates the extensive diffusion of Renais-

sance design. German workshops were renowned for their metalworking skills, especially in arms and armour, and some German founders and coiners had been employed at the Scottish court earlier in the century, but this cup was made in Germany for export and is of sufficiently high quality to have graced any royal or noble table across the entire Continent before it was adopted as a communion vessel. A simpler and more typical communion cup was made by the Edinburgh goldsmith John Mossman in 1585–6 for Rosneath Kirk, Dunbartonshire (NMS). It has a baluster stem and an

LEFT. Gold cup made by Christopher Lindenberger of Nuremberg c.1555 and later given to St John's Church, Perth, possibly by Mary, queen of Scots.

RIGHT. Silver communion cup from Rosneath Kirk, Dunbartonshire, made by John Mossman of Edinburgh in 1585–6 in a restrained but elegant style.

incised egg-and-dart pattern around the base: a form of decoration which took its inspiration from ancient Greek and Roman models.[32]

St John's, Perth, owned an important collection of early church plate (and a fine chandelier) which gives some indication of how church ritual changed after the Reformation. In the Catholic Mass the communion wine was reserved for the priests, with the lay congregation taking only the bread, thus the capacity of chalices (communion goblets) tended to be rather small, except where they were made for imposing display at prestigious sites. After the Reformation everyone partook of communion wine and so larger cups were introduced and were often adapted from secular use, as with the Nuremberg cup and some mazers (drinking bowls). Likewise, the practice at baptisms also changed (communion and baptism were the only two sacraments recognised by Protestants, as opposed to the seven sacraments of Catholicism).

LEFT. The Galloway Mazer, maplewood and silver gilt,
made by James Gray of the Canongate, 1569.

RIGHT. The Pitfirrane Goblet, probably made in the
Low Countries in the late sixteenth century.

Previously, elaborately carved stone fonts held the holy water and the priest would use a spoon or shell-shaped vessel to scoop it up and dribble it over an infant's head. Most of these fonts were regarded by the Reformers as papist and their carvings idolatrous, so they were smashed. Thus ministers in the Reformed Kirk again had to adopt vessels previously used in the secular custom of washing hands before a meal: the laver and ewer (jug and basin). The jug would have held the water, which was dribbled from the spout over a child's head to pour into the basin below. The Reformed Kirk was so denuded of sacramental plate that in 1617 an Act of Parliament required all parish kirks to provide at the very least a jug and basin for baptism and a cup for communion. This law gave a boost to the trade of the burgh goldsmiths, but sadly most plate of this period was melted down in the civil wars of the 1630s and 1640s. St John's had several early cups and a very rare surviving

baptismal basin made by David Gilbert of Edinburgh in 1591–4 and perhaps reworked in 1649 (Perth Museums). It is a partially gilded platter with a moulded edge and vandyked (zig-zag) decoration on the rim.[33]

Two other rare survivals, in the National Museum, demonstrate further the workmanship of the Scottish goldsmiths of the time. An ewer (jug) with a baluster-shaped rock-crystal body mounted on a silver-gilt base, handle, spout and lid was made between 1565 and 1567 by James Cok of Edinburgh for John Erskine, earl of Mar, whose arms are engraved on the lid. It was said to have been a present from Queen Elizabeth I at the baptism of one of his children, but the face of Bacchus (the Roman god of wine) appears on the thumbpiece, which suggests it was intended to hold wine rather than water. It is much simpler than the Perth cup but graceful and well fashioned nonetheless. More impressive is the Galloway Mazer, or drinking bowl, made of silver gilt with a maplewood cup, by James Gray of the Canongate for Archibald Stewart, later provost of Edinburgh, in 1569. This is a high-quality Renaissance design with a candelabrum or baluster stem decorated with acanthus leaves, foliage and lobes on the foot, and elegant foliage scrolls and shields of arms on the rim. Inside the bowl is a (rather ironic) biblical text: 'Ane good name is to be chosen above great riches and loving favour is above silver and above moste fyne golde.' Several other standing mazers with baluster stems and Renaissance decoration also survive from the period, showing that they were a very popular item of household plate and were characteristic of Scottish Renaissance design.[34]

Drinking glasses were very unusual in the sixteenth century, and all had to be imported because glass was not manufactured in Scotland until after 1610.[35] A rare surviving example is the Pitfirrane Goblet (NMS) which is said to be the glass from which James VI drank in Dunfermline before setting out to claim the English throne in 1603. Its delicate stem of twisted cords and scrolls supports a fine red cup. The style is known as *façon de Venise* because it was made by craftsmen from Venice (which produced the finest European glass of the period), who were at work in the Low Countries.

The final category of applied art which deserves consideration comprises the coins and medals of the period. The extensive use of carved medallion-head decoration across Renaissance Europe, noted above, was probably inspired by the example of ancient Roman coins and medals, which invariably show the head of the subject in profile or semi-profile in a realistic likeness, and these images became the models for Renaissance coins and medals too. James III was the first Scottish monarch known to have taken an interest in the idea of imperial kingship (see Chapter 1) and this concept, along with an awareness of the styles of ancient Rome, influenced the design of his coins. His silver groats and half-groats, first issued in about 1485, show the king's head in three-quarter profile and wearing an arched crown: 'the first true royal portrait on the Scottish coinage, . . . probably the earliest Renaissance coin portrait outside Italy'.[36] Certainly, Flemish and English coins do not start to use the imperial crown until a little later: 1487 and 1489 respectively, whilst the Roman style of the portrait suggests a strong Italian influence, perhaps through Anselm Adornes (see Chapter 2). However, Adornes was killed in 1483, so could not have worked on the final issue. The likeness of James III is certainly distinctive and recognisably the same man as the king portrayed

on the Trinity Altarpiece of the 1470s (see Chapter 4). Strangely, the coins of James IV reverted to the medieval, full-face, stylised king's head wearing an 'open' crown, which made Robert III, James II and James IV, for example, look almost identical. However, James IV's later coins did adopt Roman lettering, rather than the Old English lettering of earlier tradition.[37]

The finest Scottish Renaissance coin portrait is to be found on a medal commissioned by William Scheves, archbishop of St Andrews, in 1491 from Quentin Matsys (NMS). Matsys was mainly famous as a painter in Antwerp, but he trained in metalwork in his home town of Louvain and only moved to Antwerp in the same year that the medal was made. Thus it was probably in Louvain that he cast the medal for the archbishop, who also had strong connections with that city and is said to have studied at the university there. Matsys produced a finely characterised, cast bronze portrait in the Roman style, with the archbishop's name and title in a Latin inscription around the rim. It was fashionable for Italian popes and cardinals to commemorate their greatness with Roman-style portrait medals and Scheves' medal stands comparison with the best of them. Scheves had risen to prominence as a close personal servant of James III (d.1488) and had a fraught relationship with James IV, who insisted on being crowned by another bishop. Scheves had to repeatedly defend his position from rivals who had the king's favour, so the assertive self-promotion of the medal rather looks like an attempt to boost his position as primate of Scotland, a dignity which had been granted to him only in 1487 and which he never fully exercised before his death in 1497.

In 1524, another commemorative medal was struck for John, duke of Albany, regent for the

Silver groat of James III, c.1485: inspired by Italian Renaissance designs, it depicts the king wearing an arched imperial crown.

young King James V. It is thought to have been made of Scottish gold from the mines of Crawfordmuir but was probably struck in France, where Albany was one of the great nobles of the realm, and whither he returned that year, having acted as regent intermittently, and largely in the interests of France, for the previous decade. It is finely made but does not imitate the antique style as closely as the older Scheves medal. Duke John does not appear in a portrait but rather in his shields of arms: on the obverse impaled (combined) with those of his wife, Anne de la Tour d'Auvergne, and on the reverse accompanied by the French chivalric Order of St Michael. The reverse also carries an image of a dove, representing the Holy Spirit, with the pious inscription *Sub umbra Tuarum* (Under the shadow of Thy [wings]).[38]

LEFT. Quentin Matsys, portrait medal of
Archbishop William Scheves, Louvain, 1491.

RIGHT. Marriage medal of Mary, queen of Scots, and Dauphin
Francis, 1558. Mary's husband takes precedence on this medal.

Like the Albany medal, the coinage of James V's minority was essentially traditional in style, but the adult king was keen to present himself as the equal of other European monarchs and thus he adopted more fashionable, classically inspired, elements on his coins. His silver groats of 1526–39 show the king's head in profile, wearing an arched imperial crown and the design of the coin is modelled closely on those of his uncle, Henry VIII.[39] Both Henry and James might have taken inspiration for their profile portraits from an earlier German medal of Charles V: designed by Albrecht Dürer and made by Hans Krafft the Elder in 1521 to celebrate Charles's anticipated visit to Nuremberg (NGS). Dürer was one of the greatest German Renaissance artists and had studied in both Italy and the Low Countries. His image of Charles was clearly intended to portray the new Holy Roman Emperor as heir to the emperors of ancient Rome. Intriguingly, the contract to mint James V's silver groats was awarded in 1527 to a German miner and coiner, Joachim Hochstetter of Augsburg, but the arrangement did not last because Hochstetter transferred his services to Henry VIII within the year. However, a German influence on the design of the Scottish coin is a tantalising possibility.

A very striking profile portrait of James V appears on his gold ducats of 1539–42. They are commonly known as 'bonnet pieces' because the distinctive likeness of the king is shown wearing a soft cap or bonnet, rather than a crown (an imperial crown appears above his arms on the reverse). He also has his hair closely cropped and a neatly trimmed beard, which is exactly how he

was portrayed in the fine Renaissance portrait by Corneille de Lyon of 1536–7 (see Chapter 4). The bonnet pieces were made from Scottish gold and James V took an interest in the mine workings at Crawfordmuir, employing German, Dutch and French miners there and using much of the gold in refashioning his regalia (see Chapter 8). The bonnet pieces were also the first Scottish coins to bear a date, although this was not necessarily changed every year.[40]

The coins of the minority of Mary, queen of Scots, continued in the Renaissance style set by James V, with appropriate modifications to the head and royal title. During the regency of the earl of Arran (1543–54) the coins also included the Hamilton *cinqefoil* (five-petalled flower) badge. The portrait of the child queen presents her as a female version of her father and looking rather older than her age. However, the coins of Mary of Guise's regency (1554–60) introduced a distinctly French influence, as might be expected from the queen who had been made an adopted daughter of the French king before her marriage to James V. John Acheson, the master coiner, was sent to Paris to engrave new dies so that the head of Queen Mary (the younger) could be updated to match the portraits made of her at the French court, where she was being brought up to marry the heir to the throne, Dauphin Francis. When this marriage took place in 1558, Francis was granted the 'crown matrimonial', meaning that he was made king of Scots and given joint sovereignty with his wife. A new gold ducat and commemorative medal were issued which showed their two heads face to face, with the imperial crown of Scotland suspended between them. In the Latin inscription of their titles his name comes before hers, translated it reads: 'Francis and Mary, by the Grace of God

The 1565 silver ryall celebrating the marriage of Mary, queen of Scots, and Henry, Lord Darnley. Controversially, Darnley was given precedence here.

King and Queen of Scots, Dauphin [and Dauphine] of Vienne'; the reverse of the coin carries the motto, *Horum tuta fides* (Their faith [in each other] is unshakeable); whilst the reverse of the medal is inscribed, *Fecit utraque unum* (He hath made them one [flesh]). This is the first Scottish coin to bear a double portrait and was modelled on the examples set by Mary Tudor in her marriage to Philip of Spain.

When Mary married Darnley in 1565, she issued a silver ryall which was similar to the coin made for her first marriage: his name comes before hers on the inscription and he is accorded the title of 'king', although no crown is depicted over his head (however, an early medal does show him crowned). The coin was quickly withdrawn because Darnley's title was not approved by parliament. It was later

LEFT. Silver ryall of Mary, queen of Scots, 1566,
with the motto *Dat gloria vires*.

RIGHT. Gold £20 piece of James VI, 1575–6, struck to commemorate
victory over the supporters of Mary, queen of Scots.

OPPOSITE. James VI from Beza's *Icones*, published in Geneva in 1580.
The portrait has clearly been copied from the £20 coin.

reissued (along with a medal without a crown) with Mary's name placed first. The legend on the reverse reads, *Quos Deus coniunxit homo non separet* (Those whom God has joined together, let not man put asunder).[41] Mary's double-portrait coins and medals are of fine workmanship and make the medal issued for the marriage of James VI to Anna of Denmark in 1590 look rather crude by comparison, since the two heads are badly proportioned and roughly made. Another coin related to the Darnley marriage was also struck in 1565 and demonstrates again Mary's fondness for emblems and mottoes with very personal interpretations, which has already been seen in her embroi-

deries. It was another silver ryall carrying the image of a tortoise climbing a crowned palm tree, with the motto, *Dat gloria vires* (Glory gives strength), which Mary later stitched into the Oxburgh hangings. The coin was the first instance of this newly devised emblem and is thought to have initially represented Darnley (the tortoise) rising to glory through Mary (the palm tree). However, since she continued to use the image on coins and hangings long after Darnley's death, it must also have indicated a more general moral message.[42]

Despite the uninspiring marriage medal, James VI's coins were generally of a high quality and employed a mixture of traditional and Renaissance

IACOBVS · 6 · DEI · GRA · REX · SCOTOR ·

IN VTRVNQVE
PARATVS.

styles. The traditional designs included a revival of the medieval 'noble' depicting the ship of state, and a revival of the medieval 'rider' showing the king as a mounted knight. More in tune with his mother's enthusiasm for emblems were the silver 'balance' half- and quarter-merks of 1591–3. They show an image of a sword and scales (of justice) with the legend, *His differt rege tyrannus* (In these a king differs from a tyrant). The most remarkable of James VI's coins was the gold £20 piece of 1575–6. It was Scotland's largest ever gold coin, weighing one ounce, and was struck after James's ministers had defeated the last of Mary's supporters and were becoming more confident in their regime. The coin carries a half-length portrait of James crowned and wearing armour, with a naked sword in his right hand and an olive branch in his left. The motto is *In utrunque paratus* (Prepared for either [war or peace]) and the reverse carries the legend, *Parcere subiectis et debellare superbos* (To spare the conquered and defeat the proud).[43] These mottoes were probably devised by the king's tutor, George Buchanan, to encourage his royal pupil in the virtues of kingship. The coin clearly found its way abroad, since the king's portrait, complete with motto, was reproduced in 1580 when John Knox's friend Theodore Beza published his *Icones* in Geneva. The book was intended to commemorate the heroes of the European Reformation and was dedicated to King James.

The existing examples of Scottish Renaissance carvings, tapestries, embroideries, jewels, plate, coins and medals represent a tiny fraction of what was recorded in the inventories and accounts of the period, and are often chance survivals. With such sparse material evidence it is very difficult to know how far the remaining pieces were typical of the wider culture, but they are all we have left to provide a flavour of the decorative and applied arts of the time. Many of the pieces have royal connections and might be considered exceptional for that reason. However, the documentary record indicates that finely decorated items were also to be found in some profusion in the households of those of lesser (if not low) rank, such as the parson of Stobo or the laird of Sanquhar. Certainly, the exuberance of the Stirling Heads, the striking colours of the Lochleven Hangings, the obscure imagery of the Darnley Jewel and the self-promotion of the Scheves medal (amongst other pieces) collectively create a vivid impression of the material culture of the period. Despite the expense, Scottish patrons seem to have been keen to possess the most fashionable examples of the decorative and applied arts. As with the developments in architecture, their tastes combined motifs in imitation of the antique (such as cameos and portrait medals) and styles borrowed from Italy and France (such as the grotesque and arabesque designs) with an attachment to the chivalric and heraldic aspects of the Gothic tradition. The decorative use of medallion heads within roundels or wreaths is a particularly prominent feature of Scottish Renaissance design but one which clearly has parallels in many other countries; as does the fascination with emblems, mottoes and *imprese*. It seems clear that Renaissance decorative and applied arts were adapted to Scottish tastes and requirements but were also very much a part of the wider European culture of the age.

4

BRIGHT IMAGES

Renaissance Fine Arts

The scarcity of surviving examples of the decorative and applied arts of the Renaissance in Scotland is more than matched by the rarity of items from the fine arts such as illuminated manuscripts, panel paintings and murals. However, the few pieces that do survive are often of high quality, suggesting that Scottish patrons of the period were sophisticated and discerning. Indeed, the documentary record provides tantalising glimpses of a lost world of colourful, inventive, elegant and fashionable artistic endeavour, which drew inspiration from the Low Countries, Germany, France, England and Italy. In common with other countries, much Scottish artistic patronage of the period was religious, so the sacred books and paintings suffered a particularly heavy blow at the Reformation, with a second round of iconoclasm sweeping up most of the remnants during the Covenanting period. Reconstructing this lost world is thus something of a treasure hunt combined with a detective story.

Throughout the Middle Ages and into the High Renaissance, manuscript illumination was one of the most exquisite and expensive of the arts. The finest handwritten books on parchment or vellum, decorated with the most intricate designs executed in glowing colours and gold leaf, required such intensive and skilled labour that they could be afforded by only the wealthiest patrons. Many medieval monasteries had specialist workshops (*scriptoria*) which copied and illuminated both religious texts and chronicles for the luxury market. By the fifteenth century, the production of illuminated manuscripts had spread into the studios of secular artists belonging to the craft guilds of towns and cities engaged in international trade. There were skilled illuminators working in urban centres right across Europe, but the finest manuscripts of the Renaissance came from Flanders and northern France, particularly from the artists of the Ghent-Bruges school. Their books frequently included full-page illustrations which were masterpieces in miniature, easily comparable with the output of the more famous panel painters of the period, but they seldom signed their work, so even the great master illuminators are often anonymous. The development of the printing press in Germany from the 1450s and in most European

states by c.1500 made mass-produced printed books much cheaper than manuscripts, and gradually extinguished the market for handpainted illuminations, so that there were hardly any illuminators in regular work by the middle of the sixteenth century. Those few that persisted also practised in other media, such as portrait miniatures or engravings, to make a living. One of the latest artists to engage in manuscript production was Esther Inglis or Kello, who worked in Scotland and England at the turn of the sixteenth and seventeenth centuries. Her work for patrons such as the sons of James VI, princes Henry and Charles, among others, focused much more on elegant calligraphy than illumination.

Although very few survive, we know that Scottish patrons purchased books from Flanders and France and the most exalted customers would certainly have wanted illuminated manuscripts of the highest quality. In 1505, the chapel royal at Stirling had 28 manuscript volumes and ten printed books, including four great antiphoners (choir books) with 'various gilt capital letters', but no other details of illuminations are noted.[1] King James V purchased parchment manuscripts in Falkland and service books for the royal chapels from the *scriptorium* at Culross, Fife, and is also known to have bought books in Paris, Rouen and other French towns when he visited the court of Francis I in 1536–7. Sadly, the financial records do not always tell us the subject matter of volumes purchased, or even if the books were manuscripts or printed editions. However, the payments made for the elaborate covers of the books in the royal collection indicate that they were regarded as precious objects and were probably illuminated manuscripts of the finest quality. For example, in 1538, one of James V's books was covered with purple velvet and kept in a pouch decorated with cloth of gold, gold embroidery, purple silk ribbons and lined with crimson satin; whilst, in 1539, the king's matins book was given a green velvet cover and gold clasps, and a green velvet pouch lined with red damask and embroidered with gold. This matins book was a gift from the royal secretary, Sir Thomas Erskine of Brechin, who had studied at the university of Pavia and travelled extensively on diplomatic missions, giving him ample opportunity to obtain a fine royal present from the Continent.[2] Meanwhile, the 1542 inventory of the parson of Stobo, whom we met in the previous chapter, reveals that his private oratory contained an illuminated parchment missal (mass book) sitting on a cushion of cloth of silver on the altar, and a personal prayer book (a book of Hours) covered in green velvet and sitting on a velvet cushion on his prayer desk. His desk also held books of law, theology and 'science', whilst Sir William Hamilton's inventory of 1559 notes 60 books in English (as opposed to Latin), including histories and biblical translations, and a manuscript copy of *Regiam Majestatem*, a guide to Scottish law.[3] Thus we can demonstrate that manuscripts were owned by many people in the upper ranks of society and we may assume that the quality and quantity of illumination reflected the wealth of the patrons.

One example of a fine illuminated manuscript with Scottish provenance is a vellum copy of Virgil's *Bucolics*, *Georgics* and *Aeneid* (EUL) produced in Paris c.1460 for an unidentified Scottish patron. The copyist was 'Florius Infortunatus', the Italian author and scribe, Francesco Florio or Franciscus Florius (c.1428–c.1485) who worked in Paris, Tours and Bruges.[4] The opening page of the *Aeneid* includes a depiction of the royal arms of Scotland, indicating that this book was commissioned for a

Scottish royal owner. The arms are encircled by a chivalric collar, which appears to be the Order of the Broom Pod: a French honorific order recorded c.1380–c.1420, the collar of which is most famously depicted around the necks of Richard II of England and the angels on the Wilton Diptych (NG). The same page includes the mysterious initials P and L joined by lovers' knots. It has been suggested that the book was owned by Eleanor, sister of James II, and that PL stands for *Principissa Leonora*, but the knots imply that P and L were an engaged or married couple: Eleanor's husband was called Sigismund, so she seems an unlikely owner. Conventionally, the man's initial would be placed first and the royal arms are depicted in the male form (a shield and helm) rather than the female form (a lozenge), although royal ladies were sometimes represented by shields.[5] Alternatively, PL might be an abbreviation of a chivalric motto. The motto of the Order of the Broom Pod was *Exaltat Humiles* (He exalts the humble), but the motto of the contemporary Order of the Sword was *Pour Loyauté Maintenir* (To maintain loyalty). Thus, if some adaptation was going on, PL might stand for *Pour Loyauté* and the knot would then be a symbol of fidelity. The Order of the Sword belonged to the Lusignan crusading kings of Cyprus, and King James III was famously enthusiastic about the idea of a crusade, so perhaps the manuscript was his. James was still a child in 1460, but this was also the year of his accession, when he took on the dignity of kingship if not yet the full responsibility, and the book might mark that occasion. However, this is all conjecture and the true identity of the book's Scottish owner remains hidden. The borders of the pages of the manuscript are intricately decorated with twining acanthus leaves, flowers of many varieties,

fruit, birds and animals in beautiful detail. There are also four delightful miniatures, three of which depict idealised landscapes including closely observed agricultural activities (tending goats, keeping bees, harvesting grapes) and the fourth shows the reception of Aeneas by Dido at Carthage. It was certainly a manuscript fit for a king.

The illumination of manuscripts within Scotland was much more of an amateur operation, unable to compete on equal terms with the very sophisticated and specialised European studios. Nevertheless, the monasteries at Culross, Lindores, Kinloss and elsewhere produced attractive manuscripts and some impressive examples of native work exist. Sir Thomas Galbraith was a clerk of the chapel royal at Stirling c.1490–c.1513 and was recorded painting and gilding many items for James IV, including a cover for the great gun, Mons Meg, and banners, standards and shields of arms for tournaments. He was also paid for illuminating books for the king: 'the king's book' in 1506, the king's Gospels in 1508, and the great parchment 'porteous' (a breviary or service book) for the king's chapel in 1512. The only work of his to survive is the marriage contract for James IV and Margaret Tudor and the accompanying Treaty of Perpetual Peace, 1502 (National Archives, Kew). He decorated the documents with the royal arms, the intertwined initials of James and Margaret, and delicately observed depictions of symbolic flowers: roses, thistles and marguerites. His work is not as accomplished as the Flemish and French illuminations of the period, but it is in the same tradition of the Renaissance observation of nature, and of very good quality. Another example of native illumination is the presentation copy of John Bellenden's *Chronicles of Scotland*, written for James V by David Douglas c.1531 (Morgan Library). The man-

ABOVE. James Brown, dean of Aberdeen,
presented to the Virgin and Child by St Ninian
from *Dean Brown's Book of Hours*, 1498.

buskenneth Cartulary (a collection of charters) of
c.1535 (NLS) also has some illuminated pages of
vigorous native workmanship, which display greater
poise in the depiction of the royal and abbatial
arms and an awareness of the Continental fashion
of twined floral decoration.[6]

Probably the majority of the illuminated manuscripts produced in this period were religious
books. There were not large numbers of the official Latin translation of the Bible (the Vulgate) in
circulation, but smaller editions of the Gospels
were common, as were missals, breviaries, psalters
and other liturgical manuscripts. A richly illuminated psalter was made for Robert Blackadder,
archbishop of Glasgow, in France in the late
fifteenth century (NLS). It has delicate patterns of
foliage and birds in the borders, with a distinctive
repeating pattern of halved *fleurs de lys*, and contains many miniatures of Scottish saints such as
Margaret and Ninian. Archbishop Blackadder
himself appears in a portrait praying before the crucified Christ within a landscape that looks much
more French than Scottish. He certainly had a
very international outlook: he visited Rome seven
times from 1471, was a royal envoy at the courts
of England and Spain, and died at sea on a voyage
out of Venice in 1508 on an attempted pilgrimage
to Jerusalem. The only complete Scottish missal to
have survived, along with a prayer book and
psalter, is the *Arbuthnott Missal* (Paisley Library),
made for the church of Arbuthnott in the 1490s.
The manuscript is largely in the Gothic tradition,
but the floral borders owe something to the new
Renaissance style, and amongst the miniatures is
an image of St Ternan, which is said to be a portrait of Archbishop William Scheves and was made
at about the same time as his portrait medal (see
Chapter 3).[7]

uscript is lavishly illuminated with particularly fine
floral borders and decorated capital letters, but
there is also a certain naïvety to elements of the
design. For instance, the unicorn supporters of the
royal arms on the title page are placed off-centre
and in rather awkward positions, although their
smiling features are very endearing. The *Cam-*

The books of Hours (*Horae*) form by far the largest category of surviving manuscripts. These were extremely popular in the late medieval and Renaissance periods and were personal prayer books, often for lay people who wished to include elements of monastic devotions in their daily lives, or for clerics who were travelling away from their mother churches. Their popularity indicates not only rising levels of lay literacy but also a growing desire for a more individual spiritual experience. There is some variation in the precise content of the books, but conventionally they would contain a calendar of the major church feasts, extracts from the Gospels, selected psalms and cycles of prayers. The Hours of the Virgin, the Penitential Psalms and the Office of the Dead were almost always included, but other texts were optional and the books were often customised for important patrons. Amongst the surviving Scottish books of Hours are some very attractive examples. The *Book of Hours of the Virgin and St Ninian* (EUL) was produced in the Low Countries for a Scottish owner in the early sixteenth century and includes some delicate foliate borders and eleven miniatures, including a portrayal of St Ninian himself. Like the *Arbuthnott Missal*, this is a transitional text which has a mixture of Gothic and Renaissance elements in its style.[8] More accomplished is *Dean Brown's Book of Hours* (NLS), produced in the Bruges workshop of Alexander Bening (who was an expatriate Scot) in 1498 for James Brown, dean of Aberdeen. This is a northern Renaissance manuscript of very high quality and the beautifully observed flowers, birds and insects in the borders are typical of the best of the Ghent-Bruges school. Amongst the miniatures is a charming portrait of Dean Brown presented by St Ninian to the Virgin and Child.[9]

The finest and most famous Scottish book of Hours is the *Book of Hours of James IV and Margaret Tudor* (National Library of Austria). Books of Hours were often given as marriage gifts by grooms to their brides and this exquisite volume is generally thought to have been a present from the king to his new wife in 1503. However it has also been suggested that James presented the book to Margaret in 1507 after the birth of their first son.[10] Conclusive documentary evidence for either date is lacking, but the book was clearly commissioned for the royal couple because it includes their portraits at the front and back, and their arms, mottoes and twined initials throughout. It was often the case that children (even the very young or deceased) were depicted as mini-adults kneeling behind their parents in portraits showing the patrons at prayer (sons behind the father, daughters behind the mother), and the absence of an image of a child in this book might strengthen the case for the earlier date. It is usually thought that the artists included Simon Bening (eldest son of Alexander), Gerard Horenbout and the 'Master of James IV' (who might be identified with Horenbout). The portraits, sacred scenes, images of saints and decorated borders are of the finest quality of the Ghent-Bruges school of illumination and full of intriguing details, such as the two onlookers, who peer at James IV from behind a screen. It is a magnificent example of a Renaissance illuminated manuscript.

There were probably even more Flemish and French artists engaged in panel painting than in manuscript illumination, and they were working for a similar market. At this period almost all portable paintings were applied to wooden panels. Some Venetian and Florentine painters started to use canvas c.1500, but it was not in general use

until the late sixteenth century. Again, the documentary record gives us tantalising glimpses of works of art that no longer exist. An altarpiece was imported from Flanders for the abbey of Fearn in the late fifteenth century, whilst an altarpiece imported from Italy for Paisley Abbey in the 1450s was considered 'the stateliest tabernacle that was in all Scotland and the most costly'. Bishop George Brown of Dunkeld imported two Flemish altarpieces in 1505 (one for Dunkeld and one for a church in Dundee) and there were two more at Pluscarden in 1508. In 1505, the chapel royal at Stirling contained a triptych (a three-panelled altarpiece) of the Virgin and Child with two angels playing musical instruments painted by David Pratt, another triptych of the crucifixion with four saints, a single panel showing the image of Christ on St Veronica's veil, and another panel of the Virgin Mary. English, French or Flemish painters, who produced portraits and a picture of St John, are known to have visited the court of James IV; James V is known to have purchased fine Flemish pictures through his agent, John Brown of Leith, and to have owned a 'tabernacle' (altarpiece) of the Virgin Mary and a painting of Adam and Eve. Likewise, Mary of Guise owned a panel painting of the Muses, another of 'grotesques or conceits' and a series of eight panels of the 'doctors of Almaine' (German theologians, presumably of the Catholic rather than Protestant variety). None of these paintings survive.[11]

The finest surviving panel painting of the period is undoubtedly the *Trinity Altarpiece* (NGS). It was painted in 1478–9 by Hugo van der Goes of Bruges for the collegiate church of the Holy Trinity, Edinburgh, which had been founded by Queen Mary of Gueldres in 1460. The painting was probably originally a triptych: a central panel flanked by two hinged 'wings' which were painted on both sides and could be displayed open or closed. The central image is long lost and only the two outer panels have survived, probably because they held royal portraits.[12] When open, James III and Queen Margaret of Denmark are shown kneeling in prayer. James is accompanied by his son and St Andrew, Margaret by St George (or possibly St Canute), and the saints are presenting the king and queen to the lost central image, probably a Virgin and Child. The custom of depicting living patrons in the presence of saints in a realistic setting was characteristic of Flemish Renaissance art and (like the popularity of books of Hours) is connected to the growth of expressions of lay piety known as the *devotio moderna* (modern devotion), which encouraged people to develop a personal relationship with Christ. Hugo van der Goes never met James and Margaret so their portraits were probably taken from sketches, with the king's face possibly overpainted later in Scotland. However, the provost of Trinity College, Edward Bonkil, travelled to Bruges to commission the painting, so his portrait is taken from life and is of a very high quality. He appears when the 'wings' are closed, kneeling in prayer before a representation

OPPOSITE. James IV presented to Christ by St James from the *Book of Hours of James IV and Margaret Tudor*, 1503.

OVERLEAF. Hugo van der Goes, the *Trinity Altarpiece*, 1478–9.
A Renaissance masterpiece made in Bruges for a Scottish royal foundation.

(or a chapel within a church) where they could worship together. In Helsingor, their devotions focused on the altar of St Ninian in the Church of St Olai and the Scots community commissioned an altarpiece for their chapel c.1500. Known as the *Helsingor Altarpiece* (National Museum of Denmark), it is in the northern German, rather than Flemish, Renaissance style. The central panel has three sculpted and painted saints (Ninian flanked by James and Andrew) and the 'wings' have painted panels depicting scenes from the life of St Ninian and images of other saints (Martin, Erasmus, Barbara and John the Evangelist). The elaborate construction and rich decoration provide another indication of how altarpieces in Scotland might have looked at the time. Since Scots merchants often had short-term postings and would return home laden with souvenirs, German, Dutch, French and Scandinavian altarpieces are likely to have appeared in many Scottish churches, particularly those in the burghs of the east coast.[13]

Some rare surviving native panel paintings were made for the church of Foulis Easter, near Dundee, towards the end of the fifteenth century. The panels were once part of an altarpiece and a 'rood screen', which divided the choir from the nave, but were later cut into separate pieces and are now incomplete. They depict the crucifixion, the *pietà* (Mary mourning the dead Christ), the risen Christ, the Holy Trinity and a series of saints and apostles. The anonymous artist was local and employed a very earthy, direct style, which crowds the paintings with detail. This is clearly provincial work, inferior to the panels imported from Flanders but engaging nonetheless, and probably characteristic of the decoration of the lesser churches and chapels of Scotland in the period. However, aspects of the composition, such as the landscape in the back-

Helsingor Altarpiece, c.1500, made by an unknown (probably German) artist for the Scottish community in Helsingor. At some point, the 'wings' have been detached and reassembled in an incorrect position so that they open like a book rather than a door.

of the Holy Trinity: God the Father seated on a throne, holding the broken body of His crucified Son, with a dove representing the Holy Spirit hovering between them. Bonkil is shown in a church setting with two angels playing an organ, whilst the image of the Trinity is represented as an ethereal vision floating in a cloud. The altarpiece is a masterpiece of the northern Renaissance and gives some indication of a lost artistic heritage.

The only Scottish altarpiece to survive intact is in Denmark. There were small colonies of Scottish merchants in many of the major trading centres of northern Europe and the communities would generally have adopted a particular church

Crucifixion scene from the Foulis Easter panels, painted
in the late fifteenth century by an unknown Scottish artist.

ground of the crucifixion scene or the rather exotic
clothes of the onlookers in the same panel, suggest
that the artist had encountered, and taken some
inspiration from, the finer imported works. The
same painter probably produced the ceiling panels
of Guthrie Church (NMS), which depict a crucifixion and a last judgement (Christ sits victori-
ous on a rainbow at the end of the world). The
Guthrie pictures are now very badly faded and
difficult to discern.[14] A panel of St Bartholomew
painted for the altar of the Glovers' Incorpora-
tion at Perth in 1557 (Perth Museum) is also clearly
native work but shows awareness of Renaissance
style in the classical architectural details of the
background and the characterisation of the face
of the saint.[15] There was certainly one native
painter whose work was very accomplished and
sought after: Andrew Bairhum (fl.1538–41). Noth-

ing of his output survives, with the possible exception of a badly damaged mural of St John at Pluscarden Abbey. He was employed for three years
at the Abbey of Kinloss painting panels and murals
and he was clearly valued as 'outstanding in his
craft' because his apparently cantankerous and
violent temperament was tolerated. He is said to
have worked 'in the lighter style of painting which
is now customary throughout Scotland': this may
well have been the Renaissance 'grotesque' style,
which imitated the paintings of ancient Rome and
was very fashionable in Europe by the 1530s.[16]

There is some tantalising evidence of a lost
painting of Lucretia that was once in the collection
of James V and may well have been another masterpiece of the Flemish school. The painting is listed
on a warrant of January 1543 as 'the brod of
Lucres' (the panel of Lucretia) with other panel

OPPOSITE. Master of the Holy Blood of Bruges, *Lucretia*, c.1530.

ABOVE. Sketch of a lady stabbing herself, probably representing Lucretia,
from an account book of the royal household, 1534.

paintings (one of the Virgin Mary and one of Adam and Eve are named but there were others too) belonging to the recently deceased king. The editor of this document, John Harrison, finds it hard to believe that this might have been a depiction of Lucretia, but she was a very popular subject in the Flemish and German Renaissance schools, which were so closely connected with Scotland.[17] She was also conventionally one of the nine female Worthies and thus possibly appears as one of the Stirling Heads and in the 'City of Ladies' tapestries (see Chapter 3). A virtuous aristocratic lady of ancient Rome, Lucretia was raped by a member of the then ruling dynasty, the Tarquins. She made the crime known, exhorted her friends and family to avenge her and then committed suicide by stabbing herself in the heart. The subsequent public outcry led to the fall of the Tarquins and the establishment of a Roman republic. Lucretia was thus regarded as a symbol of chastity, virtue, righteous justice, liberty in defiance of tyranny, and self-sacrificing honour. Despite the Church's condemnation of self-destruction, Lucretia's suicide was sometimes even compared to the self-sacrifice of Christ and

there is one example of her image on a diptych (a two-panelled altarpiece). This piece was by the German painter Lucas Cranach c.1537 and placed Lucretia alongside the Old Testament heroine Judith, who was also one of the female Worthies. Lucretia's image is also to be found in the company of saints Jerome and Mary Magdalene in the Kinneil House murals, discussed below.[18] Paintings of Lucretia at the moment of her death were made by Dürer, Cranach (31 examples), Joos van Cleve and others. A depiction of her suicide from c.1530 is attributed to the Master of the Holy Blood of Bruges (Budapest Museum of Fine Arts). This picture exists in several versions and since it is clear that considerable Scottish artistic patronage was channelled through Bruges, it is quite likely that James V had a copy. Certainly, the clerk who wrote the accounts of the king's spice house in October–November 1534 (NRS) had seen a very similar image, since he drew a sketch of it on his page (alongside a thistle, a rose and a unicorn). The drawing is sometimes said to represent a lady (Queen Margaret has been suggested) playing the bagpipes, but it seems clear to this writer that the 'bag' is actually part of her bodice and the 'pipe' is actually a dagger piercing her breast.[19]

By far the largest numbers of surviving Scottish Renaissance panel paintings are portraits. Even during the iconoclasm of the Reformation, images of royal or noble persons and of ancestors were accorded a lot of respect, which clearly protected the *Trinity Altarpiece* panels, and probably others, from destruction. The spirit of individualism and the cult of fame, already identified as important Renaissance characteristics (see Chapter 1), prompted artists and patrons to desire realistic likenesses. Furthermore, because Protestantism encouraged a very personal and direct relation-

ship with God, great significance was attached to the strength of character and personality of individuals, which artists attempted to capture in paint. Although pre-Reformation portraits of bishops, abbots and other clerics are now quite rare, the new Kirk did not seriously retard the growth of this genre. Thus there is much more continuity in the development of portraiture in Renaissance Scotland than in many of the other arts. Nevertheless, the upheavals of religious and political change, and of warfare, have taken a toll on the portrait record too. Some important portraits from the royal collections, for example, were clearly dispersed during minorities and some went south after 1603, only to be destroyed in the civil wars or sold by Cromwell.[20]

Portraits were frequently used to assist long-distance negotiations for royal and noble marriages. We know that there was a collection of portraits at the court of James IV because a painter called Mynours is recorded arriving there from England in 1502 as part of the arrangements for the king's marriage to Margaret Tudor. Mynours brought portraits of Henry VII, his queen, Elizabeth of York, their heir, Prince Henry (the future Henry VIII) and 'our queen', Princess Margaret. Mynours stayed at the Scottish court for over a year, giving him plenty of time to paint some portraits of James and his family to take back to England. Mynours was probably the Fleming Meynnart Wewick, known in England as Maynard, who later worked with the Florentine sculptor Pietro Torrigiano on the tombs of Henry VII and Lady Margaret Beaufort. None of Mynours' Scottish portraits have survived, but an early portrait of James IV, known to have once belonged to Henry VIII, was copied for Charles I by Daniel Mytens (Private Collection). The Mytens version suggests that the original was

a very accomplished Renaissance masterpiece in the Flemish manner and might have been Mynours' work (see Chapter 1). Alternatively, Mytens might have been copying a picture by Piers, a painter sent to Scotland from Flanders by Andrew Haliburton, conservator of the privileges of the Scottish nation in the Low Countries. Piers worked for James IV between 1505 and 1508, but sadly the financial accounts which list payments for his fees and materials (and indicate that he did a lot of heraldic work) do not record the subjects of any panels he might have painted, with the possible exception of an image of St John in Edinburgh Castle.[21]

Remarkably, sketches of some early Scottish portraits, the originals of which have all been lost, found their way into a French portrait album known as the *Recueil d'Arras* (Médiathèque d'Arras). The collection was drawn by a herald, Jacques le Boucq, in the 1560s, but contains copies of portraits of eminent people of the fourteenth, fifteenth and sixteenth centuries, mainly from the Low Countries and France, but with a few from Germany, Italy, England and Scotland. As far as we know, Le Boucq never travelled to Scotland, but he obviously encountered Scottish portraits on the Continent and copied them. The originals were probably paintings kept at the princely courts visited by the herald. The *Recueil* includes subjects associated with Mynours: Henry VII, Margaret Tudor and James IV, and those from the time of Piers: Alexander Stewart (archbishop of St Andrews), Alexander Haliburton (presumably a relative of Andrew), Bernard Stuart d'Aubigny (a French noble of Scottish descent), Antoine D'Arces de La Bastie (who later became the agent of Regent Albany in Scotland) and other French knights who participated in the celebrated Scottish tournaments

of 1507 and 1508 (see Chapter 8). This group of sketches seems to have been copied from a collection of portraits of the Flemish school of the early sixteenth century and gives a fascinating glimpse of the portraiture which once emanated from the Scottish court.[22]

Even more astonishing is the presence in the *Recueil d'Arras* of a portrait labelled *Jacques Roy descoce* (James, king of Scots). The clothes and hair of the subject suggest a date in the first half of the fifteenth century and the original portrait seems to have been done in the Flemish style of the van Eyck or van der Weyden schools; it was certainly closely observed. The most recent editor of the manuscript identifies the sitter as King James II, but this is not very likely. James II had a bright red birthmark and was known as 'James of the Fiery Face'. The shading in the sketch is delicately done and there is no hint of a facial blemish. However, James I is said to have brought artists and craftsmen to Scotland from England and Flanders, so it is much more likely that the original was a realistic likeness of James I, taken from life in the 1430s. If this were so, the sketch provides us with the earliest extant lifelike portrait of a Scottish monarch and deserves to be much better known. The presence of James I's portrait in le Boucq's collection can probably be explained by the international contacts established through the marriage of his eldest daughter Margaret, to the dauphin (the future Louis XI) in 1436. Tellingly, Margaret's portrait also appears in the *Recueil* alongside her husband, although in a section some distance from her father's image (she is on folio 8 and he is on folio 21) and clearly by a different original artist. The original portraits of Louis and Margaret were perhaps taken from the 'wings' of a French or Flemish triptych of c.1440, since both

Faramÿ Roy deffoca

seem to be in the attitude of prayer and are facing each other. Had le Boucq's album not survived, these extraordinary Scottish Renaissance portraits would be completely unknown.[23]

If James I had employed a Flemish Renaissance portraitist, we might expect his son, James II, to have done something similar, especially after his marriage to a Burgundian princess, Mary of Guel-dres, in 1449. Jacques le Boucq seems not to have encountered any Scottish portraits from this period, but there are pages missing from his manuscript, which might once have contained such images. The only realistic likeness of James II was painted by a German knight, Jörg von Ehingen, who served at the court of the king's sister, Eleanor, arch-duchess of Austria, and visited Scotland in 1458. The manuscript of von Ehingen's diary includes a miniature of James II, which clearly shows the red birthmark on the left side of his face.[24] After the images on the *Trinity Altarpiece*, one of the earliest surviving Scottish panel portraits is of William Elphinstone, bishop of Aberdeen (Marischal Museum), painted c.1500–10 (see Chapter 7). The quality is good, but not of the first order, and the artist was either a minor figure from the Bruges workshops, or a painter in Scotland who had been trained in Flemish traditions and techniques. Lorne Campbell has identified him as Willem Wallinc of Bruges, who worked for Bishop George Brown of Dunkeld between 1506 and 1516.[25] We also know of the existence of two portraits of the princesses Dorothea and Christina of Denmark, which were made in Brussels and sent to James V when he was considering marrying one of them in 1531. It is likely that these lost portraits were of

a similarly high quality to the famous portrait of Christina of Denmark made by Hans Holbein for Henry VIII a few years later (NG).[26]

Three very fine Renaissance portraits were made in France in the 1530s. James V visited the court of Francis I in 1536–7, where he married Princess Madeleine. Whilst there, James and his betrothed both sat for Corneille de Lyon, who produced two small but delicately observed companion portraits, each with the same characteristic green background (NT Polesden Lacey and Château de Versailles). Corneille also painted James's second wife, Mary of Guise (SNPG), in the same style and around the same time, or a little later. All three portraits engage in the intense, almost forensic, scrutiny of the subject for which Corneille was famous, so that James appears determined, Madeleine wistful and Mary shrewd. Corneille was born in The Hague but spent virtually all his career at Lyon and was granted naturalisation after many years of producing fine portraits for the French court. The royal court had an extended stay in and near Lyon in the autumn of 1536, just as James V arrived in France and this provided the opportunity for these exquisite portraits to be made. Corneille's portrait of Mary of Guise was possibly 'the board of the picture of the Queen Regent' retrieved from France for Mary, queen of Scots, in 1563 by Sir Richard Maitland of Lethington, and the Corneille portrait of James was possibly the 'little old picture of King James the Fifth' which was recorded in the inventory of Edinburgh Castle in 1578 (along with portraits of Mary's first husband, Francis II, and the constable of France, Anne de Montmorency). In 1561, Mary, queen of Scots, certainly owned a portrait minia-

OPPOSITE. Jacques le Boucq, sketch of James I
from the *Recueil d'Arras*, 1560s.

95

LEFT. Corneille de Lyon, portrait of James V, 1536.

RIGHT. Corneille de Lyon, portrait of Mary of Guise, c.1538.

François Clouet, portrait of Mary, queen of Scots, at the time of her first marriage to Dauphin Francis, 1558.

ture of her father kept in a gold case (probably a locket) shaped like an apple, now lost.[27]

All the Scottish Renaissance portraits so far considered were painted by artists from the Continent and this trend continued into the later sixteenth century. When Mary, queen of Scots was being brought up in France, naturally she was painted by the court painters, notably François Clouet, who portrayed this celebrated beauty in a rose-pink dress at the time of her first marriage in 1558 (Royal Collection) and in the famous 'white mourning' veil (SNPG), which she wore for an extended period following the deaths of her father-in-law, Henry II, her mother, Mary of Guise, and her first husband, Francis II, in quick succession in 1559–60. A Flemish painter Hans Eworth worked mainly in England from the 1540s to the 1570s, where he was regarded as the successor of Hans Holbein. In 1561, he visited Scotland and painted companion portraits of James Stewart, earl of Moray, and Lady Agnes Keith, on the occasion of their marriage (Private Collection). They are both shown in the most fashionable black clothes, which at that time would not have been considered strange attire for a wedding. Eworth also painted portraits in England of the young Lord Darnley.

A fine pair of portrait miniatures in oils on copper disks was painted in 1566 for the marriage of James Hepburn, 4th earl of Bothwell, to Lady Jean Gordon (SNPG). The artist is unknown but was clearly working in the same Franco-Flem-

ish tradition as Eworth and Clouet, since the pictures are minutely observed and very graceful, with Lady Jean's image the finer of the two. George, 5th Lord Seton, was a loyal supporter of Mary, queen of Scots, and spent much of the 1570s in the Low Countries as her envoy. There he was painted with his children by Frans Pourbus the elder of Antwerp (NGS), and by Adrian Vanson, who depicted him in the splendid garb of master of the queen's household, which office he had held 12 or so years previously (SNPG, see Chapter 8). The tradition of engaging portraitists from Flanders was continued by James VI who employed first Arnold Bronckorst (in the early 1580s) and then Adrian Vanson (c.1584–1602) as court painters. Vanson was made a burgess of Edinburgh on the condition that he would train apprentices, but no pupils of his are known and his own son, Adam de Cologne (who took his mother's name), seems to have received his training in the Low Countries. However, de Cologne returned to work in Scotland in the 1620s, where he developed a style based on the Dutch Baroque tradition of Daniel Mytens and Frans Hals.[28]

Among the long list of portrait painters from the Low Countries and France who worked in Scotland or for Scottish patrons, we know of no native Scottish portrait painters of the Renaissance (Esther Inglis included miniature self-portraits in many of her manuscripts, but she did not paint portrait commissions). Panel portraits were made by Scottish artists, but they are all anonymous and

OPPOSITE LEFT. Hans Eworth, portrait of James Stewart, earl of Moray, 1561–2.
Moray was an illegitimate son of James V and, at this point, his sister's closest adviser.

OPPOSITE RIGHT. Hans Eworth, portrait of Lady Agnes Keith,
1561–2, at the time of her marriage to the earl of Moray.

decidedly inferior to the work of the Continental masters. The native portraits tend to be rather stiff and formulaic, giving a representation of the rank or office of the subject rather than a close likeness: what Dana Bentley-Cranch calls 'effigy-portraits'. There are dozens of examples from the sixteenth century but very few that may be dated any earlier. Among the better quality examples are a portrait of James V from c.1540 (Royal Collection), which is quite recognisable as the man portrayed by Corneille, and the double portrait of Henry Darnley and Queen Mary (NT Hardwick Hall), which was probably painted in Scotland at the time of their marriage in 1565. Here, Mary's face presents a reasonable likeness, but Darnley's image is less successful and the background is an almost medieval black and gold embossed pattern.[29]

Many of the native 'effigy-portraits' were produced to convey specific messages, often as part of a portrait sequence. For example, many of the images of Mary, queen of Scots, which were made after her death, such as the Blairs Museum 'memorial', represent her as a Catholic martyr, almost a saint. Similarly, portraits of James I to James V, but none of Mary, were displayed at James VI's royal entry into Edinburgh in 1579, clearly urging the young king to emulate his male forebears rather than his mother. The university of Edinburgh, founded in 1583 as a new Protestant college, had a whole gallery of portraits of great Reformers. This was probably inspired by Beza's publication of *Icones* (Geneva, 1580): a printed collection of etched portraits, which memorialised the heroes of the European Reformation and was dedicated

to James VI. The university later added to its collection portraits of kings, emperors and other notable figures from history, whose lives presented examples of virtue. The first known native portrait painter was George Jameson who worked in Aberdeen and Edinburgh from about 1620 to his death in 1644. He had been apprenticed to a decorative painter, and it is unclear how he developed his skills in portraiture, but perhaps the competition from Adam de Cologne provided some stimulus. Indeed, he developed a rather restrained version of the Dutch Baroque style, which became very popular with the patrons of the time, and he also continued the tradition of producing portrait sequences. He painted 107 fanciful images of the king's ancestors for the royal entry of Charles I into Edinburgh in 1633, and a series of kings, queens, ancestors and notables for Sir Colin Campbell of Glenorchy a few years later. Jamesone's portrait sequences provided the model for Jacob de Wet's gallery of Scottish monarchs, created for the Palace of Holyroodhouse in the late seventeenth century after its Baroque redevelopment.[30]

The most characteristic genre of native Scottish Renaissance painting was the decoration of interior walls, and especially the ceilings, of the homes of lords, lairds and burgesses. It is likely that the interiors of pre-Reformation churches were also similarly painted, but hardly any examples have survived: there are some badly damaged fragments at Pluscarden (of St John), Dunkeld (of the Judgement of Solomon), and very few other sites. Thus the busy, colourful and inventive schemes which remain in their domestic settings, give another

OPPOSITE. Arnold Bronckorst, portrait of James VI as a boy, 1574. The young king's pose, with a hawk on his left wrist, is reminiscent of the image of his great-grandfather, James IV, as copied by Daniel Mytens (see Chapter 1).

Mural of the Good Samaritan from Kinneil House, painted for Regent Arran c.1553. Here the wounded man lies in distress on the left, as the priest and the Levite ignore him and hurry past.

A nineteenth-century copy of a mid-sixteenth-century design from a
painted ceiling in Mary of Guise's house, Castlehill, Edinburgh.

indication of long-lost ecclesiastical interiors. The artists are usually anonymous and their work generally lacks the refined articulation and polished modelling of the Continental artists, but it also has confidence, vigour and exuberance, which is very attractive and distinctively Scottish. The artists worked in tempera paints (finely ground pigments bound with egg yolk or similar) on dry plaster or wooden panels prepared with a chalk-size ground, which gives a rather grainy, matte finish. The design was usually outlined in black with other colours filled in later: the paints are very susceptible to water damage over time and in some cases the colours have washed out leaving only the black outlines behind. Oil paints were used occasionally but infrequently, and the fresco technique (pigments applied to damp plaster so that they soak into the fabric), which was so prevalent in Italy, was hardly used in Scotland, or indeed northern Europe in general, where the climate was unhelpful.

The earliest surviving examples are the murals in two chambers at Kinneil House, which were painted for Regent Arran c.1553.[31] Arran had visited France with James V in 1536–7 and was later granted the French title, duke of Châtelherault, with an appropriate income and a residence in Paris. His eldest son was brought up at the French court of Henry II from 1548 to 1559 and was also the dedicatee of a 1549 French edition of Andrea Alciato's *Emblemata*, first published in 1531, which started the Renaissance fashion for emblem books; so the family had some credentials as patrons of the arts.[32] There are faint traces of colour in the murals at Kinneil, but essentially only the black outlines remain. The Parable Room tells the story of The Good Samaritan in six sections with three further images of St Jerome, St Mary Magdalene and Lucretia, all within a framework of a painted classical arcade, with a frieze and dado band of scrolled acanthus, grotesques and medallion roundels. The Arbour Room has roundels depicting Samson and Delilah, David and Bathsheba, Abraham and Isaac, and the Temptation of St Anthony, with the arms of Arran and his wife on the vaulted ceiling, and extensive foliage tendrils, birds and beasts connecting the design. These remarkable murals at Kinneil, which display such familiarity with Renaissance design, had been plastered over and were only rediscovered during demolition in 1936, following which they were conserved, but many others from the period have certainly been lost. For instance, it is thought that painted mural and ceiling decoration in a style which also included foliage, scrollwork, arabesques, grotesques, medallions, emblems, and heraldry had once graced Mary of Guise's palace on Castlehill, Edinburgh.[33] The building was demolished in the nineteenth century, but some drawings were made of the painted ceilings and afford a glimpse of another sumptuous and colourful scheme now lost.

Several royal sites also contain painted decoration which survives from the early seventeenth century and where we do know the names of some of the painters. The homecoming of James VI in 1617 resulted in his birthplace in Edinburgh Castle being decorated as a kind of shrine by John Anderson, whilst Matthew Goodrick of London probably painted the splendid *grisaille* (grey and white) frieze in the royal bedchamber at Holyrood, which is full of Renaissance motifs such as cornucopias (horns of plenty), although it might possibly be work from an earlier generation. Similarly, Charles I's homecoming of 1633 resulted in the ceiling of the chapel at Falkland Palace being anonymously repainted, whilst Valentine Jenkin was paid for an extensive programme of repainting throughout

Mural in the chapel royal, Stirling Castle, originally painted in 1594 and
repainted by Valentine Jenkin in 1629. The royal cipher of King James VI appears
with the Honours of Scotland either side of the *trompe l'oeil* window.

Stirling Castle in 1628–9 in anticipation of the king's return. Jenkin's heavily restored work survives only in the chapel royal, where he was instructed to do his new paintwork 'in the form it was before', which explains why he used the initials of the old king, I6R for Iacobus 6 Rex (King James VI), rather than those of the new King Charles.[34] These initials are sometimes said to represent CIR (Carolus I Rex), but no monarch is ever accorded the numerical style of 'the first' until a second one of the same name appears (Queen Victoria the first?). It is clear to this writer that the supposed roman letter 'C' is actually an arabic numeral '6'; indeed, the Scottish kings rou-

tinely used arabic, rather than roman, numerals in their ciphers. Thus the murals in the chapel royal probably preserve the scheme originally designed for the baptism of Prince Henry in 1594 (see Chapter 8), including images of the Honours of Scotland, scrollwork, strapwork and *trompe l'oeil* features (optical illusions).[35]

There are over a hundred examples of painted ceilings from the period c.1550–c.1640 which survive across Scotland and, since there have been the inevitable losses over the years, it rather looks as if this form of decoration was extremely common in the homes of the increasingly educated and urbane merchant, professional and landowning classes. We know virtually nothing of the artists, but the patrons were clearly cultivated and sophisticated people who kept up with Continental fashions. Michael Bath has demonstrated that European books of emblems, patterns, and designs imitating the antique were copied and adapted extensively in these painted ceilings, which are so characteristic of the Scottish Renaissance.[36] The schemes include images of genealogy, heraldry, piety, classical myths, allegory, and fable, with considerable stress on moral and philosophical symbolism, and often include verses, proverbs and mottoes. The styles range from the arabesque and grotesque decoration of the High Renaissance, through the strains of Mannerism, into the ornate embellishment of the Baroque. One of the finest grotesque designs was painted on a board-and-beam ceiling at Prestongrange for Mark Kerr, commendator of Newbattle, in 1581, and is now at Merchiston Tower, Edinburgh. Many of the motifs are copied directly from Hans Vredeman de Vries, *Grottesco: in diver-*

sche manieren (Antwerp, c.1565–71), but other sources include prints by Cornelis Bos and Richard Breton's *Les Songes Drolatiques de Pantagruel* (Paris, 1565), which was then thought to be a posthumously published work by Rabelais. The figures are painted in *grisaille* on a bold red background: a colour which was particularly associated with ancient Roman paintings. The design includes birds, beasts, plants and human images all rolling out along the bands between the ceiling beams in a continuous metamorphosis, which Bath has identified as a 'dreamwork', as defined by Dürer: that is, a design which mixes together elements which bear no rational connection or explanation, a pattern 'without rhyme or reason'.[37]

However, it was more common for the painted ceilings to include figures and designs which did represent values, ideas, morals, or stories. Scenes from classical myths (such as the Siege of Troy which was once at Cullen House) or the Bible (such as Abraham and Isaac from Dean House, now NMS) were popular and often took their inspiration from European prints. So too did symbolic or allegorical groupings such as the four seasons, the five senses, the twelve signs of the zodiac, or the seven planetary deities (Saturn, Jupiter, Mars, Venus, Mercury, Sun and Moon), which were seen sculpted on the walls of Stirling Palace and of the garden at Edzell in Chapter 2. The most extensive painted scheme of this type is at Crathes Castle, Aberdeenshire, built for Sir Alexander Burnett of Leys between 1553 and 1596 in the castellated style with Renaissance interiors. Here there is a ceiling of the Nine Worthies and one of the Virtues and Muses, amongst other designs of

OPPOSITE. The grotesque designs of the ceiling painted for Mark Kerr at Prestongrange House, 1581, now at Merchiston Tower, Edinburgh.

c.1599.[38] The Nine Worthies have already been considered in the discussion of the Stirling Heads in Chapter 3 and at Crathes they are depicted as full-length figures in modern armour accompanied by their shields of arms and verse inscriptions extolling their achievements. Charlemagne is given particular prominence since he is claimed to be the founder of the 'auld alliance' between France and Scotland. This ceiling has a very masculine mood, but there is no corresponding depiction of the female Worthies at Crathes. Instead, the room decorated for the lady of the house, Katherine Gordon, portrays the Virtues and the Muses, who are shown as female figures (see page ii). Traditionally there were three Theological Virtues (Faith, Hope and Charity) and four Cardinal Virtues (Temperance, Prudence, Fortitude and Justice) and they each had conventional symbols or attributes (Hope with an anchor, Justice with a sword and scales, etc.). Sometimes the seven Virtues were depicted overcoming the seven Deadly Sins, but at Crathes they are accompanied by the figure of Fame and the nine Muses, who spread the fame of the Virtues through their creative talents: Calliope (epic verse), Clio (history), Euterpe (lyric verse), Thalia (comedy), Melpomene (tragedy), Terpsichore (dance), Erato (love poetry), Polyhymnia (sacred music), and Urania (astronomy). The Crathes ceilings are a colourful, vibrant and distinctive interpretation of Renaissance designs.

The most intellectual painted scheme was devised for, and probably by, Alexander Seton, first earl of Dunfermline and chancellor of Scotland, in the long gallery at Pinkie House in 1613. Seton had been given a thoroughly classical education by Jesuits in Rome and was a lifelong exponent of the classical languages and humanities as well as being a great architectural patron (see Chapter 2).

He was a closet Catholic but made a public show of conforming to the Presbyterian Kirk, which allowed him to retain the king's favour and hold high office.[39] Seton was a great exponent of Neostoicism, a philosophy which adapted ancient Athenian ideas to the Christian context of his time. Neostoicism advocated subduing the passions in order to submit to God's will: it favoured peace over war, modesty over grandeur, restraint over exuberance, contemplation over action.[40] The pagan Stoic philosophy took its name from the *stoa poikile*, or painted gallery, in Athens where learned discussions would take place aided by visual imagery, and Seton's painted gallery at Pinkie seems to have been a conscious attempt to recreate this ancient Greek environment. The boarded and vaulted ceiling is divided into sections by a painted *trompe l'oeil* arcade and within the arches are emblematic scenes with Latin and Greek inscriptions. Many of the scenes illustrate mottoes or witty sayings from the poetry of Horace copied or adapted from Otto van Veen, *Emblemata Horatiana* (Antwerp, 1607), which stress the value of moderation in all things. One panel shows a wise man taking a small drink from a fountain, whilst a greedy man attempts to take a large drink from a river and is swept away (motto: *nihil amplius opto*, I choose nothing more), and includes Seton's portrait on the face of the wise and moderate man. The gallery is centred on a breathtaking three-tiered octagonal *trompe l'oeil* cupola (see Chapter 9), viewed from the inside, populated with *putti*, and providing glimpses of the sky beyond, which was copied from a mathematical diagram in Hans Vredeman de Vries, *Perspectiva* (Antwerp, 1604–5). Thus this remarkable collection of 'speaking pictures', which are testimony to Seton's 'conspicuous modesty', has a spectacular climax, which is anything but modest.[41]

The ceiling of the Nine Worthies at Crathes Castle, Aberdeenshire,
painted for Sir Alexander Burnett of Leys c.1599.

Thanks to the research carried out in the last 20 to 30 years, it is now possible to challenge the prejudices and assumptions which used to be voiced about Scottish art in the Renaissance. It was once held to be self-evident that there was no Renaissance in Scotland, but no longer. The destruction wrought by the Reformation clearly took its toll and the patronage of the Church in the fine arts was withdrawn after 1560. The deposition of Mary in 1567 certainly broke the 'auld alliance' which had allowed the arts and artists of France to exert such a powerful influence in Scotland. The departure of the royal court after 1603 removed another major source of artistic patronage as well as many prized pieces from the Scottish royal collection. Nevertheless, both the remarkable surviving works and the documentary traces of lost works demonstrate that the Scottish fine arts drew on European influences and developments to a considerable degree and were much more creative, vibrant and up-to date than used to be thought. The *Book of Hours of James IV and Margaret Tudor*, the *Trinity Altarpiece* and the Corneille portraits, for instance, are examples of the highest quality of northern Renaissance art. The patrons and artists of the period were sometimes hampered by Scotland's relative lack of wealth but they were cosmopolitan in their outlook, sophisticated in their tastes and cultivated in their understanding.

5

MIGHTY FOES

Renaissance Warfare

Although it is well known that, to take just one instance, Leonardo da Vinci trained as a military engineer and spent much of his career designing weapons and fortifications, the 'military revolution' of Renaissance Europe (some scholars argue more for 'evolution') is often given much less attention than developments in the arts.[1] However, for the princes of the age the development of ships, fortifications, artillery and other aspects of military technology were of the utmost importance. The Scottish Crown was not wealthy enough to engage in some key developments of the period such as the employment of professional mercenary forces or the creation of a standing army funded by regular taxation. However, an overwhelming dominance in the possession and deployment of the latest weaponry was vital to subdue rebellious or lawless magnates, to enforce the regal claim to be the source of all justice and the guarantor of peace and prosperity within the realm, to defend the kingdom from foreign threats and to uphold the prestige of the sovereign and the state. We have already seen that the Stewart monarchs had great ambitions to dominate their magnates and ensure

that the nobles were servants of the Crown rather than rivals to it; that they focused strongly on the imperial theme of the king as 'emperor in his own kingdom'; that they stressed their descent from Robert Bruce to emphasise their credentials as the guardians of Scottish independence; and that they wished to claim parity in dignity, if not in wealth, with other princes (see Chapter 1). Although the resources of the Scottish monarchs were small in comparison with other powers, the great expense of purchasing the finest and most up-to-date ships, castles and guns meant that the Stewart kings could generally (although not invariably) overpower their magnates, and a grand display of naval or ballistic force was often helpful in convincing foreign ambassadors of the value of a Scottish alliance or the danger of Scottish enmity.

One of the problems in tracing Scottish military developments in the fifteenth century is the scarcity of useful documentary sources. Crown expenditure on ships, artillery and fortifications was mainly recorded in the *Treasurer's Accounts* and these have been lost for the period before the reign of James IV, with the exception of one year of

James III's reign, 1473–4. It is from the accounts of this year that we discover that James III had established a foundry to manufacture guns at the Blackfriars in Edinburgh, and if the other records of his reign and of earlier times had survived, we would certainly know much more.[2] From the 1490s onwards the records are quite full, although there are still some significant gaps. Similarly, the accounts of the masters of works, who were often engaged in military constructions, do not begin until 1529. Absence of evidence does not necessarily equate to evidence of absence, but reconstructing the lost world of early military activity is extremely difficult. Nevertheless, there are some indications that the Scots were keeping up with some European trends in this as in other fields.

Ships were not in themselves a novelty in fifteenth- and sixteenth-century Scotland: small craft had traversed the navigable rivers, and fishing vessels gathered the harvest of the seas, for centuries. In the Western and Northern Isles the galleys or birlinns, as successors of the Viking ships, used the sea routes as major highways. The coastal burghs had merchant vessels which were long accustomed to crossing the North Sea, the Baltic, and the west coast of Ireland down to the Bay of Biscay, although the route through the English Channel was often closed to Scottish ships in times of war. Likewise, merchant ships from France, the Low Countries and Scandinavia frequently arrived in Scottish ports. Much of this medieval seafaring tradition continued unchanged into the Renaissance period. The really significant new developments came in the design and use of warships. During the fifteenth century there was something of a naval arms race when European monarchs competed to own the biggest ships capable of overpowering smaller vessels in a close engagement. By the sixteenth century the emphasis shifted from size to firepower, as ships were adapted to carry new forms of ordnance which allowed them to blast enemies out of the water at a distance without taking the risk of grappling at close quarters. At either stage the princes were concerned to protect their native shipping from piracy, to intimidate hostile powers, to impress allies, and to assert control over their coastal waters. For the newly emerging imperial powers of Spain and Portugal (and by the late sixteenth century, England, France and the Netherlands) naval power was also essential to safeguard the routes to their colonies in the Americas and the East Indies.

James I had learned the craft of kingship during his captivity (1406–24) by observing the conduct of the English, French and Burgundian rulers. Henry V of England had an early royal navy (the *Jesus*, *Trinity Royal* and *Holigost* are recorded as royal ships) and was one of the first monarchs to build an outsized warship as a matter of prestige. Following his victory at Agincourt in 1415, a great new ship, *Grâce Dieu*, was built in Southampton between 1416 and 1418, and was intended to safeguard the vital Channel crossing.[3] It was a clinker-built monster of about 1,500 tons and its remains now lie in the mud of the River Hamble, where it sank after a fire in 1439. Clinker-built ships had hulls constructed of overlapping planks, giving a stepped profile. This was the standard medieval technique of boat-building and resulted in a very strong hull, provided it was not pierced. Cutting gunports into a clinker-built vessel compromised the hull and so ships of this sort carried only a few, quite small guns which sat on the main deck and were fired over the gunwale (parapet). The *Grâce Dieu* was also provided with lofty fore and sterncastles (timber fortifications) manned by

longbowmen, and pikemen who would fight at close quarters. When he returned to Scotland, James I clearly did not have the financial resources to match the English and French kings, but he made a great effort to present himself as a monarch of European stature as far as he was able. He created a shipyard at Leith where, towards the end of his reign, a 'great barge' and a 'little ship for the queen' were built. These sound like royal yachts for ceremonial display rather than warfare. However, James launched a raid on the Western Isles in 1429 and royal warships might well have been used for that campaign, although it was also common practice for kings to hire merchant vessels and arm them for military service.[4]

In the mid-fifteenth century the grandest Scottish ship on record belonged not to a king but to a prelate. James Kennedy, bishop of St Andrews, was a grandson of King Robert III, a councillor to James II, and a guardian of James III in his minority. He founded St Salvator's College at St Andrews in 1450, created a magnificent tomb for himself in the late-Gothic style in the college chapel, and was a regular traveller abroad. He studied at the university of Louvain, made the pilgrimage to Rome for the papal jubilee of 1450 and often visited France and Flanders. His ship, the *Salvator*, was large at about 500 tons, was said to have cost him £10,000, and was considered a marvel of the age. A few years after his death it was wrecked off the coast of Northumberland and we cannot say exactly what form it took or how it might have been armed, but it regularly crossed the North Sea and the Baltic and seems to have been strong enough to deter pirate attacks. A document which noted the presence of the *Salvator* at the port of Sluys in 1457 also recorded other Scottish ships alongside vessels of other nations: a carvel of 140

tons owned by the bishop of Aberdeen, a barge of 150 tons under Bartholomew Buton and a 350-ton barge captained by Robert Barton. These references indicate that Scottish ships were firmly engaged with Continental trade and that the king had a choice of large vessels he could hire in times of need. Two other famous ships of the period, the *Yellow Carvel* and the *Flower*, were captained by James III's loyal servant, Andrew Wood of Largo, but might have been royal vessels. However, Scottish ships still struggled to hold their own against English depredations or occasional acts of piracy by Danes or Portuguese. It was common for ships and their cargoes to be captured and ransomed, and the English sometimes raided coastal settlements in Lothian and the Firth of Forth, such as the attack on Leith, Kinghorn, Pittenweem and Blackness in 1481. On the other hand, Scottish captains such as the Bartons of Leith also preyed on foreign vessels, sometimes licensed by royal letters of reprisal or letters of marque, and sometimes not.[5]

By the end of the fifteenth century clinker-built hulls were increasingly giving way to carvels, which were built with planks attached edge to edge in a smooth profile. It thus became possible to cut gun-ports into these hulls so that artillery could be installed at several levels. The heaviest guns still required big ships but firepower and manoeuvrability gradually took priority over size *per se*. It has already been shown how James IV became a more active patron of Renaissance arts and architecture after his marriage of 1503, and his naval programme also expanded hugely in the last decade of his reign, to the extent that Norman Macdougall considers it a 'royal obsession'. Macdougall also stresses that the navy was built with the help of French master shipwrights, using timber imported

A model of the *Yellow Carvel*, a late-fifteenth-century ship,
captained by Andrew Wood of Largo in the service of James III.

from France (and Norway) and that it provided James with closer ties to the French king as an alternative and balancing strategy to the 1502 Treaty of Perpetual Peace with England.[6] At its height, annual expenditure on ships reached about a third of the royal income, with the total bill for the reign amounting to around £100,000. James had clearly identified the navy as a matter of personal interest and royal prestige, and a shift of emphasis from the west coast to the east might also

indicate concern with his international status. Royal shipbuilding was still undertaken at Dumbarton as late as 1507, but much more investment now went into the Forth dockyards at Leith, a new dock at Pool of Airth, and at Newhaven which, as its name suggests, was also a new dockyard created especially for the construction of the royal flagship, the *Michael*. During the course of his reign, James IV created a fleet of some 38 ships. The great ships at the core were the *Margaret* (a four-master of about 600 tons launched in 1506), the *Treasurer* (built for the king in Brittany but wrecked off the English coast in 1507) and the *James* (purchased in 1511). The *Margaret* was such an impressive ship that Henry VIII felt compelled to build something similar: the *Mary Rose*, launched in 1511 and named after Margaret and Henry Tudor's sister. However, the pride of the Scottish fleet was undoubtedly the *Michael*, named after the archangel who was one of the patron saints of the royal Stewarts.

The *Michael* was later described by an enthusiastic chronicler as 'the greatest ship and the strongest that ever sailed in England or France'.[7] This was something of an exaggeration, but at about 1,000 tons she was probably the largest vessel of her day, was specifically designed to carry the latest artillery, and represented an extraordinary boost to the prestige of the realm. Henry VIII was so jealous, he ordered an equivalent ship of his own: the *Henri Grâce à Dieu* was built between 1512 and 1514 and was variously reported as 1,000 tons or 1,500 tons with many heavy guns. The *Michael* cost James about £30,000, carried a crew of about 300 men, and was armed with 24 bronze cannon, 3 great 'basilisks' (heavy bronze cannon) and probably 300 pieces of small arms. She was launched in 1511 and fully fitted for service by 1512. In the summer of 1513, as Henry VIII launched an invasion of France, a plan was hatched for the Scottish fleet, led by the *Michael*, to sail north out of the Forth, through the Pentland Firth, and down the west coast of Ireland to join with the French fleet in harrying English shipping in their vital cross-Channel supply routes. Perhaps the *Michael* and the other ships might have proved themselves effective in battle had they been given the chance. Unfortunately, the earl of Arran, as admiral, broke his journey with a futile siege of Carrickfergus and bad weather also delayed progress. The Scottish fleet thus arrived in France in mid-September, too late to disrupt the main thrust of the English campaign and just in time to hear the news of the disaster at Flodden.[8] In 1514, the *Michael* was sold to the king of France for only £18,000. Renamed *La Grande Nef d'Ecosse* (the Great Ship of Scotland), she probably continued to serve in the French fleet for some years afterwards, although the evidence is patchy. The *Margaret* and the *James* returned to Scotland and were back in Dumbarton by 1515, but James IV's expensive and impressive fleet was quickly sold, dispersed or otherwise lost during his son's minority.

When James V started to rule in his own right in 1528, he seems to have possessed no ships of his own but hired vessels from Scottish captains when necessary. Once James had established himself as master of the realm by about 1532, he certainly began to take an interest in recreating a royal fleet like his father's. In 1533, he was presented with two ships captured from the English during hostilities: the *Mary Willoughby* was taken by Hector Maclean of Duart from the Isle of Man and the *Lion* was captured by one of the king's captains, Robert Fogo. It is not quite clear if the latter

A model of the *Michael*, launched in 1511 as the flagship of
James IV's navy and one of the greatest ships of the age.

ship joined the royal fleet or operated as a privateer (i.e. a privately owned ship licensed to take
action against enemy ships, including the capture
of prizes). *Mary Willoughby* was named after one
of Katherine of Aragon's ladies and the *Lion* after
the English royal heraldic beast: both ships had
been recorded in English navy lists of 1522 as
about 150 tons each.[9] In the summer of 1536,

James set sail on his first major voyage, leaving Pittenweem on 23 July heading north, through the Pentland Firth and back down the west coast landing at Whithorn on 4 August. We don't know which ships took part in this expedition, but the leading captains were all involved including Robert Barton of Overbarnton, Andrew Wood of Largo and Wood's brothers, John and Robert. The trip was a swift one and James was obviously not engaged in any major policing of the Highlands and Islands at this stage. He seems to have been making friendly visits to outlying locations, reviewing the extent of his territories ('beating the bounds' of his realm in Roger Mason's phrase) and perhaps was using the voyage as a test run for his next venture, which was a trip to France in pursuit of a marriage alliance. English spies were confused and reported that James had been intending to visit France by the westerly route and had been foiled in the attempt.[10]

James set sail again from Kirkcaldy on 1 September 1536 and landed at Dieppe eight days later. He spent the next eight months as the honoured guest of King Francis I, whose daughter he married on 1 January 1537. The *Mary Willoughby* and the *Lion* were part of the king's outward fleet and were accompanied by other ships hired from Scottish captains such as Thomas Richardson, Patrick Barcar and John Lawson. As soon as he landed, James sent two men to purchase a new ship for him and by October the *Moriset* or *Morischer* had joined the Scottish royal navy. Francis I later decided to cover all of his guest's expenses so the purchase became a gift alongside another present, the *Salamander* of about 300 tons (named after Francis's personal badge), which had been built at Honfleur and entered Scottish service by March 1537. By 1538, the king was building new

ships in Leith using timber from Lochaber. They are described in the accounts as 'galleys' or 'row boats', but they were also provided with sails so were technically galleasses, which could use either oars or sails as conditions dictated. Perhaps James was inspired by his visit to the Western Isles in 1536, for galleys were the mainstay of Gaelic seafaring, or more likely he was emulating the French fleet which also relied heavily on such vessels: two French galleys, *Perforce* and *Monsieur de Roy* had escorted the king and the new queen on their return to Scotland in May 1537. It is likely that both the *Moriset* and *Salamander* were also galleasses and provided the models for the native-built ships. In July 1539, the *Great Unicorn* of about 250 tons was launched, followed by the *Little Unicorn* in August. The *Little Unicorn* was provided with richly carved cabins for the king and queen, her masts, sails and oars were painted and gilded with arms and 'faces' and she had many colourful banners, flags and pennants, so she seems to have been intended as a royal yacht, as well as having military uses. In 1541, another royal ship appears in the records: the *Little Forfar*, which implies that there must have been a *Great Forfar* in service too.[11]

In June 1540, James V made his second major voyage to the Western and Northern Isles, shortly after the birth of his short-lived son and heir, Prince James, at St Andrews. The king was at sea between 12 June and 6 July and again his route took him from Fife north to Orkney, then down the west coast, calling at Lewis, Skye and other islands and peninsulas before landing at Dumbarton. James was keen to secure the obedience of the clan chiefs and took hostages or pledges (usually sons and heirs) who were subsequently detained in honourable captivity in Dunbar, Tantallon and the

Bass. This policy secured the payment of Crown revenues for the rest of the reign; a matter of some importance since the newly crowned queen, Mary of Guise, had the earldoms of Orkney and Ross and the lordships of Ardmeanach and the Isles (amongst other lands) as part of her jointure (marriage portion), whilst the newly baptised prince was duke of Rothesay, amongst other titles. To be sure of imposing his will on the clans, James travelled with a substantial and impressive fleet which included the *Lion*, *Great Unicorn*, *Little Unicorn*, *Salamander*, *Mary Willoughby* and a dozen other ships, all armed with the latest artillery. According to English accounts, his party numbered over 2,000 men, including the great magnates of the region: the earls of Argyll, Huntly, Arran, Atholl, Erroll, Cassillis and the Earl Marischal, as well as Lord Maxwell (lord admiral), the Master of Glencairn, and Cardinal Beaton. It was customary for naval commanders to use whistles to issue orders whilst at sea and James was provided with a gold whistle on a long chain for this voyage, whilst the 'patron' of the king's ships had a silver whistle and chain. Both James IV and Henry VIII before him are also known to have carried golden whistles when at sea.[12]

James V was so interested in naval matters that he commissioned the first rudimentary navigational manual for the Scottish coastline, which was drawn up either on his 1536 voyage or the 1540 expedition. This was a 'rutter' of the Scottish seas (known in France as a *routier*, and in the Mediterranean as a 'portolan'), drawn up by a pilot, Alexander Lindsay, who was probably from Kinghorn. A rutter was a list of instructions for navigating coastal waters by sailing from one headland to the next using basic navigational aids such as compass and lead-line. Rutters included information on tides, currents, winds and soundings, with descriptions of the main landmarks, harbours and dangers to be encountered. Courses were set by compass points and distances calculated very roughly in miles or 'kennings' (which meant about as far as the eye could see). The earliest English rutters and French *routiers* were available in manuscript from the late fifteenth century and in print from the 1520s. Proper charts were not made until the late sixteenth century. Lindsay's rutter describes an entire 'circumnavigation' of the Scottish coast from the mouth of the Humber in the south-east, north to Orkney and back down the west coast to the Solway Firth. It is likely that he drew on earlier local rutters which have since been lost, and Lindsay's original manuscript has not survived either. We know of its existence from English copies made c.1546 to assist the Rough Wooing and a French translation of c.1547 by Nicholas de Nicolay, sieur d'Arfeville and cosmographer to the king of France, published in 1559 and 1583.[13]

After the death of James V in December 1542, the Scottish royal navy again fell into decline and the losses of the Rough Wooing were significant. A major English assault on Scotland was launched in 1544 by the earl of Hertford, who would later become Lord Protector Somerset. In April 1544, the privateer, *Little Martin*, was captured by English ships and in May the *Salamander* and the *Great Unicorn* were captured at Leith, along with several other 'worthy' Scottish ships, and taken into English service. The Scots put up no defence of the pride of James V's fleet and the earl of Bothwell, hereditary admiral, seems to have been guilty of incompetence at best, or collusion at worst.[14] In about 1546, Anthony Anthony, an overseer at the English ordnance office, compiled an illustrated list

NAVIGATION DV ROY D'ESCOSSE

IACQVES CINQVIESME DV NOM,

autour de son Royaume, & Isles Hebrides & Orchades, sous la
conduite d'Alexandre Lyndsay excellent Pilote Escossois.

LE CONTENV EN CETTE NAVIGATION.

Cette Nauigation est diuisée en quatre parties.
La premiere contient le passage depuu le Havre du Lyth, iusques aux principales parties d'Escosse tirant au fleuue Humbre.
La deuxiesme partie, du mesme Havre du Lyth, iusques à Dungesby en Cathnes.
La troisiesme partie, de Dungesby en Cathnes, iusques à la Mule de Kinteir.
Et la quatriesme partie, de la Mule de Kinteir, iusques à la Mule de Gallouvay, & au fleuue de Solvay.

En chacune desdites Nauigations sont declarées cinq choses.

La premiere, est la course de la marée.
La seconde, le temps que la mer entre & sort.
La troisiesme, l'approchement des costes.
La quatriesme, la veue d'vne terre à l'autre.
Et la cinquiesme, les Havres, Raddes, profonditez & dangers.

COVRSES DES FLOTS DE MER DEPVIS LE
Havre du Lyth, iusques aux principales parties d'Escosse,
tirant au fleuue Humbre.

V Havre du Lyth la marée court quand regnent les vents Sud-Sud-Oest, & Nort-Nort-Est.
De la pointe Sainte Ebbes iusques au fleuue Humbre deux mille loing de terre, la matée court, Oest Sud-Oest, & Est Sud-Est: & sept mille loing de terre elle court de l'Est à l'Oest.

Entrées & sorties de Mer, depuis le Havre du Lyth iusques au fleuue Humbre.

Du petit Lyth à la pointe Sainte Ebbes, quand la Lune est au Sud vn quart au Sud-Oest, il y est pleine Mer.
De Bambourg iusques à la pointe de Flambourg la Lune estant au Sud vn quart à l'Oest, il est pleine Mer.
De Flambourg iusques au fleuue Humbre, la Lune estant à l'Est & Oest il est pleine Mer.

Courses depuis le Havre du Lyth iusques au fleuue Humbre.

Tirant au Nort entre le Lyth & Kingorne iusques à Basse, faut aller du Nort quart à l'Est, & du Sud quart à l'Oest.
De Basse iusques à la pointe Sainte Ebbes, Est Sud-Est, & Oest Nort-Oest.
La pointe Sainte Ebbes & la sainte Isle, gisent Sud quart à l'Est, & Nort quart à l'Oest.
La course de la sainte Isle passage iusques à ce que l'on a passé le lieu nommé Plux, & le lieu appellé Suagmonde, sera Sud Sud-est. Et quand vous serez droit dedans le canal entre le Plux & Gouldestone, qui signifie Pierre dorée, le Chasteau de Bambourg sera de vous au Sud Sud-Oest.
De Suagmonde par le canal, entre Byndelnes & Ferne Illande, la course sera Sud-Est, & quelquefois du Sud vn quarre à l'Est.
Byndelnes & Houthlisith, gisent Sud-est, vn quart au Sud, & Nort-Oest, vn quart au Nort.
De la pointe Sainte Ebbes, pour fuit le danger d'Staples, la course sera Est Sud-Est.

Ppp

---

of all the ships in Henry VIII's navy. Amongst the 58 ships listed on the *Anthony Roll* are pictures of both the *Salamander* and the *Unicorn*, each with a distinctive figurehead, and described as galleasses of about 300 tons. The *Unicorn* was sold in 1555, but the *Salamander* was part of the fleet which supported the next major English attack, the Pinkie campaign of 1547, and continued in English service possibly until 1574. The Scottish navy was so depleted by 1547 that it required a fleet of French galleys under the Italian commander Leon Strozzi to break the siege of St Andrews and take the murderers of Cardinal Beaton and their supporters (including a young John Knox) into servitude at the oars. In that same year, the *Lion* was sunk in a skirmish off Dover, and the *Mary Willoughby* was taken off Blackness (again unopposed) and returned to service in the English navy. In the Blackness action seven other Scottish ships were captured or burned and six more were burned at Leith a few days later. Thus within five years of the death of James V all the great ships of his navy, and many smaller vessels, had been lost. Only the *Little Unicorn* was still in Scottish hands by 1550.[15]

In 1559, Henry II of France was killed in a jousting accident and in 1560 Mary of Guise died. The Scots then completely reversed their foreign and religious policy. The anti-Catholic, anti-French, pro-Protestant, pro-English Lords of the Congregation took control of the Scottish government and an English fleet was now used to support the Scottish authorities in driving out French troops. Thus, the Anglo-Scottish wars ended and the need for a Scottish royal navy was significantly reduced:

Title page of Nicholas de Nicolay's *Navigation du Roy d'Ecosse*, published in Paris in 1583, as a translation of a Scottish text of 1536 or 1540.

piracy and reprisals were still issues, but naval warfare was not, since the old enemy had become a (somewhat uneasy) new ally. During the personal reigns of Mary and James VI the Scottish Crown had many ways of projecting its dignity and power, but the creation and maintenance of an impressive royal navy was no longer one of them. Both Mary and her son focused strongly on their claims to the English succession, so the traditional stance of naval opposition to English ships was not deemed appropriate. Only after the Union of the Crowns in 1603 did James VI take an interest in naval matters. He wished to create a united British fleet flying the Union flag, but in the end the Lord High Admiral of Scotland continued to exercise authority, albeit in cooperation with the ships of the (English-based) Royal Navy. The ships available to the Scottish admiral by this time seem to have been hired merchant vessels, although the Scottish Crown seems to have owned one ship called the *Charles* between 1614 and 1621. There was no attempt to revive the glory days of the *Michael* and the *Salamander*.[16]

The naval policy of James IV and James V was aimed primarily at the prestige of the Crown and the defence of the realm from English seaborne attacks. Both objectives were also served by the creation of a sequence of modern coastal fortifications, especially in the strategically important Firth of Forth. The loss of Berwick to the English for the final time in 1482 meant that English ships had a secure base from which to launch naval raids on Scotland so coastal defences needed urgent improvements. Between 1497 and 1501, the medieval castle of Dunbar underwent a programme of repairs and modifications under a new keeper, Sir Andrew Wood, who was also one of the most experienced Scottish naval captains and therefore

Fortifications at Ravenscraig Castle, built for Mary of Gueldres in the 1460s and completed in the 1470s for the earl of Caithness.

very well suited to the task. Wood had already contributed to the Forth defences by building his own fortified base on the Fife coast at Largo. The Largo fort received a retrospective royal licence in 1491, and in the same year James IV granted the small rocky island of Inchgarvie to John Dundas and his heirs with instructions to build a fort there. Inchgarvie lies where the Forth narrows at Queensferry so the site was well chosen to defend the settlements upstream from that point. The Inchgarvie fortress seems to have been completed by about 1516 with funds from the royal treasury and between 1515 and 1523, the defences at Dunbar were strengthened by Regent Albany. English reports suggested that the new works made Dunbar impregnable. James V also made improvements to the fortifications at Blackness and Kinghorn, and founded a new harbour and royal burgh at Burntisland in 1541. The new harbour was protected by three blockhouses well supplied with guns and was able to accommodate the great ships of James's navy, as English spies reported to their master. However, it is fair to say that the chain of Forth forts pales into insignificance in comparison with the extensive English coastal defences constructed for Henry VIII from 1538 when he was expecting a Franco-Imperial invasion.[17]

The design of fortifications in this period responded rapidly to developments in artillery. In the late fifteenth century, as heavy field guns were increasingly deployed in siege warfare, castles were provided with massively thick stone walls to withstand bombardment, and extensive outer ditches and earthworks to keep attacking artillery out of range. Gradually, the possibilities of using artillery mounted on platforms at parapets and casemates were also developed. One of the earliest and most impressive Scottish castles built to both utilise and withstand artillery fire was at Ravenscraig near Dysart. It was built for Queen Mary of Gueldres between 1460 and her death in 1463 and completed by William Sinclair, earl of Caithness, in the 1470s. The castle is naturally defended from the sea by rocky cliffs and so the fortifications are all focused on the landward side. The first line of defence is a deep ditch, behind which are two massive towers with walls more than 4 metres thick. Between the towers is a gatehouse range supporting an artillery platform from which to return fire. The castle has the earliest Scottish examples of inverted key-hole gunholes, which later became a standard feature of Renaissance fortifications, and were sometimes modified into a dumbbell shape.[18] At Dunbar, the new blockhouse built for Regent Albany c.1520 also had massively thick walls (over 6 metres in places) and included a new wide-mouthed style of gunport, so that artillery and small arms could be used more effectively for all-round defence. Its squat shape and angular ground-plan is somewhat reminiscent of the Italian developments of the period, although not as complex as many Italian forts. It was probably one of the first such structures in the British Isles and it has even been claimed that the inspiration for the design came from Antonio da Sangallo the younger. Albany, his captain of Dunbar, Antoine de la Bastie, and probably many of the French gunners employed there had all served in the French armies of the Italian wars so this early appearance of Italian-inspired fortifications in Scotland is quite explicable. After Albany's death in June 1536, Dunbar Castle reverted to the Crown and this innovative blockhouse probably provided inspiration for some of James V's later fortifications, which included work at Blackness, Tantallon, Kinghorn, Crawfordjohn and Hermitage, much of which involved strengthening walls and inserting gun-ports.[19]

The defensive works carried out between 1536 and 1542 at Blackness Castle certainly appear to owe some inspiration to the French blockhouse at Dunbar, and until 1540 were under the supervision of Sir James Hamilton of Finnart. The existing castle walls were thickened to over 5 metres in places, the south tower was heightened and vaulted gun emplacements were constructed. Like Dunbar, the resulting bulwark has a rather angular plan and deep casemates opening to wide-mouthed gunports. A heavy gun could also be mounted at the window of the great hall and small arms could be used from the parapet. In the 1560s, a 'spur' was added to the castle entrance, which also housed flanking gun emplacements and a caponier (a covered gallery for firing small arms through angled gunports), which could rake the approach to the inner gateway with gunfire. Caponiers had been in use in Italy from the end of the fifteenth century and the earliest known Scottish example was built at Craignethan Castle in the 1530s for Hamilton of Finnart, where a deep, stone-lined ditch could be raked from a caponier accessible only from the castle. The curtain wall at Craignethan is also a massive masonry barrier and the ramparts and tower were also provided with wide-mouthed gunports for small arms whilst larger guns could be mounted on the parapets. The castle at Craignethan was a beautifully proportioned country residence for gracious living with a display of sculpted heraldic beasts (Hamilton antelopes) at the roofline, but it was also provided with the most up-to-date Franco-Italian-style defences on a double courtyard design. Finnart was a very influential figure at the royal court in the 1530s until his fall in July 1540 on charges of

TOP. The south tower at Blackness Castle where the fortifications were enhanced in the 1530s and 1560s.

ABOVE. The caponier at Craignethan Castle, an Italian military innovation introduced to Scotland by Sir James Hamilton of Finnart in the 1530s.

treason, which were probably trumped up for the benefit of his resentful half-brother and ward, the second earl of Arran, who had just attained his majority. Finnart had French connections, sophisticated tastes, and he has some claim to be the first major architect in Scotland. His masterpiece was probably the palace block at Stirling Castle (see Chapter 2), but he also worked on Linlithgow Palace and contributed to the modern fortifications at Tantallon, Blackness, Crawfordjohn, Cadzow and elsewhere.[20]

The Italian wars of the late fifteenth and early sixteenth centuries provided a powerful impulse for the development of military technology. A new style of fortification was created known as *trace italienne*, sometimes called 'star forts'. The essential features of *trace italienne* forts were that the walls were low and squat, often buttressed with extensive mounds of earth that could absorb artillery fire without shattering. Projecting from the walls were sharply pointed 'angle bastions' or bulwarks, also often reinforced with earthworks. They would have bristled from the fort in a formation that would have allowed the defenders to fire large guns or small arms at attackers at any point around the perimeter: there would have been no 'blind spots' providing refuge for the enemy. Finally, the whole edifice would have been encircled by a network of ditches and earthen ramparts. Such castles took into account the ease with which modern field guns could smash through the lofty towers or thinner curtain walls of medieval tradition and gave the defenders optimum defensive use of their own artillery. With adequate supplies of food, water, powder and shot, such forts could withstand a heavy siege for months, even years. A chain of these forts located at strategic points could allow an occupying army to command the terrain for miles around.

English forces had adopted modern *trace italienne* techniques to defend Boulogne after taking it from France in 1544 and when the earl of Hertford returned to Scotland as duke of Somerset for the second phase of the Rough Wooing in 1547, he brought the new designs with him.[21] Somerset's strategy was to occupy the Scottish Marches and the Firths of Forth and Tay by placing permanent English garrisons into modern forts and gradually force increasing numbers of Scots (especially the major magnates) to 'assure', i.e. to switch allegiance to the English Crown and support the main objective: the marriage of the infant Mary, queen of Scots, to the young King Edward VI. The plan failed because the Scottish government was so desperate to resist English domination that it instead accepted French protection in the Treaty of Haddington of 1548. The terms of the treaty included the immediate departure of the queen to be brought up at the French court as the future consort of Dauphin Francis (later King Francis II) and, if Mary and Francis had had heirs, it would have made Scotland effectively a French colony. The English also discovered that their garrison strategy was ruinously expensive and its failure contributed to Somerset's fall from power in 1549.[22]

The new forts for the English garrisons of the Rough Wooing were constructed under the direction of Sir Richard Lee and Sir Thomas Palmer, who had Italian engineers such as Giovanni di Rossetti on their staff. The first was built at Eyemouth between September 1547 and January 1548 and included a full Italian bastion with flanking walls about 55 feet thick with an outer ditch and rampart. The fort was demolished when England, France and Scotland made peace in 1550, then rebuilt with a double bastion to house a French garrison in the 1550s and demolished again after the expulsion of the French in 1560. Only marks on the ground now remain. English garrisons were placed into adapted strongholds and new fortifications at Castlemilk, Lauder, Dunglass, Haddington, Roxburgh, Inchcolm and elsewhere. At Broughty Craig near Dundee, an existing fifteenth-century castle was handed over to the English forces by an assured Scot, Patrick, Lord Gray, in September 1547 and its defences were extended by the addition of a massive ditch and earthworks. A new fort overlooking Broughty Castle and consisting of extensive earthwork ditches and ramparts was also constructed nearby at Balgillo. The English fortifications at Broughty protected a garrison which dominated Dundee, menaced Perth and other Tay settlements, and resisted two Scottish attacks in November 1547 and January 1548. The castle was eventually recovered by a combined Franco-Scottish force with French artillery in February 1550.[23]

The Scottish resistance to the Rough Wooing received major support from Henry II of France and new fortifications were built by the French armies in Scotland to harry the English and defend the Scots at Dunbar, Aberlady, Inveresk, Leith and elsewhere. Furthermore, in 1548, Henry sent to Scotland a 'famous captain', Migliorino Ubaldini, to devise new defences for the main Scottish castles at Edinburgh, Dunbar and probably Stirling. Ubaldini was assisted briefly at Dunbar by another Italian military specialist, Pietro Strozzi, who had also worked on the new *trace italienne* fortifications at Leith, where a great defensive citadel was planned from 1548 and completed in ten years. There is no documentary proof that Ubaldini worked at Stirling, but Marcus Merriman made a strong case that he did so. If Merriman was right, Ubaldini designed the *trace italienne* 'French

Broughty Castle: Italian-inspired earthwork defences were added to the medieval tower by the English garrison in the late 1540s.

spur' with a demi-bastion or 'orillon' to augment the defences of James IV's forework. Archaeological work at the castle in 2010–11 located traces of some of the works of this period. At Edinburgh, Ubaldini certainly built a *trace italienne* spur with related walls and gun platforms and these have also been identified in an archaeological dig on the esplanade in 2009–10.[24] So effective were the defences at Edinburgh Castle that the queen's men (supporters of Mary, queen of Scots) were able to resist the Lang Siege by the king's men (supporters of James VI) from 1571 to 1573. The siege was broken only when English troops brought heavy guns from Berwick and battered the castle into submission, demolishing the fourteenth-century David's Tower in the process. James VI's vic-

torious regent, James Douglas, earl of Morton, reconstructed the castle's defences in the 1570s. He encased the stump of David's Tower in the formidable half-moon battery, which was based upon design principles expounded in the 1520s by Albrecht Dürer. He also commissioned the portcullis gate with its graceful Renaissance decoration of delicate pilasters and string-courses, built by William McDowell from 1577. A pedimented recess (aedicule) framing the royal arms was added by William Schaw in 1584.[25] Again, as with the navy, by the late sixteenth century, the onset of first peace and then regal union with England meant that there was no further need for major innovations in fortifications until the outbreak of the Covenanting wars in 1638.

The other major technical innovation of the 'military revolution' of the Renaissance period was the development of artillery and ballistics. All the warships of James IV and James V and all the fortresses discussed above were specifically designed to carry the latest guns and firearms. Such developments did not mean that medieval weapons were instantly superseded: for many years the new guns were used alongside longbows, crossbows, pikes, axes, bills, halberds, swords and other traditional weapons. This was particularly impor-

LEFT. Morton's Gateway, Edinburgh Castle, built in 1577–84 as part of the reconstruction of the castle's defences after the Lang Siege.

OPPOSITE. Arnold Bronckorst, portrait of James Douglas, earl of Morton, 1580. Morton commissioned the rebuilding of the defences at Edinburgh Castle in the 1570s. The castle shown in the background of this painting is probably a rather fanciful depiction of Morton's own seat of Tantallon.

Mons Meg, forged in the Low Countries in 1449 and presented to James II in 1457. The great gun has been kept in Edinburgh Castle for centuries.

foundries in Flanders. His 'great bombard' (giant siege gun) proclaimed the king's might and status in an inscription on the barrel:

> For the illustrious James, worthy prince of the Scots. Magnificent king, when I sound off I reduce castles. I was made at his order, therefore I am called *Lion*.

This and the other royal guns were operated by hired German gunners under Johannes Paule 'master of the king's engines'.[26] More famous than *Lion* and its fellows, partly because of its size and partly because it has survived to this day in Edinburgh Castle, is *Mons Meg*. As its name suggests, it was forged in the Flemish town of Mons in 1449 by Jean Cambier and presented to James II in 1457 by the uncle of the queen, Philip, duke of Burgundy. At 6 tonnes and firing gunstones of 200 kilograms, *Mons Meg* was a remarkable status symbol, the heaviest piece of artillery in the British Isles until the eighteenth century, potentially a devastating weapon but also very cumbersome. It could be hauled only three miles a day and could fire only about ten shots a day before it overheated. *Lion*, *Mons Meg* and the other guns of this period were made of wrought iron, which was brittle and had a tendency to burst, as James II discovered to his cost, when one of his own guns exploded and killed him at the siege of Roxburgh in 1460.[27]

By the 1470s and 1480s, forged and cast-iron guns were being manufactured in Scotland for James III and James IV and from about 1505, French, Flemish and Dutch or German gunsmiths were employed to cast bronze guns which were more reliable, accurate, had a longer range than their iron predecessors, and could fire iron shot which was more penetrating than gunstones. The

tant in the early stages of artillery development when both the big siege and field guns and the smaller handguns were inaccurate, unreliable and slow to reload. As the accuracy, reliability and loading speeds improved during the sixteenth century, archery became largely obsolete, but the other weapons were still required for close engagement with an enemy, especially when the supply of shot had been exhausted. The great siege guns of the period were so expensive that only the Crown could really afford to buy them, and at first they all had to be imported. In 1430, James I ordered 'bombards, engines and instruments of war' from

TOP. A cast bronze field gun, known as a hagbut, probably
made in Edinburgh Castle by David Rouen in 1553. This is a
rare surviving example from the royal arsenal.

ABOVE. The Breadalbane Gun, made by Patrick Ramsay
of Dundee for Sir Duncan Campbell of Glenorchy in 1595.

iron guns were usually loaded at the breech by
the insertion of a 'chamber' or canister containing shot and powder, which created a weak spot
in the barrel, whilst the newer cast-bronze guns
tended to be muzzle-loaded and therefore had
greater resilience. The latter ranged in size from
the large cannon and culverins (which were bat-
tering guns), through the smaller culverins and
large falcons (which were carriage-mounted field
guns), down to the smaller falcons and hagbuts
(which could be mounted on parapets or used as
handguns).[28] The main centre for artillery manufacture was established in Edinburgh Castle by
1511 under a Scottish specialist, Robert Borth-
wick, and his successors, the Frenchmen Piers and
David Rouen, and continued in operation until
1558 but ceased thereafter, as the Scots dropped
out of the arms race in cannon casting.

By the end of James IV's reign, the Crown arsenal was well stocked, but many artillery pieces
went to France with the navy or were captured by
the English at Flodden in 1513 (having been badly
deployed) so a new programme of rearmament
was needed. Regent Albany imported guns from
his home in France (some returned with him in
1524) and kept his own French garrison at Dunbar
well supplied, but when James V attempted to
arrest his hated step-father, the 6th earl of Angus,
by a siege of Tantallon Castle in 1528, he found
his artillery stocks to be quite inadequate. Having
borrowed guns and shot from the captain of
Dunbar and requisitioned powder in Leith belonging to King Christian II of Denmark, he still failed
to take his prize. James was humiliated and made
strenuous efforts to restock his arsenal in the
1530s. Guns, shot and powder were imported
from Denmark, Flanders and France; French and
Flemish founders, gunsmiths and gunners were

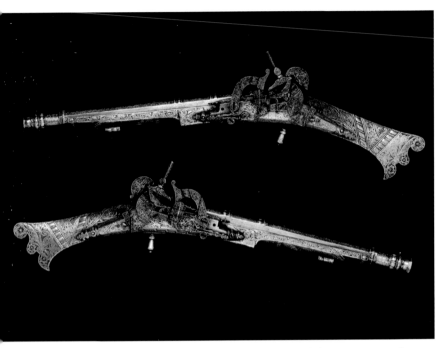

Pair of brass pistols made by James Low of
Dundee for Louis XIII of France, 1611.

1560, the royal foundry in Edinburgh Castle ceased
to manufacture heavy guns, although gun founders
in some burghs, such as Aberdeen, continued to
produce medium-sized pieces for noble patrons.
At Edinburgh Castle the surviving weapons, sup-
plemented by some imported pieces, were maintained at the fortress throughout the reigns of
Mary and James VI.

In time, the Scots did become very proficient
at the manufacture of modern handguns, as the
burgh craftsmen realised that small, affordable
pieces could find a ready market; indeed the finest
Scottish pieces were in demand for export by about
1600. The earliest handguns (hagbuts and culverins) of c.1500 were essentially miniature cannon
fired by a smouldering match-cord and were first
manufactured in Scotland by French, Flemish and
Dutch or German gunmakers employed by the
Crown. By the mid-sixteenth century pistols and
muskets were being made in Edinburgh, the Canongate and Dundee, as clockmakers and locksmiths
adapted their skills to develop new types of firing
mechanism (matchlock, wheel-lock, snaphance
lock, etc.). By the end of the century some very elegant pieces were produced. The earliest surviving
complete Scottish firearm is the Breadalbane gun
(NMS) made by Patrick Ramsay of Dundee for Sir
Duncan Campbell of Glenorchy in 1595. It has a
snaphance mechanism in which a piece of flint on
a sprung lever creates sparks to ignite the charge
when the trigger is pulled. One of the finest surviving examples is a pair of brass pistols made by
James Low of Dundee in 1611 for Louis XIII of
France (NMS). They also have snaphance locks
with fishtail butts and are engraved with the king's
arms.[30]

On the Continent from the mid-sixteenth century the new handguns were effectively deployed

employed, and bronze cannon of all sizes were
cast in large numbers. The only piece that survives from this industrious period is a small 'falcon'
of 50-millimetre bore with James V's arms and
initials on the barrel (Glasgow Museums). James
also invested in other arms and armour, employing specialists to make swords, bows and plate
armour at a new armoury established under a
French master craftsman at Holyrood in 1532.[29]
Again, there were losses after the death of James
V in 1542: many of his larger guns were captured
along with the great ships or otherwise became
casualties of the Rough Wooing. At this period
the Scots became very reliant on French guns and
gunners, whose resources and skills they now
could not match. After the peace settlement of

by massed ranks of infantry in the new professional armies alongside formations of pikemen. Many Scots of the period served as mercenaries overseas, but it does not appear that many returned to Scotland and brought their expertise and weaponry with them. Companies of Scots soldiers and archers had formed the elite *Garde Ecossaise* of the French kings from 1418, but the kings of Scots struggled to finance any bands of professional and permanent troops, even a royal guard. In the 1520s, Queen Margaret had created a royal guard for the young James V, which was supported by English funds. In the 1550s, French money had financed bands of professional soldiers in Scotland, and in the 1560s, Mary had used her income as queen dowager of France to pay for a royal guard of Scots archers. Between the 1580s and the 1620s, the English state financed a royal guard for James VI, but funds were not paid regularly and money was always short. Indeed, it was quite clear that the Scottish government could not afford to pay for regular troops of its own. Essentially the Crown continued to rely on the amateur levies of the 'common army', which could not be properly drilled in the latest infantry techniques. This had left the Scots at a huge disadvantage at the Battle of Pinkie in 1547, where English smallarms fire did considerable damage. The Scots 'common army' was organised through local musters called wapinshawings where men would turn out under the leadership of their feudal overlords or senior burgesses. The men were expected to provide their own weapons and this duty was only patchily fulfilled. In the wapinshawing of Cunningham in 1532 more men were absent than present, and as late as 1596 in the wapinshawing of Moray 42 per cent of those who did turn out had no arms or armour. It was not until the Covenanting wars

after 1638 that Scottish armies were able to adopt the most modern military methods.[31]

Alongside the 'military revolution' of the period there was also a 'cartographic revolution' and the two developments were connected (indeed, the definitive maps of modern Britain are produced by an agency still called Ordnance Survey). In 1500, maps were extremely rare, although not unknown, right across Europe and those that were drawn were often very impressionistic without scale or detail. By 1600, maps were in common use across the Continent, including Scotland, to help landholders manage their estates, to support legal cases in the courts, to reinforce a sense of identity and belonging, and to help the political and military powers in their planning and administration.[32] The importance of the military imperative behind the development of cartography has already been illustrated by the fact that the only surviving copies of Alexander Lindsay's 'rutter' of the Scottish seas of about 1540 were made for the English and French governments during the Rough Wooing. Some of the earliest English maps were drawn in the 1530s by military engineers, several of whom were Italian, to help Henry VIII plan his defences. In the Rough Wooing, new English fortifications were built in Scotland and the maps, plans and sketches drawn at this time provide some of the earliest visual records of parts of Scotland, including Edinburgh. The earliest English maps drawn to scale depicting the defences of Calais, Guisnes, Boulogne, Hull, Carlisle and Dover were also made in the 1540s.[33]

In the 1540s and 1550s, some rather rudimentary maps of Scotland were produced by Italian publishers and they seem to have relied heavily on information from an English Catholic exile George Lily. One of the best surviving early maps

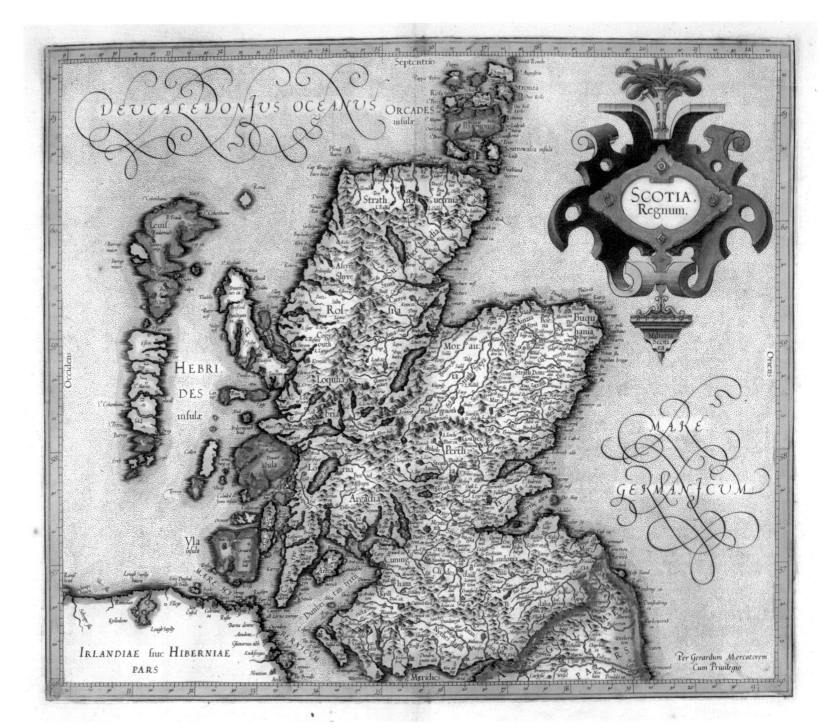

of Scotland is in a manuscript produced in the 1560s by an English cartographer Lawrence Nowell. Nowell never visited Scotland and must have used earlier, unidentified maps as sources. His version of Scotland is considerably more detailed and accurate than a map of 1564 produced by the famous Flemish cartographer Gerard Mercator, which received much wider publication than Nowell's work.[34] Mercator, famous for his 'projection' (a representation of a sphere on a flat surface), seems to have drawn on information provided by an exiled Scottish cleric John Elder, who had drawn the first map of Scotland in 1543 to assist Henry VIII's invasion plans. Elder's original map is now lost. Mercator's map of 1564 was reproduced in the *Atlas* published by his heirs in 1595, which in turn became the model for the beautifully decorated map of Scotland published in John Speed's atlas, *The Theatre of the Empire of Great Britaine*, published in London in 1611–12, which includes portraits of James VI, Queen Anna, and their sons Henry and Charles.[35]

The most detailed mapping of Scotland, accompanied by written descriptions of its geography, history and economy, was carried out between 1583 and 1596 by Timothy Pont, who later became a minister of the Kirk. It is not clear why he undertook this task. He does not seem to have been officially commissioned, but his father, Robert, was an eminent clergyman (six times Moderator of the General Assembly, amongst other distinctions) and arranged funding from Church resources for his son. Thus Pont's work might be seen as part of the Kirk's attempt to extend its authority throughout the land. Timothy Pont spent these 13 years (and possibly more) travelling the country, compiling detailed information and drawing sketch maps, many of which were later revised into fair copies. Some of his manuscripts have been lost, but 78 of his maps survive on 38 sheets in the National Library of Scotland. Technically, his work is classed as chorography (illustrated topographical description) rather than cartography, but his manuscripts later formed the basis of a major new cartographical publication. After Pont's death, his maps (with some revisions and additions in the 1630s by Robert Gordon of Straloch and his son, James Gordon of Rothiemay) were published in Amsterdam by Joan Blaeu as 47 regional maps, with a new map of the whole country, in the fifth volume of *Atlas Novus* (1654), at which point Scotland became one of the best mapped countries in seventeenth-century Europe. No other comparable collection of primary source material survives for any of the other countries mapped in Blaeu's monumental work, which gives the Pont manuscripts unique significance in the history of cartography.[36]

In the popular imagination, the military history of Scotland in the fifteenth and sixteenth centuries is usually seen as a series of dismal defeats and humiliations: the loss of Berwick in 1482, Flodden 1513, Solway Moss 1542, Pinkie 1547, the domination by French armies in the 1550s, and the dependence on English money from the 1560s onwards. However, the really remarkable aspect of this story is that Scotland was not overrun and conquered. English forces often enjoyed superi-

OPPOSITE. Mercator's map of Scotland, published in Duisberg in 1595 and based on earlier maps, now lost.

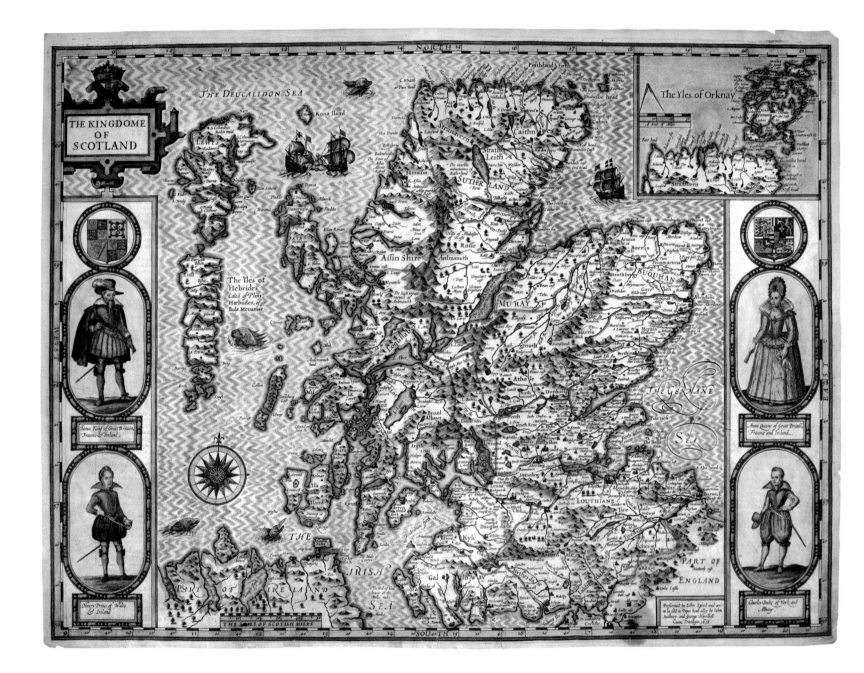

THE KINGDOME OF SCOTLAND

The Yles of Orknay

The Deucalidon Sea

The Yles of Hebrides Caled of Pliny Hæbudes, of Beda Meuaniæ

James King of Great Britain, Fraunce & Ireland.

Henry Prince of Wales & Ireland.

Anna Queene of Great Brittaine, Fraunce and Ireland.

Charles Duke of York and Albany.

THE SCALE OF SCOTISH MILES

Performed by John Speed and are to be sold at Popes head alley by John Sudbury and George Humble Cum Privilegio 1676

THE GERMANE SEA

THE IRISH SEA

PART OF IRELAND

PART OF ENGLAND

OPPOSITE. John Speed's map of Scotland, published in London in 1611 and based on Mercator's map.

ABOVE. Timothy Pont's view of Dundee from his maps of the 1580s and 1590s.

RIGHT. Timothy Pont's view of Stirling from his maps of the 1580s and 1590s.

ority of numbers and resources, yet the battles of Flodden and Pinkie did not lead to subjugation by the English Crown. The harsh Scottish weather and terrain and the English distractions in France certainly contributed to this reprieve, but so did dogged Scottish resistance and a determination to make the most of what limited military resources were available. For about a century between the 1440s and the 1540s, the Scottish Crown worked a minor miracle as it managed to keep up with European developments in ballistics, fortifications and naval power and to 'punch above its weight' in international relations. However, by the time of the Treaty of Haddington in 1548, the Scottish government was so overwhelmed by the massive financial strains of modern warfare that it was forced to choose between becoming a satellite state of either England or France. Initially, the French seemed to offer the better deal but the religious and political upheavals of the Reformation of 1559–60 eventually settled the matter in favour of peace with England and the tempting prospect of a Stewart succession to the Tudor throne. Thus there was no longer any point in trying to compete with the greater powers in military developments and Scotland dropped out of the Renaissance arms race.

6

SOUNDS CELESTIAL

Renaissance Music

Having established that the visual arts and military sciences in Renaissance Scotland, as in many other countries, were strongly shaped by foreign influences which were adapted to Scottish needs, it should be no surprise to find similar trends in the development of the art of music. Of course there was a vibrant tradition of Scottish folk music which, because it was almost entirely orally and aurally transmitted, is exceedingly difficult to trace in the historical record. It was probably quite distinctively provincial rather than international in outlook and, therefore, important though the folk heritage is for Scottish culture in general, it cannot be considered a part of the cultural movement of the European Renaissance. However, Scottish musicians of the period were also exponents of the more 'highbrow' pursuit of art music or 'musick fyne', which was deliberately composed, written down in musical notation, and performed by trained practitioners for cultivated patrons. Here, Scottish music was clearly a part of the cultural mainstream of the northern Renaissance.[1] As with the fine arts considered in Chapter 4, the Reformation of 1559–60 was particularly destructive of

music books and manuscripts, almost all of which, having been designed for liturgical use, perished in the bonfires which purged Scotland of Catholicism. The surviving evidence is so fragmentary that, yet again, we have to piece together a jigsaw with many of the parts missing and make informed guesses about what has been lost.

For centuries the medieval Church had been the wellspring of fine music. The daily round of masses, prayers and psalms was usually sung rather than spoken and most clerics were expected to have a basic vocal facility. Most of the greater Scottish monasteries, cathedrals, burgh churches, collegiate churches, university chapels and the chapel royal maintained choral establishments under the direction of a precentor or chanter, which consisted of professional singing men (vicars choral) and boy trebles, who were educated in the 'song schools' attached to their churches. In Aberdeen, for instance, there was lavish provision for choral services at St Machar's Cathedral, the parish church of St Nicholas, and the chapel of King's College.[2] King James IV refounded the chapel royal at Stirling Castle in 1501 as a collegiate church with a large

choral establishment to enhance his regal dignity and prestige: it had 16 singing men (canons) and 6 boy trebles. There were probably at least 58 song schools in pre-Reformation Scotland, assuming that there were schools attached to all 12 cathedrals and the 46 collegiate churches, and not counting those at the greater abbeys and parish churches. Most of them were located to the south and east of the Highland line, but they were well distributed right across Lowland Scotland.[3] Boy choristers were recruited on merit, sometimes from relatively humble backgrounds, taught Latin, divinity and music in the song schools, often sent to university when their voices broke, and might return to their mother churches or other establishments as vicars choral, chaplains, or priests.[4] Thus there was a clear career progression for talented male singers, organists and composers within the Church, which passed musical skills down the generations and provided opportunities for some social mobility.

The liturgy observed in the churches of pre-Reformation Scotland was a variant of the Sarum (or Salisbury) rite or 'use' of medieval England, which was itself an elaboration of the Roman rite. The Use of Sarum was originally devised for services in Salisbury Cathedral and formed the standard observance in both England and Scotland by the twelfth century. At this period the Scottish and Anglo-Norman churches and royal families were very closely connected and it seemed natural to adopt a common liturgy. The Roman rite and some other Continental liturgies were also known in Scotland, but do not seem to have been widely practised.[5] To the Sarum framework was added the veneration of local saints and shrines and the absorption of some aspects of religious observance from the Low Countries, such as the adoption of the cult of the Holy Blood of Bruges and the use of the rosary to assist private devotions. William Elphinstone, bishop of Aberdeen, planned to codify and standardise the Scottish liturgy, in an attempt to foster a distinctively Scottish Church within the wider Catholic communion. Since English and French publishers would not usually print books solely for the Scottish market, this initiative required the establishment of a native printing press, for which he gained royal support. In 1507, James IV granted a licence to Walter Chepman and Andrew Myllar, burgesses of Edinburgh, for the monopoly printing in Scotland of 'books of our laws, acts of parliament, chronicles, mass books and porteouses [breviaries] after the use of our realm, with additions and legends of the Scottish saints now gathered and added thereto'.[6] The patent went on to commend Elphinstone's collation of books in 'our own Scottish use' and to ban the importation of books of the Use of Sarum. Accordingly, in 1510, the fledgling Edinburgh press published Elphinstone's *Aberdeen Breviary*. Based on the Sarum rite, the breviary removes or downgrades the feasts of many English saints, while promoting the commemoration of over 90 Scottish saints, complete with their *Legenda*, i.e. the liturgically recited stories of their lives. Some were major figures such as St Kentigern (Mungo) and St Ninian; others were more obscure such as St Modoc (the evangelist of the Hebrides) and St Bean (the founding bishop of Mortlach). However, the first Scottish press struggled to compete with cheap imported books (the official ban was ineffective) and was short-lived (Elphinstone's *Breviary* is its last known publication), so the unchanged Sarum rite continued to be employed until Henry VIII's assertion of the Royal Supremacy in England in 1534. Between 1534 and the temporary restoration of English Catholicism in 1554,

The feast of St Kentigern in the *Aberdeen Breviary*, printed by Chepman and Myllar in Edinburgh in 1510. Early printers used 'black letter' type, which imitated medieval handwriting.

the French presses stopped producing books for the Sarum rite and the English presses engaged in increasingly Protestant liturgical innovations, which were unacceptable in Catholic Scotland. However, instead of reverting to Elphinstone's grand plan, the Scottish Church of the 1530s and 1540s seems to have turned to the revised Roman liturgy developed by Cardinal Quignonez, since several examples of his work with Scottish provenance have survived from this period.[7]

In the later Middle Ages, the predominant choral technique in western Europe was the plainsong (a single melody sung in unison) of Gregorian chant. Gradually, variations and elaborations of plainchant began to develop and were given rather exotic names, such as organum and fauxbourdon. Over time, composers became more inventive and adventurous. From the thirteenth century, polyphony (two or more independent melodies intertwined) became common in western Christendom and by the fifteenth century, choral writing for four, five, or more independent voice parts was standard at prestigious sites. Plainsong still formed the core of the services, with polyphony used to decorate and highlight particularly important texts. However elaborate and sumptuous the polyphony became, the original chant could be found underpinning the entire creation (*cantus firmus*), usually in the tenor part. Elaborately composed sacred music had long been familiar in the greater Scottish churches. For example, the mid-thirteenth century *St Andrews Music Book* (Ducal Library, Wolfenbüttel) which was presumably used by the cathedral choir, is an album of pieces for two, three, or four voices from a variety of liturgical traditions. Much of the music originates from the school of Notre-Dame in Paris, but there are also examples of pieces for the Dominican rite, the English Use

of Sarum, and some remarkable pieces probably by unknown Scottish composers.[8] If the choir at St Andrews was familiar with the musical traditions of France and England in the thirteenth century, we may reasonably deduce that the same could be said of major Scottish choirs in the fifteenth century, even though there are no surviving Scottish musical manuscripts of this period.

The surviving evidence for the art of music in fifteenth-century Scotland is scanty indeed. According to Walter Bower, abbot of Inchcolm, who was a great admirer of James I, the king was a distinguished musician ('another Orpheus') both as a singer and instrumentalist, who drew talented musicians to his court from abroad.[9] According to the chroniclers Ferrerio and Pitscottie, James III also had a great interest in music. He was apparently a patron of William Roger, an English musician who was hanged at Lauder Bridge in 1482 by disgruntled nobles who objected to the king's familiarity with favourites of lower birth. Roger is said to have established an accomplished school of musicians and composers centred on the chapel royal, who treasured his memory for years afterwards. Thus he might have laid the foundations of the musical 'Golden Age' identified by John Purser as c.1490–c.1550.[10] According to Gavin Douglas in his poem 'The Palice of Honour' (c.1501), the full range of polyphonic techniques was known in Scotland:

> In modulation heard I play and sing
> Fauxbourdon, pricksong, descant, countering,
> Cant Organe, figuration and gimmel.

The 'countering' and 'cant organe' mentioned here seem to have been particularly Scottish polyphonic practices, the latter probably derived from earlier improvisational traditions.[11] However, the other techniques mentioned by Douglas were also well known in England, the Low Countries and France. Since Queen Mary of Gueldres established Trinity College, Edinburgh, as a prestigious choral foundation in 1460, a strong Flemish influence on Scottish fifteenth-century music is to be expected (and the importance of music at Trinity College is emphasised by the appearance of organ-playing angels on the magnificent altarpiece; see Chapter 4). Likewise, the marriage of James IV to Margaret Tudor in 1503 (who retained at least one English musician in her service) provided a channel for the highly ornate English polyphonic style of the *Eton Choir Book* (c.1500), also known as the 'English Decorated' style, to enter the Scottish repertoire. This style was characterised by rhythmic complexity, cross-relations (where voice parts briefly 'clash' and then resolve) and soaring, high treble lines. All of these features appear in the music of the Scottish master composer Robert Carver.

The most important surviving Scottish musical manuscript of the Renaissance is the *Carver Choirbook* (NLS, copied c.1503–c.1560), a collection of polyphonic masses and motets in which the influences of the English and Franco-Flemish schools are readily apparent. The book was compiled by Robert Carver, a canon (possibly precentor) of the Augustinian abbey of Scone, and it probably survived simply because he managed to keep it safe amongst his personal possessions when the abbey was burned down by a furious mob in 1559. Carver was one of the most accomplished Scottish composers of his time and the manuscript contains all of his known works: five masses and two motets.[12] One suspects that he must have written much more in his long career, but, if the manuscript had not survived the Reformation, we would now know nothing at all of Carver's inventive, expressive and expansive music. The *Carver Choirbook* contains copies of pieces by some English and Flemish composers of the late fifteenth and early sixteenth centuries, who clearly influenced the development of Carver's style. The manuscript includes works by Walter Lambe, William Cornysh, Robert Fayrfax, John Nesbett, and possibly Walter Frye. Both Nesbett and Frye are usually said to be English, but there are suspicions that they might have been Scots. The book also includes a copy of a mass based on the popular song, '*L'homme armé*' (The armed man) by Guillaume Dufay. Dufay was one of the finest and most influential composers of the fifteenth-century Burgundian Low Countries. It was common for composers to write music for masses by taking a *cantus firmus* from a secular song or plainsong melody, the opening words of which would then form the 'title' of the mass setting. There was a tradition at the Burgundian court of using the '*L'homme armé*' tune, which was

A sketch from the *Carver Choirbook*, compiled by Robert Carver of Scone in the early sixteenth century.

closely associated with the Order of the Golden Fleece and the crusading ideal, and seems to have appealed to Scottish tastes.

Robert Carver is a rather shadowy figure. He was born c.1487–8, possibly in Aberdeen, entered Scone Abbey as a novice c.1500, and may have studied at the university of Louvain c.1504. He was a canon at Scone by 1505 and still living at the site of the derelict abbey in 1568 (so some buildings must have survived the conflagration of 1559). We do not know precisely when he died, but it was presumably sometime soon after his last documented appearance in August 1568. Carver occasionally used the alias 'Arnot' and this has led to great confusion, since a man called Robert Arnot was a burgess of Stirling between 1516 and 1551 and a man of the same name was a canon of the chapel royal from 1543. For some time, the Stirling records were thought to refer to the composer, but a recent discovery of Scone documents shows that Carver was still in Scone whilst Arnot was in Stirling and they were therefore two, or even three, distinct people.[13]

Carver's works are difficult to date with any precision, but it is likely that three of the masses and the two motets were written between c.1506 and 1513 and the remaining two masses seem to date from the 1540s. The gap in output probably indicates that a portion of the manuscript has been lost, rather than the existence of a 30-year crisis in Scottish music. Much of the discussion about possible dates for Carver's pieces has focused on events at the royal court and chapel royal on the assumption that Carver had strong connections with Stirling. Since this now appears less likely, some of the suggested dates might need to be reconsidered. However, this author can attest from personal experience of singing some of Carver's music that

it is vocally extremely demanding and virtuosic. Furthermore, the scoring can also be very ambitious (the Mass *Dum Sacrum Mysterium* is scored for ten voices and the motet *O Bone Jesu* for 19, including 11 tenors) so it is highly probable that the music was intended for performance by the superior forces of the chapel royal, even if Carver himself stayed in his abbey at Scone. One of Carver's masses is based on the '*L'homme armé*' tune, the only such work from the British Isles, and its crusading and chivalric connotations have led to it being associated with the would-be crusader king, James IV, and dated to c.1506 or c.1509. An untitled six-part mass uses fanfare-type elements and might have been written for the launch of the *Great Michael* in October 1511. The Mass *Dum Sacrum Mysterium* (While John Beheld the Holy Mystery) was written for the feast of St Michael (29 September) probably in 1508, and was recycled for the coronation of James V at Stirling in 1513. The motets *Gaude Flore Virginali* (Rejoice, Virgin Flower: setting the text of a popular late-medieval hymn to the Virgin Mary) and *O Bone Jesu* (O Good Jesus: setting a version of a prayer to the Holy Name of Jesus) probably also date from the last years of the reign of James IV. The latter with its 19 parts might have marked the nineteenth anniversary of the king's accession (1507) or Queen Margaret's nineteenth birthday (1508). The Masses *Fera Pessima* (A Wild Beast: a text relating how Jacob found Joseph's blood-stained coat) and *Pater Creator Omnium* (Father, Creator of All Things: another Latin hymn) probably date from the mid-1540s.[14]

It is thought that Carver's works incorporate hidden meanings and symbolism in the scoring and structure, as was the practice of the time. Numerology, which ascribed mystical significance to certain numbers or patterns of numbers, was a familiar aspect of Renaissance culture. Along with astrology and alchemy, numerology was considered to be part of natural science and to provide a means of understanding the divine order of the universe. So, for example, the Mass *Dum Sacrum Mysterium* takes its *cantus firmus* from the plainsong for the feast of St Michael and All Angels. The ten-part scoring therefore recalls the traditional nine orders of the angels plus a tenth category, mankind, created to replace the lost tenth order of angels (those who fell with Satan). Thus Carver suggests that ultimately humanity may join the heavenly chorus. The number seven was also considered to have great mystical power (seven deadly sins, seven cardinal virtues, etc.). The seven stanzas of the motet *Gaude Flore Virginali* reflect the Virgin Mary's seven 'joys' (the Annunciation, Visitation, Nativity, Adoration, Presentation, Christ disputing with the doctors, and the Assumption). Likewise, the motet *O Bone Jesu* sets a text associated with the veneration of the Holy Name of Jesus, a devotion which was introduced to Scotland in 1493 by Andrew Grey, chaplain of the altar of St Michael at the parish church of St Nicholas, Aberdeen, who was Robert Carver's uncle. It is in five sections, perhaps recalling the five wounds of Christ, and the choice of 19 voice parts may also be significant. The number 19 was regarded as a 'perfect' number: it represented the ideal balance between the male and the female, as the difference between three cubed and two cubed. On each occasion when the name of Jesus is sung by all 19 parts, there is a pause or 'corona', so that Jesus, the perfect man, is metaphorically 'crowned' by the music. The pauses are also grouped into threes, probably representing the Holy Trinity.[15]

The other major source of pre-Reformation music in Scotland is the *Dunkeld Antiphonary* or *Dowglas-Fischar Partbooks* (EUL). Despite the name, the manuscript has no clear connections with Dunkeld and was probably created for or by Robert Douglas, who was provost of the collegiate church of Lincluden from 1547. It consists of five out of an original set of six partbooks containing a collection of sacred music probably compiled c.1553. It contains a copy of a motet by Josquin des Prez, an early sixteenth-century Franco-Flemish composer, who pioneered the technique of imitation, where a musical phrase would be passed from one part to another in quick succession, often at a different pitch, creating a strongly homogeneous sound. The manuscript also contains works by later Franco-Flemish composers such as Claudin de Sermisy, Adrian Willaert and Pierre Certon. Furthermore, it includes two anonymous six-part masses by Scottish composers: *Cantate Domino* (Sing to the Lord) and *Felix Namque* (Thou Art Truly Happy). The Mass *Cantate Domino* is thought to date from the late 1540s and has been attributed to Carver because it seems to be musically related to his Mass *Fera Pessima*. However, *Felix Namque* is largely written in a different idiom, that of the mid-century High Renaissance, which involves not only homophonic passages of great textual clarity (where all the voices are singing the same syllable at the same time) but also a much more thorough use of imitation than is usually found in Carver. The mass also deploys very smooth vocal lines, gradually constructed textures, and the exquisite tension of the technique of suspension (where a note is prolonged beyond its 'proper' place in the harmony, creating a dissonance that has to be resolved). Several speculative suggestions have been made for the composer of *Felix Namque* including Robert Douglas himself, or David Peebles, but James Ross makes a strong case for the mass being a late work of the mature Robert Carver, who was changing his style to respond to the trends of the time.[16]

The few surviving works of Robert Carver appear to reflect his ability to adapt to changing tastes over a long career. His early masses and motets contain much highly ornate and complex decoration, and are perhaps analogous to the transitional late-Gothic/early-Renaissance art discussed in Chapters 3 and 4. Once the forces of religious change started operating widely in the 1520s, reformers in both the Catholic and Protestant camps began to criticise composers who obscured sacred texts in layers of musical elaboration and pressure grew for greater clarity, simplicity and more syllabic settings. An early Scottish denunciation of over-elaborate sacred music was made by Robert Richardson, a canon of Cambuskenneth who was studying in Paris in 1530, when he wrote a *Commentary on the Rule of St Augustine*. As a fellow Augustinian, Carver might well have been aware that Richardson regarded complex and extended polyphony as a form of vanity which served to glorify the composer rather than God. Carver's Mass *Pater Creator Omnium* of 1546 may have been a response to such views because it is a much simpler, more chordal and syllabic setting than most of his other works, although there were possibly other more practical reasons why Carver might have adopted a restrained style at this point. The Mass *Cantate Domino* also seems to embody a concern for greater textual clarity and if Ross is correct that the Mass *Felix Namque* was by Carver, it would represent the next stage in this process of stylistic refinement.[17]

Apart from Robert Carver, there are very few

pre-Reformation Scottish composers known to us. The first Scottish Protestant martyr, Patrick Hamilton (1504?–1528), abbot of Fearn, is said to have composed a mass in nine parts (representing the nine orders of the angels) on the plainsong *Benedicant Dominum omnes angeli* (Bless the Lord all ye angels), which was performed in the cathedral at St Andrews, but no copy survives. In the mid-1550s Patrick Douglas, a prebendary of St Giles, Edinburgh, wrote a five-part motet, *In convertendo* (When the Lord turned: a setting of Psalm 125), in a beautiful High Renaissance imitative style, but no other pieces by him are known. Sir John Fethy (fl.1498–c.1568) was precentor of the chapel royal from 1545 and successively master of the song schools at Dundee, St Nicholas, Aberdeen, and St Giles, Edinburgh. He was most famous as an organist and is said to have introduced a new Continental style of fingering to Scotland, involving the use of four or five fingers, rather than just the middle three which had been customary. In his long career he must have written a lot of music, but only one post-Reformation piece survives: 'O God Abufe', which was recorded in the *Wode Partbooks*.[18] Thomas Wode was a former monk of Lindores, who became a Protestant minister in St Andrews. Between 1562 and his death in 1592, he compiled a remarkable collection of Scottish music in the eight surviving volumes of his manuscript, a unique source of information on sixteenth-century Scottish music and musicians. What started as a simple collection of psalm settings gradually turned into something much more wide-ranging. Wode consciously set about trying to save what he could of Scotland's musical heritage and added many pieces to his collection until his death in 1592 (other hands also continued the collection for some years after

this). It is not clear whether or not the *Wode Partbooks* were originally intended for publication, but the psalm harmonisations certainly circulated beyond St Andrews. The books were never printed and the manuscripts are thus precious documents indeed. Wode wrote extensive marginal comments which provide valuable information about many of his composers and their works and he included vivid and colourful illustrations, which make his books a joy to behold. They constitute the only known source of many pieces of Scottish music.[19]

According to Thomas Wode, Robert Johnson (c.1500–c.1560) came from Duns and fled to England after being accused of heresy. Almost all of his known works appear in English sources and he is considered to have influenced English composers such as Sheppard and Tallis. It is thought that a small number of two- and five-part pieces might have been written before he left Scotland. Two appear in the *Wode Partbooks* and others in English sources. He is also sometimes suggested as the composer of an anonymous Scottish motet, *Descendi in Hortum Meum* (I went down into my garden) of c.1520, which is in a delicate and restrained High Renaissance style worthy of Josquin. Wode is the only source to claim Robert Johnson as a Scot and there are suspicions that he was actually an Englishman. David Peebles (fl.1530–1576), an Augustinian canon of St Andrews, was considered to be one of the finest Scottish composers of his time, but only one pre-Reformation piece of his survives, recorded in the *Wode Partbooks*: the sonorous, ethereal motet *Si quis diligit me* (If ye love me) of c.1530. Wode tells us that the piece was presented to King James V who, as a musician himself, greatly appreciated its qualities. Wode also records that in 1576 Peebles made a dramatic polyphonic setting of Psalm

Ye may be knawi be zowr tewin[...]
I a one-ma of metill cipdistic
And yairfor bringis my part if noire
most trew.
As it offeris bnto my facultici

TENNOWR.

3 in an anonymous Renaissance Latin text (not the Catholic Vulgate). '*Quam Multi Domine*' (Lord, how are they increased) was written for James VI's kinsman, Robert Stewart, Protestant bishop of Caithness, titular prior of St Andrews and later earl of Lennox, then earl of March. The psalm is set in a refined imitative style reminiscent of the work of Orlande de Lassus, the leading light of the Franco-Flemish school in the late sixteenth century.[20] There must have been many other Scottish composers of the period who have simply vanished from the historical record.

Even the great critic of sacred polyphony Robert Richardson accepted that it was appropriate to use some restrained ornamentation of plainsong and to employ organs for special celebrations, but the views of the leaders of the reformed Scottish Kirk after 1560, shaped by Knox's and Goodman's experience of Calvin's Geneva, were much more severe. The mass and the veneration of saints were seen as idolatrous and forbidden. Liturgical and biblical Latin texts were entirely replaced by the use of the vernacular so that everyone could understand the word of God for themselves. Organs and other instruments were banned from services, and many were destroyed, and the only texts to be sung in the Kirk were the psalms, sung by the entire congregation in unison. The rich and outward-looking corpus of Scottish sacred music, with a tradition stretching back many centuries, was declared obsolete and abominable at a stroke, and the nation's churches were purged of their liturgical and musical books. One of the leading Lords of the Congregation was Lord James Stew-

art, half-brother of Mary, queen of Scots, prior of St Andrews *in commendam* (i.e. holding an ecclesiastical position 'in care' and taking the relevant revenues without actually carrying out the job), who later became earl of Moray and regent for James VI. Initially, he defended his sister's right to hold Catholic services in her private chapel, but was later recorded personally burning six mass books from the chapel royal after her fall. Lord James had cultivated tastes (witness the Eworth portraits considered in Chapter 4) and he took a personal interest in providing high-quality psalm settings for the reformed kirk.[21]

Whilst in Geneva, John Knox and his English friend Christopher Goodman (later minister of St Andrews, 1560–5) would have been familiar with the French psalm paraphrases of Clément Marot and Theodore Beza in the *Huguenot Psalter*, which was in the process of compilation during Knox's exile, and was published in full in 1562. The French psalm translations were poetically distinguished, metrically varied and sung to a set of 'proper' tunes (i.e. standard tunes for psalms in certain metres), many of which had very lively dance-like rhythms. The community of English Protestant exiles in Geneva was also in the process of producing its own metrical psalter with verses and tunes that were rather less impressive. The reformed Kirk of Scotland took the decision to create its own metrical psalter, drawing on the Genevan models, using psalm paraphrases in the English language rather than Scots, yet taking some inspiration from the varied metre of the French psalter. The Scottish metrical psalter of 1564 had 105

OPPOSITE. A sketch of a shawm player from the *Wode Partbooks*, compiled by Thomas Wode of St Andrews in the late sixteenth century. The shawm was a double-reed instrument, a precursor of the modern oboe.

'proper' tunes for the psalms, many of which were borrowed from the Huguenot (French Protestant) and Anglo-Genevan traditions: they are very striking melodies.[22]

Lord James, whilst titular prior of St Andrews, desired that the 'proper' psalm tunes should be harmonised into four parts with the tune in the tenor and he commissioned one of his own canons, the accomplished composer, David Peebles, to provide the new musical settings in a simple homophonic style. Peebles was instructed to avoid the 'curiosity' of polyphony and to produce music that was 'plain and sweet'. Peebles was clearly much attached to the polyphonic style of his Catholic past and was rather lukewarm about the project, so the music-loving Thomas Wode took it upon himself to encourage him in the task. Despite his reluctance, Peebles rose to the challenge magnificently. His psalm settings are taut, elegant and melodious, but also very simple. Wode copied the new pieces into his *Partbooks* as they were completed over several years from the mid-1560s. Wode also recruited other composers to provide settings for the metrical canticles and hymns he added to the psalms. Andrew Blackhall (a former canon of Holyrood), Andrew Kemp (master of the St Andrews song school) and John Angus (a former monk of Dunfermline) all made notable contributions. Most of the 18 canticles are the work of John Angus, including some particularly graceful settings of the *Nunc Dimittis* (Song of Simeon) and the Lord's Prayer.[23] Wode also recorded Andrew Kemp's four-part polyphonic setting of a remarkable English sonnet by

Mrs Anne Locke, 'Have mercy, God, for thy great mercies sake'. Originally from London, Mrs Locke had been an exile in Geneva with Knox and Goodman and continued to correspond with both ministers after the Reformation. In 1560, she published an accomplished sequence of 26 penitential sonnets: the first sonnet-sequence in the English language, from which Goodman took one poem and asked Kemp to set it to music. Kemp's setting is beautiful and quite complex; Wode commented that it needed to be rehearsed three or four times before it could be sung well. The *Wode Partbooks* also include three fine polyphonic settings of metrical psalms by Andrew Blackhall, which seem to have been commissioned by a cultured patron, the earl of Morton, and were probably used to support his political programme of promoting James VI's claim to the English succession.[24]

The Reformation destroyed not only most of the manuscripts containing the musical heritage of the nation, but also the patronage opportunities and career structure for musicians within the Scottish Church. The song schools were virtually all closed down, the specialist choirs were disbanded, and church composers were largely restricted to simple, homophonic settings of metrical psalms and canticles. In time, a slightly more evolved style of writing 'in reports' (a type of imitative technique, like a primitive fugue) was adopted from the Huguenot practice, but it was with some justification that Thomas Wode feared that 'music shall perish in this land utterly'. In 1579, a Geneva-based Huguenot polyphonist, Jean Servin, published settings of George Buchanan's celebrated

OPPOSITE. Musical instruments from the *Wode Partbooks*. Thomas Wode decorated his manuscripts with many beautiful illustrations. This border shows harps hanging upon the willows, as described in psalm 137.

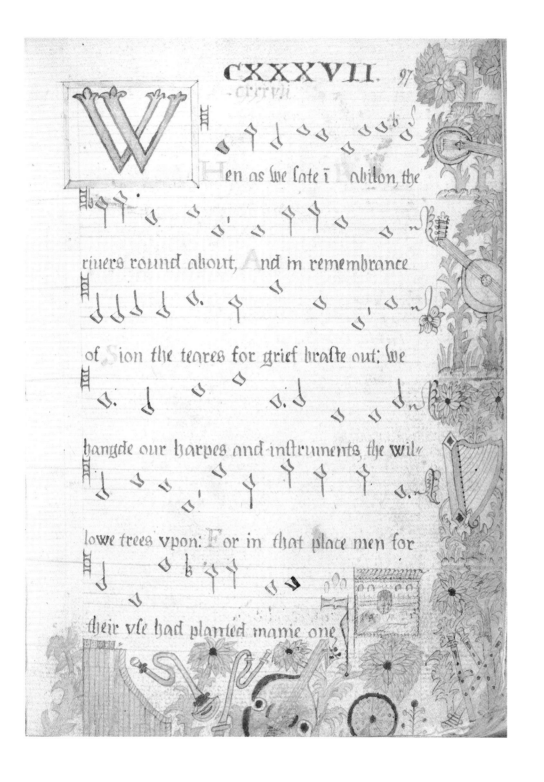

W

Hen as we sate ī abilon, the

riuers round about, And in remembrance

of Sion the teares for grief braste out: we

hangde our harpes and instruments, the wil-

lowe trees vpon: For in that place men for

their vse had planted manie one

poetic Latin psalm paraphrases, which he dedicated to James VI. In August, Servin came to visit the Scottish court with a presentation edition for the king. He probably expected to find a chapel royal establishment capable of performing his music, and perhaps offering him a job, but he was to be disappointed because the chapel royal had been thoroughly 'purged' after Mary's fall. It may not be a coincidence that in November 1579 James VI initiated a revival of song schools in the major burghs, with his Act of 'tymous remeid' (timely remedy).[25]

It may have been in connection with this development that a curious textbook on musical techniques was produced c.1580. Entitled *The Art of Music Collecit out of all Ancient Doctouris of Music* (BL), but also known as 'Scottish Anonymous', it includes many musical examples taken from Latin church music and instructions for writing fauxbourdon and countering amongst other things. It certainly set high standards for students of musical composition. It was clearly collated from pre-Reformation sources, but its confusions and obscurities show that this was done by someone who no longer fully understood those sources. King James seems to have been keen to revive polyphonic choral music at the chapel royal and he appointed his chief (secular) musician, Thomas Hudson, to be master of the music there in 1586: a post he held until his death in 1605. At the baptism of Prince Henry in 1594, Psalm 21 was reportedly sung 'according to the art of music', (i.e. either in reports or polyphony) and Psalm 128 was sung in a seven-part setting (which strongly suggests polyphony). However, after the royal court moved to England in 1603, the Scottish chapel royal went into such a decline that the king brought the English chapel royal establishment to serve him on

his homecoming tour of 1617. Organs were transported to Scotland to accompany the services (the organs of the Scottish chapel royal had been destroyed by the earl of Mar in 1567) and music was written by the English composer Orlando Gibbons especially for the occasion. Likewise, Charles I brought the English chapel royal with him for his Scottish coronation of 1633, and the Scottish chapel royal was finally abolished along with episcopacy in 1638.[26]

To an extent, the musicians who were largely deprived of patronage by the Church after 1560 could find creative outlets in writing and performing instrumental music and songs at the court (until 1603) and in the houses of the increasingly sophisticated professional and landed classes. Very little written Scottish secular music is extant from before the seventeenth century, so again it is very difficult to establish the dates and provenance of many of the surviving pieces. Some Scottish Renaissance instrumental music appears in Wode's own hand in his partbooks but most of what survives is recorded in later sources. Several country-house collections preserved lively Scottish airs and dances alongside foreign works. Duncan Burnett's music book (NLS, c.1600–10) contains the majority of the surviving examples of early Scottish keyboard music (alongside some pieces by the English master William Byrd), whilst the lute books compiled for William Mure of Rowallan (EUL, c.1612–28), Robert Gordon of Straloch (1627–9, now lost but partially copied in the nineteenth century) and John Skene of Hallyards (NLS, 1615–35) are particularly important manuscripts. The traditions of music for dances, feasts, celebrations and private entertainments were probably as deeply rooted as the heritage of sacred music, for there are records of trumpets, drums, pipes,

lutes, harps, clavichords, fiddles and many other instruments in frequent use in the fifteenth and early sixteenth centuries. Much of the early repertoire would surely have included traditional or folk music. For instance, the medieval epic 'Greysteil' was sung to James IV in 1498 by two men who accompanied themselves on fiddles and the music for this performance has been reconstructed from a tune in the Straloch manuscript.[27] Robert Wedderburn's *Complaynt of Scotland* (c.1550) includes long lists of song and dance titles, which he clearly expected would be familiar to his readers, but, unfortunately, most are now lost. Many appear to be very traditional, but there are also some more 'courtly' pieces included, as befits an age which did not recognise the later categories of 'high' and 'low' cultures. The list starts with Henry VIII's 'Pastime with Good Company' and goes on to mention over 30 other songs and a further 30 dances, a few of which have survived, such as 'Alas, that Same Sueit Face' and 'O Lusty May'.[28]

By the 1530s there is more evidence of the 'art music' of the Renaissance in Scotland. The French influence was very strong, which is understandable following James V's visit to France in 1536–7 and his two French marriages. The French were pioneers of printing musical notation. In 1528, Pierre Attaignant of Paris developed a technique for printing music in one, rather than several, impressions, which meant that French music became as cheap and accessible as any other printed text; and from 1532 to 1547, Jacques Moderne, who was originally from Italy, was also printing music at Lyon. Both Paris and Lyon were on James V's itinerary. At the French court of this period, *chansons rustiques* (country songs) were very popular. These were adaptations of traditional songs which were often woven into medleys (*fricassées*). Three spirited Scottish examples of the genre survive: 'The Pleugh Sang' (c.1500), 'Trip and Goe, Hey' (c.1530) and 'All Sons of Adam' (c.1540). The first may have been used in a theatrical parody of rural life presented at court (with the faint possibility of some satirical overtones), the second was suitable for May Day celebrations, and the third is a Christmas song.[29] Other French *chansons* of the period were settings of more courtly verses by writers such as Clément Marot or Pierre de Ronsard, with music by composers including Pierre Certon, Claudin de Sermisy, or Clément Janequin. Typically, they were written for three or four parts, with the melody in the tenor, in a simple, chordal style with repeated refrains and dance-like rhythms. The French *chansons* also exerted some influence on the early madrigal form, which was pioneered in Italy by Franco-Flemish composers such as Philippe Verdelot and Adrian Willaert. Marot wrote a *chant nuptial* to celebrate James V's marriage to Princess Madeleine and the young Ronsard came to Scotland briefly as a page in the new queen's train. Scottish partsongs with French influences include 'Richt Soir Opprest' (anon.), 'O Lusty May' (anon.) and 'Departe, Departe' (words, and possibly music also, by Alexander Scott, c.1547), which are akin to the style of Claudin, whilst 'Support your Servand' (words possibly by George Steil, d. 1542, music anon.) is a Scottish version of Marot's 'Secourez Moy Ma Dame', a poem which was also set to music by Claudin. Perhaps the most haunting of these songs is 'Departe, Departe', inspired by the Master of Erskine's courtly leave-taking from Mary of Guise on the eve of the Battle of Pinkie, where he was killed. The *chanson* tradition continued at the Francophile court of Mary and also at the court of James VI,

which after the arrival of the king's French-born cousin, Esmé Stuart, in 1579 was also heavily influenced by French tastes. A spirited drinking song, 'Nou let us sing' (anon.), was probably performed for the young king's 'joyous entry' into Edinburgh in 1579, and some 20 elegant settings of the lyric poetry of Alexander Montgomerie survive; most are anonymous, but one, 'Adieu, O Desie [daisy] of Delyt', is by Andrew Blackhall.[30]

Also in the 1530s, consorts of viols first appeared in Scotland. The viol was the most fashionable bowed instrument of the sixteenth-century Italian and French courts and was often played in ensembles (consorts) of four or six instruments of different sizes and pitches. Violars played what later ages would think of as 'chamber' music: intimate recitals to soothe or entertain a select audience in the private rooms of palaces and houses. The viol is not to be confused with the violin, since the two instruments were quite distinct: the viol had a fretted finger-board, usually six (rather than four) strings, a less resonant sound than the violin and was placed in the lap rather than on the arm. From 1538 a consort of four viols led by the Frenchman, Jacques Columbell, was employed at the royal court and payments to violars continue to be recorded in the royal accounts for the rest of the century. There is no record of the viol repertoire of this time, but Columbell would certainly have drawn on his French heritage, and by 1538 the Attaignant press had published several volumes of instrumental music and dances by Claudin and his contemporaries. The consort of four violars serving James V's grandson, James VI, were members of the English Hudson family, who had originally come to Scotland with Darnley and retained the favour of his son. The Hudson brothers were talented and versatile and it is likely that

Queen Mary's Clarsach c.1500, said to have been played by Mary, queen of Scots.

some of them wrote music, but nothing can be definitely ascribed to them. However, Helena Mennie Shire suggested that a pair of dances known as 'Hutchison's Pavan and Galliard' might have been written by one of them.[31]

Chamber music was also played on harps, lutes and small keyboard instruments such as clavichords, spinets and virginals. The Highland harp or clarsach appears in the records of the courts of James IV and James V, but as time went on it tended to be replaced by the lute. David Lindsay played the lute to the young James V and the adult

king was himself an accomplished player, as were his father and daughter. There seems to have been some considerable sharing of music for the harp and the lute and many of the songs and dances recorded in the seventeenth-century lute books might have originated in the earlier harp repertoire. Mary, queen of Scots, loved music and dancing; she is said to have had a sweet singing voice and to have played the harp, lute and virginals. Two early clarsachs from c.1500 have survived and are now in the National Museum; one of them is known as 'Queen Mary's Clarsach' and is said to have been given by her to Beatrice Gardyn of Banchory in 1563. Its hornbeam frame is decorated with intricate incised patterns.[32] The National Museum also houses a Scottish virginals of c.1560–c.1660 said to have been owned by Lady Marie Stuart, countess of Mar, a daughter of James VI's favourite, Esmé, duke of Lennox. The lid of the virginals is decorated with painted scenes including Orpheus playing music to wild animals. It has recently been restored but is in quite a fragile state.

Amongst Queen Mary's most loyal servants were the musicians James and John Lauder, father and son. John continued to serve her in her English captivity, but James returned to Scotland and the court of James VI. Some of the dances in the *Wode Partbooks* might be by James Lauder, but the only piece definitely ascribed to him is 'My Lorde of Marche Paven' (1584) written for the same Robert Stewart who commissioned Peebles' '*Quam Multi Domine*'. Stewart was clearly a discerning patron, since the pavane is probably the finest surviving piece of Scottish consort music of the period. A pavane was a stately, processional dance, which was often used as a prelude to an allemande or galliard, which were lighter, more

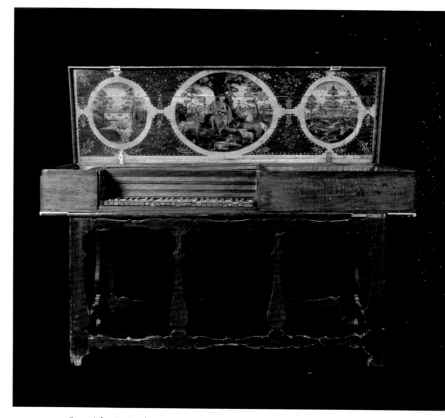

Scottish virginals, c.1560–c.1660.
Scenes from the legend of Orpheus
decorate the lid.

sprightly dances. These dances were very fashionable in the English, Continental, and Scottish courts of the period. William Hudson took 'extraordinary pains' teaching the king to dance, so that he should exhibit all the accomplishments of a gentleman. James VI much preferred to hunt, but dancing seems to have been popular in the wider court circle. The elusive figure of William Kinloch is also associated with James Lauder at the court of James VI c.1582. He wrote much of Scotland's earliest surviving keyboard music and his fantasia, the 'Battel of Pavie', calls for a virtuosic play-

ing technique. It paints a musical picture of a furious battle in the Italian wars, when Francis I was captured by the forces of his great rival Charles V in 1525. Kinloch is known to have travelled between England and Scotland (there is a suspicion that he was engaged in espionage) and it is possible that he studied with the great William Byrd in the 1570s and 1580s. Byrd, Kinloch's fellow Catholic recusant, had also written a keyboard piece on the theme of the Battle of Pavia and Kinloch's work might be seen as a compliment by a pupil to his master, and from one Catholic to another.[33] Tobias Hume (c.1569–1645) was a mercenary soldier and virtuoso player of the lyra viol (small bass viol), which he claimed was superior to the lute in chamber performance. His works contain very early examples of techniques such as plucking the strings of a bowed instrument (*pizzicato*) and striking the strings with the wood of the bow (*col legno*), and his compositions, which are strikingly original and innovative, have been viewed as anticipating elements of the Baroque style of Bach. He sought patronage from Anna of Denmark at the English court and all his known works were published in England in 1605 and 1607.[34]

The fragmentary surviving evidence suggests very strongly that before the Reformation, Renaissance sacred polyphony flourished in Scotland. Robert Carver was clearly a master of the art: his early works are fine examples of the highly decorated, rhythmic style of c.1500 and by the 1540s he was demonstrating the ability to adapt to the more restrained, elegant idiom of the mid-sixteenth century. Likewise, the polyphonic music of David Peebles seems to have evolved to match European trends between the 1530s and 1570s. Sadly, the unique beauty of the contrasting polyphonic styles of Carver and Peebles provides but a glimpse into a lost world of wonderful Scottish music. It is to be hoped that further examples may yet be unearthed in obscure manuscripts which have hitherto been overlooked. The severity of Scottish Calvinist practice was a massive obstacle to the development of Scottish sacred music after the Reformation, and it is a testament to the talents and versatility of Peebles, Blackhall, Angus, Kemp and their anonymous brethren that anything of any quality was written at all. In the circumstances, their dignified and graceful settings of the metrical psalms and canticles were remarkable achievements. Yet these men had all been trained in the art of polyphony before the Reformation and, with their deaths, original composition of church music seems essentially to have ceased. Renaissance secular music in Scotland was heavily influenced by French *chansons* and consort music and developed in line with European trends to a considerable degree. The keyboard works of Kinloch and the viol pieces of Hume were particularly innovative and inventive, and in some respects may be considered to prefigure the later developments of the Baroque style. However, the quintessentially Baroque art form of opera, which began to develop in Italy from 1597, would find no place in Calvinist Scotland.

7

THE LEARNED MUSE

Renaissance Education and Literature

One of the most important cultural developments of the Renaissance was the expansion of literacy and education beyond the clergy into a new lay elite. In the early fifteenth century the Church controlled almost all aspects of education, and the language of literature, philosophy, government and law was Latin. Of course, Latin continued to be the language of the intelligentsia for many generations to come, but by the sixteenth century a thriving vernacular culture was also developing, with the Scots language used in legal and administrative records and in literature, especially poetry. A new class of literate and often highly educated burgesses, lairds and lay professionals was also emerging. The process was assisted in many ways by the influences of both humanism and Protestantism. Humanism had Italian roots but by c.1500 was embedding itself in the universities and courts of northern Europe: the most famous humanist of the early sixteenth century was Desiderius Erasmus of Rotterdam, who travelled widely in France, England and Italy. Erasmus and his fellows promoted the study of classical texts and ancient eloquence in the belief that this would have a civilising effect on society. As was noted in Chapter 1, humanists sought to create a body of virtuous and rational active citizens who would prioritise the common good over private benefit in their public careers. At the Reformation, the desire to promote virtue and civility through lay education was echoed by the wish to create a godly people through greater knowledge of the scriptures. Both ambitions required the provision of schools and universities open to laymen as well as clerics and the establishment of printing presses in Scotland. Furthermore, the desire to create an all-graduate ministry also stimulated educational developments. The intellectual climate fostered considerable literary creativity. Indeed, the literary culture of the period was so prolific and diverse that only some examples of the most significant works can be considered in this chapter.

The origins of Scottish Renaissance humanism are rather obscure and difficult to identify with any precision but seem to lie in the fifteenth-century royal court and universities. There was little direct Italian influence, although some inspiration might have been provided by the occasional visitor, such

as in 1435 when the celebrated humanist and future Pope Pius II, Aeneas Sylvius Piccolomini, came on an embassy to the court of James I. His visit is commemorated in a fresco by Pinturicchio in the Piccolomini library at Siena Cathedral, which portrays James I in a fanciful Italianate setting as the archetypal Renaissance prince: wise, solemn and magnificent. By 1484 the royal secretary, Archibald Whitelaw, who had taught at the universities of St Andrews and Cologne, was sufficiently well versed in the classics to give an elegant Latin oration, incorporating references to Cicero, Virgil, Seneca and Livy, before Richard III of England at a diplomatic conference. This seems to have been the first substantial piece of humanist prose written by a Scot. Whitelaw also had a fine library, which included works by Lucan, Horace and Sallust, and he was a tutor to the young James III. Another Scottish cleric with an impressive library was Archbishop William Scheves, who presumably had a particular interest in history, since he commissioned his own copies of the *Scotichronicon* and the *Liber Pluscardensis* (Scottish chronicles from the 1440s and 1460s respectively). He was also well aware of his own historical importance, judging from his Renaissance portrait medal of 1491 (see Chapter 3).[1]

The records of the fifteenth-century university libraries have survived only in fragments, but St Andrews, Glasgow and Aberdeen are likely to have had considerable collections of humanist works, since Scottish students and teachers shuttled regularly to and from the Continental universities. An example that suggests this is the bequest to the library at St Andrews by Alexander Inglis, dean of Dunkeld, in 1496. His books were a thoroughly humanist collection, including works by Virgil, Ovid, Cicero, Seneca and Horace, many of which had been printed in Italy, and there is no reason to imagine that his legacy was exceptional. Indeed, classical and humanist texts appeared in many Scottish libraries of the period.[2] In the early sixteenth century, Alexander Stewart, archbishop of St Andrews, studied under Erasmus at Siena, Padua and Rome and was later remembered by his great teacher with some affection. Had he not been killed tragically young at the Battle of Flodden in 1513, he might have provided considerable intellectual and cultural leadership. The omens were good since, shortly before his death, he and Prior John Hepburn founded a new college for 'poor 'clerks', which became St Leonard's College, at the university of St Andrews. By this time, William Elphinstone, bishop of Aberdeen and keeper of the privy seal, was promoting a thoroughly humanist programme in Scotland. He founded a new university at Aberdeen in 1495, with the express intention of encouraging laymen, as well as clerics, to study the liberal arts, canon and civil law and medicine (the faculty of theology was still expected to train the clergy rather than the laity), in the hope that this would improve the standards of Scottish political and legal administration. His university was established *pro patria* (for the country). Elphinstone was probably also the prime mover behind the 1496 Education Act, discussed below, and was certainly the driving force behind the establishment of the first Scottish printing press in Edinburgh in 1507, and the attempt to create a

OPPOSITE. Portrait of William Elphinstone, bishop of Aberdeen, c.1500–c.1510, by an unknown artist.

distinctive Scottish liturgy through the publication of the *Aberdeen Breviary* in 1510 (see Chapter 6).[3]

It is often thought that the systematic provision of schooling in Scotland began only at the Reformation but this was not the case. The song schools discussed in the previous chapter, which educated the choristers at cathedrals, abbeys, collegiate churches and some parish churches, were part of a much wider network of medieval Scottish schools. Schools providing basic tuition in reading and writing were often attached to parish churches or monasteries and staffed by chaplains or monks. In many burghs, grammar schools provided boys with the education required for university entrance and the masters there were clerics too, usually secular priests. The Dominican friars, whose houses were invariably in urban centres and whose order had a special vocation for preaching and teaching, perhaps provided the masters for some grammar schools, such as those at Ayr and Glasgow, but more commonly they seem to have focused on educating their own postulants and novices, often to very high standards. There were even some 'sewing schools' for girls in a few burghs, although by the 1620s, the Kirk was getting suspicious that they were nests of 'papistry'. Before the Reformation, there were schools for girls from elite families in nunneries such as Elcho, Aberdour and Haddington, though women could not progress to university at this period.[4]

We know of the existence of about a hundred Scottish schools of various types before 1560 and there were certainly many more which have escaped the documentary record. Amongst the most difficult to identify are the informal 'household' schools which formed in the homes of the landed elite: private tutors would have been engaged to edu-cate the sons and wards of the household along with other boys who were often fostered from families with ties of kinship or clientage. For example, John Carswell, future superintendent of Argyll and bishop of the Isles, was employed in the 1550s by the 4th earl of Argyll as tutor to the future 5th earl, in whom he instilled fixed evangelical views. In some households, girls were educated too. For example, the daughters of Sir Richard Maitland of Lethington were highly literate and cultured, and Marie seems to have been an accomplished poet (discussed below). The education provided in these domestic schools depended entirely on the quality of the tutor but could be very advanced. One of the finest Scottish humanists, George Buchanan, served as tutor to the young third earl of Cassillis, then to an illegitimate son of James V, and later to King James VI. Some of the burgh grammar schools also reached very high standards. For instance, the famous Protestant academic, cleric and controversialist Andrew Melville had been educated before the Reformation at the grammar school of Montrose, where he learned to read Greek, and the schoolmaster at Dunfermline in the 1470s and 1480s was Robert Henryson, the learned and distinguished poet. For much of the period, the standard textbooks for Latin grammar used in Scottish schools were those of Aelius Donatus (a Roman writer of the fourth century) or Johannes Despauterius (a Flemish humanist, d.1520). However, there was also a native Latin grammar written by John Vaus of Aberdeen, first printed in Paris in 1522 and reprinted in Edinburgh in 1566. In 1533, George Buchanan translated Thomas Linacre's *Rudiments of Grammar* from English into Latin and this became a 'bestseller'. After the Reformation, a flurry of new native grammars appeared. Scottish schooling could thus easily stand com-

parison with the provision made in other countries of the period.⁵

The humanist idea that the promotion of lay education was of public benefit was most clearly encapsulated in the 1496 Education Act, which stipulated

> that all barons and freeholders that are of substance put their eldest sons and heirs to the schools from the age of eight or nine years, and to remain at the grammar schools until they be competently founded [educated] and have perfect Latin. And thereafter to remain three years at the schools of arts and law [at the universities] that they may have knowledge and understanding of the laws. Through the which, Justice may reign universally through all the realm . . .⁶

This was an official challenge to the general assumption made by many nobles and lairds that they had the natural birthright to be royal counsellors, administrators and judges without any training, other than in military skills. The act was supported by James IV, but is usually ascribed to the influence of William Elphinstone, as already mentioned. Elphinstone had just established his new humanist university at Aberdeen with faculties of arts and law (amongst others) and if it were not for the fact that he is invariably regarded as a high-minded and sincere reformer, the act might be interpreted as a private recruitment drive.⁷ The new law was never systematically enforced, but it promoted important principles and was unusually enlightened for its time: there was no comparable legislation in France or England. Certainly, the quality of the education of the lay professionals providing legal and administrative services to

the Crown in the following generation rose markedly. For example, James Foulis of Colinton, clerk register in the 1530s and 1540s, was a graduate of the universities of Paris and Orléans and wrote stylish neo-Latin poetry, whilst James V's royal secretary, Sir Thomas Erskine of Brechin, had studied at Pavia. It is likely that the rising quality and quantity of educated lay professionals, especially lawyers, made possible the establishment of the College of Justice as a central civil court in 1532. The original foundation consisted of equal numbers of clerical and secular judges and an attempt was made to disqualify the ecclesiastics after the Reformation, but some continued to serve until the late seventeenth century. Sir Thomas Erskine contributed to the arrangements for the new College of Justice and possibly used Italian models.⁸

The Education Act of 1496 also demonstrates that the movement for educational reform within the Catholic Church was already in evidence many years before the start of the Protestant Reformation, and was inspired to an extent by the idealism of the humanists. However, the criticisms subsequently voiced by the Protestants about poor levels of literacy, education and religious knowledge undoubtedly stung and prompted more urgent action. The provincial council of the Scottish Church which met in 1549 expressed the need for a school in every parish, thus anticipating in this respect the Protestant *First Book of Discipline*. The provincial council of 1552 authorised the publication of Archbishop Hamilton's *Catechism*, an instruction manual for the Catholic faith, and demanded that extracts from it should be read in parish churches every Sunday. The *Catechism* (which was actually written by an English Dominican called Richard Marshall) was intended as

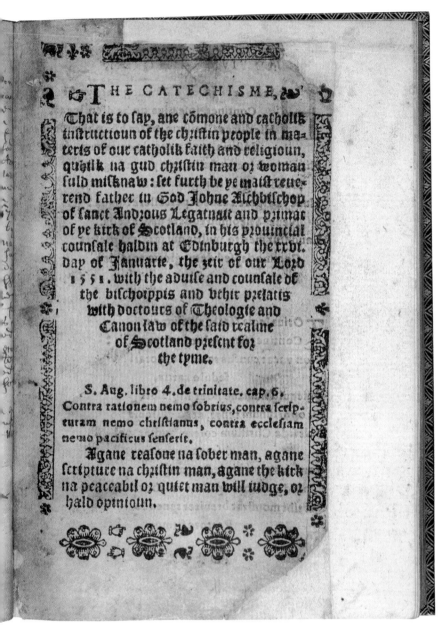

Title page of Archbishop Hamilton's *Catechism*, printed by John Scot in St Andrews in 1552.

much to raise the educational standards of the clergy as of the laity and showed some awareness of, and respect for, the Protestant critique of clerical laxity. It was the first book printed in St Andrews by the newly established press of John Scot. The *Catechism* was followed in 1559 by a short pamphlet aimed at simple lay folk, known from its price as the *Twapenny Faith*, which was also printed by Scot.[9] Thus the official focus on Scottish schooling after the Reformation did not establish an education system from scratch, but rather tried to extend and improve existing provision and to infuse Protestant doctrine. Taking some inspiration from the educational decrees of the Catholic Council of Trent but also building on the model of Calvin's Geneva, the *First Book of Discipline* of 1561 envisaged a primary school in every parish, with 'schools of full exercise' (grammar schools) in the major burghs. It also insisted that the education of the poor should be paid for out of public funds. Lack of financial support meant that the vision was never fully implemented, but by the 1630s there were about 800 schools of various types across the country. Scotland had a school system that was impressive by international standards and which had fostered one of the most literate societies in Europe.[10]

The authors of the *First Book of Discipline* (the six Johns: Knox, Spottiswoode, Willock, Row, Douglas and Winram) were also acutely aware that the new Kirk required a large number of new ministers, many of whom would need a university education. Before the fifteenth century, Scottish students had had to go abroad for their higher education. Then came a sequence of university foundations by Scottish bishops under papal bulls: St Andrews by Henry Wardlaw in 1411, Glasgow by William Turnbull in 1451, and Aberdeen by

William Elphinstone in 1495. In addition there were new colleges created within the university of St Andrews: St Salvator's by Bishop James Kennedy in 1450, St Leonard's by Prior John Hepburn and Archbishop Alexander Stewart in 1512, and St Mary's by the Beaton archbishops, James and David, in 1537–44. The creation and expansion of Scottish universities in the fifteenth and early sixteenth centuries suggests very strongly that the grammar schools were producing increasing numbers of students qualified and eager for higher education. Humanist influences were felt to an extent in all the universities from the late fifteenth century. However, only Aberdeen and St Mary's College had any overtly humanist objectives and the St Mary's foundation was rather unstable until its refoundation in 1579. At Aberdeen, the key figure was Hector Boece, who was originally from Dundee and had been educated at Paris alongside Erasmus. Boece was recruited by Elphinstone in 1497 initially to teach the liberal arts, and in 1505 was appointed principal of King's College, which was the sole university college. He was already well known as a writer of elegant Renaissance Latin verse and prose and promoted the humanist study of the classics at Aberdeen. Some of his students became very fine Latinists: the philosopher Florence Wilson is a good example.[11] There is an intriguing possibility that Boece even used the recommendations of the Florentine humanist Marsilio Ficino to arrange the layout of the new buildings at King's College for the benefit of the health of the students.[12] At St Mary's, Archibald Hay was appointed from Paris as the new principal in 1546. He was an accomplished exponent of Renaissance scholarship in Latin, Greek and Hebrew and might have made a great impact on Scottish education, had

he not been killed at the Battle of Pinkie in 1547. There was also a humanist academy established in the 1530s and 1540s at the abbey of Kinloss by Giovanni Ferrerio, a scholar from Piedmont. There he created a fine library and taught the monks a curriculum based on classical writers such as Cicero, Terence, and Virgil, and humanists such as Erasmus, Jacques Lefèvre d'Etaples, and Philip Melanchthon. Ferrerio also wrote several works of Scottish history and biography in an expansive rhetorical style.[13]

Thus, as with the school system, the reform and expansion of Scottish university education after the Reformation was built on well-established foundations, although the combination of political and religious strife and outbreaks of epidemic disease in the 1550s and 1560s brought the Scottish universities to a low ebb. The *First Book of Discipline* proposed a scheme for university reform which was not implemented by the Kirk and there was considerable inertia in the university system. The standard medieval theological textbook, Peter Lombard's *Sentences*, was abandoned as too 'papist', but little else changed in the curricula or teaching methods. However, new and Protestant, civic foundations were established with Edinburgh's 'Tounis College' in 1583 and Marischal College, New Aberdeen, in 1593 (which merged with King's College in the nineteenth century to form the modern university of Aberdeen). There was also a short-lived attempt to set up a new university at Fraserburgh in the 1590s. Furthermore, the civic authorities started to take responsibility for the provision of libraries. In 1585, the 'Common Library of New Aberdeen' was founded by ministers, lawyers and burgesses of the town and housed in the parish church of St Nicholas (the library later passed to Marischal

College). The library of St Mary's Church, Dundee, which later became the town library, was founded in 1599. In 1580, the advocate Clement Little left in his will a collection of 268 books to the town and the kirk of Edinburgh, which subsequently formed the kernel of the university library. Edinburgh University actually had pre-Reformation roots in that Robert Reid, bishop of Orkney, who as abbot of Kinloss had brought Ferrerio to Scotland, encouraged Mary of Guise to establish town lectureships in law, Greek, Latin and philosophy in Edinburgh in the 1550s. The scheme was probably modelled on Francis I's Parisian *lecteurs royaux* of 1530 and it provided a great boost to the education of the laity. At his death in 1558, Reid left money in his will to establish a new college in Edinburgh and part of this legacy was eventually salvaged in 1583 to help fund the new Protestant university.[14]

The traditional liberal arts (primarily grammar, logic and rhetoric) continued to be taught but with an increasing emphasis on studying texts, such as those of Aristotle, in the original languages. The study of the Bible in its original languages (Hebrew, Syriac and Chaldaic for the Old Testament; Greek and Syriac for the New) also became gradually embedded in the schools of divinity. An expert in these biblical languages who had established a scholarly reputation at Geneva, Andrew Melville, returned to Scotland in 1574 and virtually single-handedly revived the almost moribund university of Glasgow. He introduced specialist teaching to replace the medieval system of 'regents' (where one tutor would take a class through their entire liberal arts course) and adopted the Ramist 'method' of teaching, blending it with more traditional Aristotelian and humanist approaches in a very practical educational strategy. The Ramist

'method', named after Peter Ramus of Paris (with whom Melville had studied), was a way of breaking down complex ideas into manageable sections which could then be taught quickly and effectively to students. It was particularly applied to the teaching of logic and theology. Elements of the 'Melvillian' approach seeped into the other Scottish universities too (Robert Rollock, the first principal at Edinburgh, adopted it) but did not generally have a very durable impact: its influence was on the wane by the early seventeenth century. Melville also made St Mary's into a particularly rigorous theological college when he moved to St Andrews in 1580. Although his methods aroused fierce opposition in some quarters, his graduates formed a formidably erudite and forthright pool of ministers for the Kirk. Melville also had a very active role in the leadership of the Kirk, once famously telling James VI that he was 'God's sillie [weak] vassall'. Thus his energies were spread thinly and ultimately his success was mixed. Having offended the king, amongst others, he ended his life as an exile in the Huguenot academy at Sedan.[15]

The expansion of lay education and literacy meant that there was increasing demand for books of all sorts and Scottish booksellers and publishers emerged to meet it. It has already been shown that manuscripts were produced in the monastic *scriptoria* at Culross, Lindores, Kinloss, and elsewhere, and that manuscripts were imported from England and the Continent in the late-medieval period (see Chapter 4). By the fifteenth century, books were being sold from stalls at burgh fairs and at the universities, and manuscripts were increasingly being replaced by printed editions from the newly established European presses. From the 1450s, the Gutenberg press in Mainz was printing with moveable type and so the mass production of relatively cheap volumes became possible for the first time. The new technology quickly spread to Cologne, Basel, Venice, Lyon, Paris, Antwerp, and elsewhere. Scottish merchants and travellers imported books from all of these centres: Venice was the main source in the late fifteenth century, Paris in the early sixteenth century, and Antwerp, Amsterdam and London after the Reformation. The first books by a Scot printed during his lifetime were probably two Latin volumes by the Aberdonian philosopher James Liddell, printed in Paris in the 1490s. The first book of Scots poetry to be printed (and translated) was William of Touris' *Contemplacioun of Synnaris*, which was published in an anglicised form at Westminster in 1499. At this period, it was often the case that the roles of printer, publisher, bookbinder and bookseller were combined. After a shaky start in 1507, it took about a century for Scottish printers and booksellers to become well established in Edinburgh. There was also some printing in Stirling and St Andrews. During the course of the seventeenth century all the major burghs acquired their own booktraders.[16]

As noted in Chapter 6, the first Scottish printing press of Chepman and Myllar was established in Edinburgh in 1507 under royal patent, specifically to print books for the government and the Church. Walter Chepman was a well-connected and wealthy merchant who provided the business acumen for the venture and the premises in the Southgait (now the Cowgate). Andrew Myllar was a bookseller, who had already had two books printed for him in Rouen, and he seems to have obtained the tools and techniques of the printing trade from there, along with some skilled workmen. Both men used personal devices or badges to identify their work. Myllar's device includes

the royal arms of France, and his own initials on a shield, then makes a pun on his name by showing a miller climbing a ladder into a windmill. Chepman's device shows his initials on a shield and depicts an oak tree, perhaps the tree of knowledge (more usually shown as an apple tree), flanked by some rather outlandish figures, which may represent Adam and Eve, or perhaps the mythical wild people of the woods. The main elements of this design were copied from the device of a Parisian printer active in the 1480s and 1490s, Philippe Pigouchet. The works of the Southgait press date from between 1508 and 1510, by which latter year Chepman seems to have been operating without his partner, who perhaps had died. As well as the two volumes of Elphinstone's *Aberdeen Breviary* (see Chapter 6), the first Scottish press printed 11 books in Scots and English. The first dated publication of 4 April 1508 was *The Maying or Disport of Chaucer* (actually a work by Chaucer's admirer John Lydgate) and this was followed by further volumes of poetry including William Dunbar's *Golden Targe* (shield) and Robert Henryson's *Tale of Orpheus and Eurydice*. These Chepman and Myllar prints include the only known copies of some important works of Scottish literature. There are also some fragments of other Southgait prints surviving, and there may well have been many other works that have been lost to us.[17]

After 1510, there is a gap in the history of Scottish printing. There was a certain John Story who printed an undated devotional tract in Edinburgh, which has been tentatively dated to c.1520, but the next attested Scottish press was that of Thomas Davidson in the 1530s. Davidson's device was very similar to Chepman's: it depicted a tree of knowledge (this time bearing strange globular

Walter Chepman's device, taken from Dunbar's *Golden Targe*,
printed in Edinburgh, 1508–10. The design was borrowed
from the device of a Parisian printer.

fruits and with owls perched in the branches)
flanked by two 'wild men'. Davidson seems to
have been a native of Aberdeen and to have learned
his trade in Louvain in the 1520s. He became
king's printer to James V in the 1530s. Very few
of his publications have survived and there must
have been many others, since lost. The known
works are a Latin poem celebrating the king's
accession to power in 1528 by James Foulis, *The
Palice of Honour* by Gavin Douglas (1530s), a
Scots translation by John Bellenden of a Latin history of Scotland by Hector Boece (c.1536), and an
edition of James V's Acts of Parliament (c.1541).
The history and the statutes are the earliest known
examples of books of their genre printed in Scotland. Both were royal commissions, which suggests
that James V had similar priorities to those of
James IV in his 1507 patent. The first full edition
of all the acts of the parliament of Scotland was
not printed until 1566, for Mary. Davidson was
the first Scottish printer to use roman and italic type
as well as the older 'black letter', which mimics
medieval handwriting (Chepman and Myllar had
used only 'black letter' type). The title page of the
1541 Acts of Parliament has a particularly fine
print of the royal arms and the book concludes with
a graceful woodcut of the crucified Christ shown
within a rosary.[18] After the last known work by
Davidson, there is another ten-year gap (presumably works have been lost) before John Scot's publication of Hamilton's *Catechism* in St Andrews in
1552, noted above. Scot seems to have learned
his trade in Edinburgh and he returned there to
work sometime in the late 1550s. After the Reformation, a number of rival presses were established in Edinburgh, and the burgh became the
centre of Scottish printing. However, Robert
Lekpreuik, who was the king's printer from 1568,

worked for a while in Stirling and St Andrews in 1571–3.

It is notable that the key texts of the Scottish Reformation, the Geneva Bible of 1560, the Book of Common Order of 1562, and the metrical Psalter of 1564, were actually written in English not Scots, and thus contributed greatly to a creeping anglicisation of Scottish culture. The Geneva Bible was originally produced for and by the community of English Protestant exiles in Calvin's godly republic, with only a limited contribution from John Knox. The Geneva New Testament of 1557, for instance, was substantially based on the earlier English translation of William Tyndale. Indeed, all the vernacular bibles of the early Scottish Reformation were printed abroad in the English language and imported. Robert Lekpreuik produced several editions of the psalms and the liturgy (Book of Common Order) and was granted a licence to print the full Geneva Bible in Scotland, but he never exercised this right. In 1575, the General Assembly tried again and granted a licence to the printing partnership of Thomas Bassandyne and Alexander Arbuthnet to produce a Scottish edition of the Geneva Bible. Bassandyne had brought out the New Testament by 1576 and then died in 1577. Arbuthnet completed the publication of the Bible in 1579. His edition of the Old Testament has some flaws, but the achievement earned him the appointment of king's printer in succession to Lekpreuik, who had been imprisoned in 1574 for printing unauthorised material. However, Arbuthnet struggled to keep up with demand and bibles were still imported for many years afterwards. Scots had to wait until 1610 for a really accurate printing: the Geneva Bible of Andro Hart was so highly regarded that it was copied by many Dutch printers of the seventeenth century. The

Title page of Thomas Davidson's edition of the *Acts of Parliament of James V*, printed in Edinburgh c.1541.

growing anglicisation of Scottish culture was reinforced by the appointment of an expatriate Englishman, Robert Waldegrave, to the post of king's printer in 1590. Waldegrave printed James VI's own books, amongst others, until 1603.[19]

The literary culture of Renaissance Scotland was highly Latinate and fluency in Latin continued to be greatly prized, even as writing in the Scots vernacular (and later, English) was also increasing. Among the earliest examples of Renaissance Latin, or neo-Latin, writing by Scots is a sequence of history books. Medieval writers of history had worked in the narrative tradition of the 'chronicle' (a description of events, usually without analysis or comment) and used a style of Latin which had departed somewhat from classical models. However, the writers of the Renaissance, inspired by Petrarch and his Italian admirers, aspired to emulate the elegant Latin style of Cicero, Virgil and Livy, amongst others. For the Renaissance writers, history was a branch of rhetoric. There was always an underlying message or moral to be drawn from the study of the past, and to be expressed with the greatest eloquence; scenes would be described for dramatic effect and dialogue invented for historical figures. However, the Renaissance historians did not entirely dispense with the medieval tradition, but rather built on the work of their predecessors to a considerable extent. The great medieval writers of Scottish history were John of Fordun and Walter Bower. Fordun's *Chronica Gentis Scotorum* (Chronicle of the Nation of the Scots) of c.1363 included some rather fanciful legends about the origins of the Scottish nation. The community was supposedly founded in the time of Moses by an exiled Egyptian princess called Scota (hence *Scoti* or Scots) with her Greek husband, Gathelos. It was then ruled by an unbroken line of kings descending from the mythical Fergus MacFerquhard in 330 BC. Fordun was writing shortly after the Wars of Independence, which helped forge the Scottish national consciousness. These myths were therefore intended to counteract the English claims to overlordship over all of Britain, which stemmed from the supposed originator of the ancient Britons (according to Geoffrey of Monmouth), Brutus the Trojan. Bower's *Scotichronicon* (A History Book for Scots, 1440s) adopted Fordun's version of events and continued the story from the death of David I in 1153, where Fordun stopped, to the murder of King James I in 1437.[20]

In 1521, John Major (or Mair) published in Paris his *Historia Majoris Britanniae* (History of Greater Britain or, punning on his name, Major's History of Britain). Major was an extremely well-respected scholastic logician and theologian who had taught at the universities of Glasgow, St Andrews and Paris. He was conservative by instinct, but was also critical of the shortcomings of the established institutions of his day. This book was his only foray into history. He did not adopt the classically inspired Latin style of the humanists and was quite critical of their rhetorical concerns: 'it is of more moment to understand aright, and clearly to lay down the truth of any matter, than to use elegant and highly-coloured language'.[21] However, some of the themes he explored had quite humanist overtones. His concern with factual accuracy led him to dismiss as nonsense the origin myths of Geoffrey of Monmouth, Fordun and Bower. His book was dedicated to the young James V in the hope that the prince might learn from it how to be a good king. Major was critical of the poorly educated, chivalry-obsessed Scottish nobility, who failed to maintain peace and

civil order. He approved of Elphinstone's plan to educate the Scottish landowning classes to make them more peaceful, law-abiding and serviceable to the community. He also stressed that those who exercised authority should rule for the common good rather than private profit, but he had an unusual notion of how this might best be achieved. For Major, stability and prosperity would be most effectively gained by the dynastic union of the two realms of England and Scotland, and James V, the son of a Stewart king and a Tudor princess, would be the person most likely to achieve it. Major also had a political philosophy steeped in the theory of conciliarism: the challenge posed to the authority of the papacy by medieval church councils. He believed that sovereignty resided in the will of the people or rather, the 'worthier part' of the people (he was not a democrat), who therefore had the collective right to depose tyrants. Major's book was not initially popular in Scotland but was very influential on writers such as Knox and Buchanan (both of whom had been pupils of Major) after the Reformation.[22]

The historian who responded to Major's challenge most promptly was Hector Boece, the humanist principal of the university of Aberdeen. He had already written a neo-Latin history of the bishops of Aberdeen, which was primarily a hymn of praise to William Elphinstone. In 1527, his *Scotorum Historia* (History of the Scots) was published in Paris. This was a flowing and eloquent piece of Renaissance Latin, restating the case for Scottish independence from England. Boece accepted the legends of Fordun and Bower because they suited his purpose and he tried to add greater authenticity to the stories by citing a mysterious medieval writer called Veremund, whose work, if it ever existed, has since been lost. For Boece, the

history of the Scots was one of persistent and noble resistance to the expansionist ambitions of the English kings. Far from advocating a union of the realms, he presented the kings of Scots as the most important focus of heroic national independence. This book was dedicated to James V, who was so pleased with it that he commissioned one of his clerks, John Bellenden, to translate it into Scots, and Thomas Davidson to print it, as we have seen, so that it would have wider circulation. Bellenden's work (the first of several versions of Boece's history) was a rather free translation, with some of his own ideas injected into the narrative, but it was lively, colourful and direct. It was the first vernacular history of the Scots in prose and print. Since Boece's history was available in printed editions in both Latin and Scots, and because it was a very pacy and readable text, the *Scotorum Historia* was popular and influential in the later sixteenth and early seventeenth centuries (Ferrerio wrote a continuation in Latin, and Pitscottie in Scots). Via the English historian, Holinshed, it even informed Shakespeare's idea of Scottish history. Having acquired a taste for historical translation, Bellenden went on to make a translation of the first five books of Livy's *History of Rome*, which was also dedicated to James V in the hope that he would emulate the martial prowess of the ancient Romans.[23]

After the Reformation, a new pair of Latin versions of Scottish history appeared, and this time they were both humanist texts of rhetorical and polemical force. John Leslie, bishop of Ross, published *De Origine, Moribus et Rebus Gestis Scotorum* (On the Origins, Character and Achievements of the Scots) in Rome in 1578. Leslie was a loyal servant of both the Catholic Church and Mary, queen of Scots, so his history stresses

Title page of Hector Boece's *Scotorum Historia*,
published in Paris in 1527. The design includes a
depiction of a Renaissance printing press.

the faithfulness of the Scottish people to the papacy
for many centuries, and sees the greatest dangers
in the destructive forces of heresy and rebellion.
He hoped to urge his fellow Scots to return to
Catholicism and to promote what he saw as Mary's
legitimate claim to the English throne. Leslie's
Latin history was translated into Scots in 1596
by another Scottish Catholic exile Father James
Dalrymple, so it was well known in circles sympathetic to Mary's memory. In contrast, the greatest Scottish humanist of the age, George Buchanan,
wrote scathingly of Mary after her downfall as a
heretic, a tyrant and a murderess, justifiably
deposed by her godly people who had a long history of resisting bad monarchs. He pursued his
case first in his *Detectio Mariae Reginae Scotorum*
(Detection of Mary, Queen of Scots) of 1568, then
in *De Iure Regni apud Scotos* (On the Law of
Kingship among the Scots) of 1579, and finally in
Rerum Scoticarum Historia (The Matter of Scottish History) of 1582. Like its precursors,
Buchanan's history was dedicated to the king, with
the intention that the latter should profit from the
lessons of history. In particular, James VI was
asked to remember that royal power was legiti-
mately constrained by the will of the people.
Although Buchanan was more sceptical than Boece
about Fordun's legendary version of Scottish origins, he found the stories of the deposition of some
of the early Celtic kings rhetorically useful. In
Buchanan's history, the full panoply of neo-Latin
scholarship and eloquence is deployed in the service of a passionately partisan argument. His royal
pupil, James VI, owed much of his formidable

intellectual development to Buchanan's influence, but he would reject this radical political philosophy outright (see below).[24]

These Latin texts on Scottish history are just a small sample of the Latin prose literature of the period, which anchored Scottish literary culture firmly within the European Renaissance. Because they are in Latin, they have been somewhat neglected in modern times, although they are now becoming increasingly accessible in translation.[25] In the same way, George Buchanan's status has suffered despite his outstanding Latinity. Today he is chiefly remembered for besmirching the reputation of Mary, queen of Scots, and as the tutor of James VI who did not spare the rod on his royal pupil. At the time, Buchanan was a prolific neo-Latin author of poetry, plays, masques, and tracts, who had a towering scholarly and literary reputation of European proportions. He taught at universities in France and Portugal and translated many texts from Greek and Hebrew into Latin. His poetic paraphrases of the psalms ran to 26 European editions over 150 years. Buchanan's French publisher, the classical scholar Henri Estienne, considered him 'easily the first poet of his own age' and his plays, *Jephthes* and *Baptistes* (written in France, 1539–43), were very influential in the later development of European Renaissance drama. Although they take biblical subjects from the Old Testament tale of Jephtha and the New Testament story of John the Baptist, they are constructed as neo-classical tragedies modelled on Euripides and Seneca. Buchanan could also produce light-hearted works for the royal court. In 1558, he wrote a joyful *epithalamium* (wedding hymn) to celebrate Mary's marriage to the Dauphin and he later provided Latin verses for court pageants and masques at Holyrood, with Darnley

depicted as a particularly heroic figure compared to Apollo. In 1566, Buchanan wrote a *genethliacon* (birthday ode) for the birth of the future James VI. He presented the baby prince in Virgilian terms, as a child of prophecy who would restore the classical Golden Age, and as a philosopher king modelled on the biblical Solomon. Thus it rather looks as if James's later fondness for describing himself as 'Great Britain's Solomon' has roots in his infancy. Buchanan's mastery of neo-Latin poetry inspired a whole generation of followers, so that Sir John Scot of Scotstarvit and Arthur Johnston were able to collect the works of 37 of them (not including Buchanan) in the remarkable anthology, *Delitiae Poetarum Scotorum* (Delightful Offerings of the Scottish Poets), published in two volumes in Amsterdam in 1637.[26]

The vernacular literature of Scotland was also developing rapidly at this period. The poetic counterparts of the histories of Fordun and Bower were the epic chivalric poems, John Barbour's *The Bruce* (c.1375) and Blind Harry's *The Wallace* (c.1477). They use the technique of rhyming couplets, which had been popular in French medieval romances and, like the Scottish prose chroniclers, they focus on the heroic resistance to English invasion. *The Wallace* became one of the most influential works in all of Scottish literature. It was printed by Chepman and Myllar and was a 'bestseller' from the sixteenth to the eighteenth century. Major and Boece referred to it, Burns and Scott were inspired by it, and the poem even shaped the story of the film *Braveheart* (1995). Of the author, Blind Harry, we know very little except that he was clearly well educated and wrote his poem for a faction opposed to James III's policy of peace with England.[27] In parallel with the lingering attachment to aspects of Gothic style in the visual arts (see Chapters 2,

3 and 4), the concern with honour, virtue and martial prowess, which characterised medieval chivalric romance, continued to be popular in literature well into the fifteenth and sixteenth centuries. The styles of the great English poets, Chaucer, Gower and Lydgate, were hugely admired and imitated in Middle Scots literature. Indeed, the Scots poets themselves, or 'makars', often called their language 'Inglis' and were proud to claim kinship with the Chaucerian tradition. The genres of 'advice to princes', 'dream-vision', 'courtly love' and the allegorical 'beast fable' all had medieval roots but continued to inspire writers in England, France and Scotland well into the early modern period. There are many examples of such works, but among the most notable are Gilbert Hay's chivalric romance, *The Buik of King Alexander the Conquerour* (c.1460), and his advice-to-princes tract, *The Buke of the Gouernance of Princis* (1456). The latter was a translation into Scots of a Latin text (via French), which at the time was thought to have been written by Aristotle for the guidance of Alexander the Great. Sir Richard Holland's alliterative *Buke of the Howlat* (owl) (c.1448) is a lively beast fable which draws the moral that 'pride goes before a fall' and may have been inspired by Chaucer's *Parliament of Fowls*. Likewise, Chaucer's tale of love blighted by tragic fate, *Troilus and Criseyde*, inspired the pathos and virtuosity of Robert Henryson's *Testament of Cresseid* (c.1480s), which in many ways surpassed its model.[28]

The early stirrings of the Renaissance in Scottish literature can be traced in the vernacular works, as well as in the neo-Latin, humanist developments considered above. *The Kingis Quair* (King's Book) of c.1424 is a case in point. The only surviving poem by King James I, it was written around the time that he married Joan Beaufort, was released from English captivity, and returned home to rule in his own right. The poem is the first in a long line of Scots courtly love poems combined with a dream-vision, and reflects upon the inconstancy of fortune and the nature of liberty. The poet willingly makes his heart captive to his lady and, through marriage, secures release from his physical imprisonment. *The Kingis Quair* is usually classified as a medieval poem because its main influences are Chaucer, Gower, Lydgate and Boethius (a late-classical author who was very widely read in the Middle Ages), but in its autobiographical nature it seems to have captured something of the Renaissance spirit. It was also one of the earliest Scots poems written by a layman, rather than a cleric. The classical influence is more overt in Henryson's *Orpheus and Eurydice*, where the poet draws inspiration from Ovid and Virgil, as well as Boethius, in his retelling of the ancient Greek legend; and also in Henryson's *Morall Fabillis of Esope the Phrygian*, which likewise draws on the work of an ancient writer, mixed with a sprinkling of medieval sources. Gavin Douglas also drew on Ovid and Virgil for his allegorical dream-vision *The Palice of Honour* (c.1501). It is a conspicuously learned poem, with references to classical history, mythology and topography, alongside biblical and theological themes. Probably the greatest classically inspired poem from this period

OPPOSITE. Arnold Bronckorst, portrait of George Buchanan, 1581. Buchanan was the greatest Scottish humanist of the age.

SIC BVCHANANVS ORA. SIC VVLTVM TVLIT.
PETE SCRIPTA ET ASTRA. NOOSSE SI MENTEM CVPIS.

ÆTATIS. 76.
AN°. 1581.

is Douglas's translation of Virgil's *Aeneid* into Scots: *Eneados* (1513). This is the earliest British vernacular translation of a major classical work, and still today remains one of the finest. Douglas is faithful to the original and renders the whole epic (including the continuation of 1428 by the Italian humanist Maphaeus Vegius) in elegant verse. Moreover, he includes poetic prologues to each book, which are sensitive, original and fittingly complementary to the translation. *Eneados* is undoubtedly a masterpiece of the Scottish Renaissance. It is surely to be regretted that after 1513 Douglas devoted himself to political and ecclesiastical intrigue and seems to have abandoned poetry.[29]

The most famous vernacular poets of the early sixteenth century were William Dunbar and Sir David Lindsay of the Mount, who wrote works commemorating the spectacles of the Renaissance courts of James IV and James V respectively. Both poets display great versatility and variety in the styles and genres they employ. There are traditional pieces presenting dream-visions, beast fables, petitions, and offering advice to princes. There is humour, pathos, allegory, satire, devotional fervour, and the distinctively Scottish practice of 'flyting': a verbal duel where poets hurl elaborate abuse at each other. There are also works displaying influences from English, French and Flemish court literature and an awareness of humanist learning. Dunbar's 'Thrissill and the Rois' celebrates the triumphant marriage of James IV to Margaret Tudor in 1503, by depicting 'Dame Nature' awarding crowns to the thistle and the rose, as the king and queen of the flowers. His 'Blyth Aberdeane' describes the impressive pageantry when Queen Margaret made her official entry into the burgh in 1511, and 'The Ballade of Barnard Stewart' heaps elaborate praise on a French nobleman of

Scottish descent, who visited James IV's court in 1508. Stewart is compared to Achilles, Hector, Arthur, Agamemnon, Hannibal and Julius Caesar, and each verse ends with a refrain wishing him 'glory and honour, laud [praise] and reverence'. Stewart died shortly after this poem was written and Dunbar penned an elegy to him as the 'flower of chivalry'. Sir David Lindsay had been a close household servant of James V from the moment of the king's birth, and in the 1530s was the senior Scottish herald (officially appointed Lyon King of Arms in 1542), which meant that he visited the courts of England, France and the Low Countries on formal embassies. His poems of c.1526–42 are all set in the royal court and combine celebration, commemoration and humour with some stern criticism of the venal, self-serving world of the courtier. 'The Testament and Complaynt of our Soverane Lordis Papyngo' (parrot) and the 'Complaint and Publict Confessioun of the Kingis Auld Hound, callit Bagshe' are both beast fables which urge greater virtue and morality on clerics and courtiers and employ the device of real pets, known to have been owned by the king, as protagonists. 'The Deploratioun of the Deith of Quene Magdalene' is a formal, elaborate and touching tribute to the young queen who died so shortly after her marriage; whilst 'The Justing betwix James Watsoun and Jhone Barbour' is a comic parody of a chivalric tournament in which the combatants are not glorious nobles but rather humble, clumsy and cowardly servants. Thus, through the vivid, varied and engaging poetry of Dunbar and Lindsay, the Renaissance courts of James IV and James V may be reanimated for modern readers.[30]

After the death of James V in December 1542, Lindsay presided over the king's funeral in January 1543; thereafter he had some difficulty navi-

gating the stormy waters of Mary's minority. Though he retained his position as senior herald, he increasingly retreated to his Fifeshire estates, where his verses took on a much more humanistic and moral tone, focused on the theme of the commonweal: what has been termed 'vernacular humanism'. Here, he refashioned a dramatic work that had originally been written as a court entertainment in 1540, and developed it into the first surviving Scottish play, *Ane Satyre of the Thrie Estaitis*. Lindsay skilfully combined the traditional form of a morality play with influences from the English court poet John Skelton, the French comic *sottie* genre, and the humanist moral agenda. *Ane Satyre* was first performed in the burgh of Cupar in 1552 and was revived for Mary of Guise in Edinburgh in 1554, just as she was embarking on her regency. The essential message is the humanist theme that for justice and good government to prevail, rulers should cultivate virtue, avoid vice and promote the common good. The vices and virtues are represented by allegorical figures, who receive their just desserts at a session of parliament (the three estates of the title), so that 'King Humanity' may rule well and 'John the Commonweal' have peace and prosperity.[31]

Ane Satyre is the earliest known text of a Scottish play, but it obviously grew out of an established tradition of court entertainments, burgh plays for town festivals, religious or mystery plays for sacred feasts, Robin Hood plays for May Day, and more learned clerks' plays at the universities. All of these dramas are noted in the documentary record, but no texts have survived. After the Reformation, dramatic productions continued at the royal court and some noble residences, but most of the other forms of plays and dramas faced increasing official disapproval and suppression. Appearances by

Robin Hood and some of his fellows were still enacted in some towns into the seventeenth century and James VI gave his patronage to some English theatre companies who performed in public in 1599 and 1601. However, there was no commercial, public theatre in Scotland and therefore no opportunities for Scottish playwrights to develop careers comparable to those of Shakespeare and Marlowe.[32] One other rare surviving Scots Renaissance play, the anonymous *Philotus*, was not published until 1603 and is usually dated to the 1580s or 1590s, but there is a strong possibility that it was written for the court of Mary. It is a sparkling comedy inspired by Italian and French courtly sources and the classical models of Plautus and Terence. It involves star-crossed lovers, long-lost siblings, and cross-dressing disguises amongst other devices, and romps along with remarkable dramatic verve. The only other surviving Scottish play of the period was a translation by John Burel of a twelfth-century verse drama inspired by Ovid, *Pamphilus* (c.1591). It seems to have been written as a closet drama, i.e. a play intended to be read, perhaps out loud, but not performed on stage. It is a very assured translation which presents a rhetorically powerful story of lust, seduction and rape. It appears to have been written within a context of courtly intrigue, as part of a campaign to urge the 16-year-old duke of Lennox to abandon his adolescent infatuation for Lilias Ruthven. Whatever the literary merits of the play, and there are many, it failed in its purpose, for shortly afterwards Lennox abducted Lilias Ruthven and married her.[33]

In the later sixteenth century, Scottish vernacular poets took considerable inspiration from French and Italian literature. French *élégies* and *chansons*, often inspired by Italian verse, had been written for

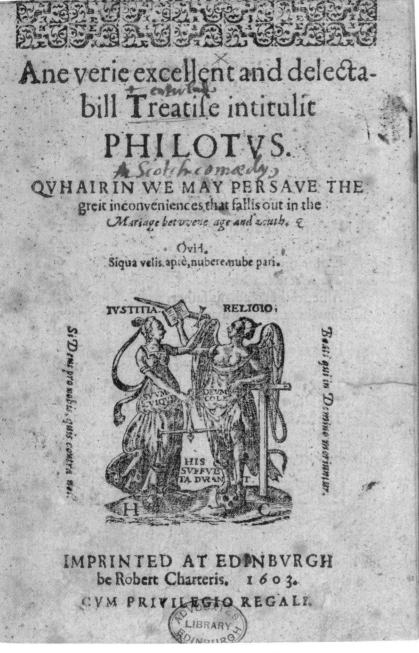

Title page of *Philotus*, a Renaissance
play by an unknown Scottish author, printed
in Edinburgh in 1603.

James V when he was in France, and were immediately imitated and popularised by Scots poets,
who swiftly developed a versatile tradition of lyric
poetry, in the sense, that is, of short poems, often
set to music, focusing on emotional themes, especially love. Even with the absence of a monarch in
the 1550s, there was still an interest in vernacular
literature, particularly poetry, from the educated
urban professional and merchant classes, especially
in Edinburgh. In the mid-1560s George Bannatyne
was able to collect hundreds of examples of Scots
vernacular poems, many of which were lyrics from
the pen of Alexander Scott. The famous Bannatyne
Manuscript also preserved many of the masterpieces of the age of the makars. Some of the love
lyrics of the Bannatyne Manuscript are very intro-
spective. They often present love as a moral ques-
tion of self-governance, rather than a passionate
abandonment, linking the notion of self-knowl-
edge and self-discipline to the Renaissance theme
of individualism and virtuous service to the common
good. Amongst the finest of Alexander Scott's
poems, which was actually an advice-to-princes
piece rather than a love lyric, was his 'New Yeir Gift'
to Mary, queen of Scots. This was presented to her
in January 1562 at Seton Palace, as she celebrated
her first Christmas in Scotland after her return
from France. It offers her praise and greetings and
expresses the hope that she will cultivate the virtues,
promote justice and the commonweal, and bear a
son who would rule over all Britain.[34]

George Bannatyne claimed to have completed
his manuscript in 1568, at the start of a lean time
for the culture of the royal court, between the deposition of Mary in 1567 and the emergence of
James VI as an adult in the 1580s. The arrival of
the king's French-born cousin and favourite, Esmé
Stuart, in 1579 stimulated cultural interest in all

Brass book stamp of James VI, late sixteenth century. James had an extensive and impressive royal library.

things French, including a revival of Scottish appreciation of the courtly poetry of the *Pléiade* circle (Mary had been a great admirer of the poetry of Ronsard). As the king entered manhood, he drew around him a group of inventive and versatile Scottish poets, who have traditionally been known as the Castalian Band (named after a spring on the mythical Mount Parnassus, dedicated to the Muses), although this is a term they did not use of themselves. James's *Essayes of a Prentise in the Diuine Arte of Poesie* (1584) was a manifesto for rejuvenating Scots literature by seeking inspiration in French and Italian rhetorical and metaphorical poetry. The 'master' to the young king's 'apprentice' (and a distant relation) was Alexander Montgomerie, an accomplished lyricist, versatile in his use of poetic forms, who was eventually disgraced in 1597 by his involvement in Catholic plotting. The Castalians responded enthusiastically to James's encouragement. William Fowler translated Petrarch's *I Trionfi* (Triumphs) and *Il Principe* (The Prince) of Machiavelli, John Stewart of Baldynneis translated a French version of Ariosto's *Orlando Furioso*, Thomas Hudson and the king translated works by du Bartas, and Alexander Montgomerie produced some of the finest lyrics of the age. James was delighted to welcome du Bartas as a visitor to his court in 1587 and relished as a great compliment the fact that the Huguenot poet translated the king's own epic poem, *Lepanto*. As with the visual arts of the period, it is possible to detect in Castalian poetry

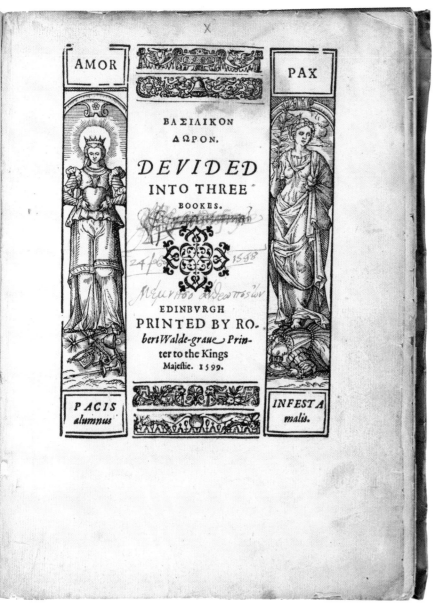

Title page of James VI's *Basilikon Doron*, printed in Edinburgh by Robert Waldegrave in 1599. This was a private printing of only seven copies. A public printing followed in 1603. The allegorical figures proclaim that Love fosters Peace, and Peace drives out Danger.

an awareness of the Mannerist aesthetic, with its emphasis on self-conscious artifice. Mannerists particularly prized the highly contrived verse-form of the sonnet, and the Castalians wrote many sonnets, sometimes in sequences such as Fowler's *Tarantula of Love*. Montgomerie's poems, such as 'The Cherrie and the Slae' (sloe), were also highly stylised and witty in the Mannerist fashion. In other European countries, Mannerist poetry, art and music were rapidly developing at this time and would lead Renaissance culture into the Baroque of the seventeenth century. The Mannerist inclinations became even more pronounced in the post-Union works of Robert Ayton, William Drummond of Hawthornden and William Alexander, earl of Stirling, who all wrote in the English idiom, and arguably might be seen as poets of the Baroque.[35]

In the 1590s, James VI began to take more interest in theology and politics than poetry. His *Trew Law of Free Monarchies* (1598) presents a philosophy of divine monarchy and rejects the resistance theories of Knox, Buchanan and Melville. However, James's *Basilikon Doron* (kingly gift) of 1599 was a handbook on kingship for his eldest son, Henry, which was much more pragmatic about the realities of rule. James VI's many learned tracts included a study of witchcraft (*Daemonologie*, 1597) and a denunciation of the new habit of smoking (*Counterblaste to Tobacco*, 1604), amongst many others. These works were the products of a studious, stoical prince, who in many ways embodied the virtues of Renaissance humanism. He once remarked wryly that he was forced to speak Latin before he could speak Scots. His tutor, George Buchanan, had certainly instilled in him a thorough appreciation of Latin, Greek and even Hebrew literature. James also exhibited the

grandiose ambitions of his Stewart forbears in his desire to rule united kingdoms as God's anointed. Furthermore, he cultivated his image in Europe, since he also had ambitions to become a leader of Christendom. Thus, with this agenda in mind, many of his prose works were translated for English or Continental consumption.[36]

The culture of the court of James VI was very male dominated and there were few female writers at this time. From the early sixteenth century, many humanists had promoted literacy and education for women as profitable to the common good. The Spanish scholar Juan Luis Vives served Katherine of Aragon in the 1520s and briefly acted as tutor to the then heiress to the English throne, Princess Mary Tudor. He wrote two Latin books dedicated to Katherine and Mary, which promoted the scholarly education of girls, and his works were known in Scotland. Furthermore, Marguerite of Navarre, a princess of the Valois dynasty (into which Mary, queen of Scots, married), was a prolific and published author of the early sixteenth century. After the Reformation, there was a desire in some quarters that women should be fully part of the godly community and therefore be able to read and understand scripture. Many of John Knox's most devoted disciples and correspondents were women. Nevertheless, there was also a strongly misogynist streak in the culture, which regarded female sexuality as a dangerous threat to social order and demanded that a woman, however learned, should be modest, submissive and take no public role. The view is most famously represented by Knox's polemic, *The First Blast of the Trumpet against the Monstrous Regiment* [rule] *of Women* (1558), which insisted that it was unnatural and ungodly for women to wield political power. In such a climate it is hardly surprising

that women writers were scarce and if they published at all, were often anonymous. The fact that Mary, queen of Scots, who had been well educated at the French court, wrote poetry in French, Italian and Latin was regarded as highly suspicious in some quarters, and a sequence of French sonnets, supposedly declaring her passion for Bothwell, formed part of the notorious Casket Letters. The authenticity of the letters has been highly contested, since they were used by Mary's enemies to try to establish her complicity in the murder of Darnley. However, the poems constitute the first sonnet sequence written in Scotland, a poetic form which was particularly characteristic of the late Renaissance. We should probably regard these poems as purely literary exercises rather than personal testimony.[37]

One of the few female poets of the period was Marie Maitland, daughter of Sir Richard Maitland of Lethington. She seems to have acted as a kind of secretary to her father and was the scribe for substantial portions of the Maitland quarto manuscript (c.1586), a collection of poetry associated with her family. One of the poems compares her to the ancient Greek lyricist Sappho and to the sixteenth-century Italian classical scholar Olimpia Morata. Maitland is thought to be the author of several anonymous poems in the quarto manuscript, all accomplished love lyrics. Another female poet of the time was Christian Lindsay, who seems to have been on the fringes of the Castalian circle. One well-crafted sonnet has been attributed to her in which she accuses Robert Hudson of being unfriendly to Alexander Montgomerie: 'Oft have I heard, but ofter found it true', probably of the late 1580s. She is mentioned in one of James VI's poems and Montgomerie also expresses the hope that when he and his poetic brethren are dead,

she will write their epitaphs. It has been suggested that 'Christian Lindsay' might have been a poetic persona rather than a real woman poet. If this were so, it would at least indicate a Castalian interest in the female 'voice'.[38] Probably the most accomplished female poet of the Renaissance in Scotland was Elizabeth Melville, Lady Culross. Melville was a devout Calvinist, who was friendly with some of the more radical preachers of her day. In 1603, she became the first woman author to have work printed in Scotland, when her devotional poem, *Ane Godlie Dreame*, was published in Edinburgh. This is an intense and allegorical dream-vision, which suggests she was familiar with this tradition in classical and Scottish poetry. All of her poems are spiritual works; some are sonnets, some sacred parodies of secular pieces. She displays a deep knowledge of the Geneva Bible and the metrical psalms, and a skilful command of her language and metre. Many of her poems have recently been discovered in manuscript and a selection has just been published. At the time of writing, a modern edition of her complete works is in preparation. She was a remarkable Renaissance talent and it is a most welcome development that her work is now emerging from obscurity.[39]

The intellectual culture of Renaissance Scotland was very impressive in many respects. Scottish scholars and writers had very close connections to the universities and courts of Continental Europe and participated in most of the educational and literary developments of the period. Printing seems to have developed in Scotland rather tentatively and later than in many other countries. Scottish drama seems to have been somewhat restricted in scope, when compared to the theatrical developments in other realms. Yet Scots were quick to adopt Renaissance humanism, to promote educational reform, and to develop a rich heritage of prose and poetry in Latin and Scots. Indeed, through figures such as Boece and Buchanan, the Scottish Latinate intelligentsia commanded European admiration. By the end of the period it is clear that Scots were well aware of their progress in scholarship and literature and were proud of their achievements. We have already seen that the Latin poets were celebrated in the publication of *Deli-tiae Poetarum Scotorum* in Amsterdam in 1637. In a similar vein, in 1627 Thomas Dempster, a Catholic exile and Professor of Humanities at the university of Bologna, published *Historia Eccle-siastica Gentis Scotorum* (An Ecclesiastical History of the Scots People). Despite its title, this is actually a biographical catalogue which describes the lives of Scottish writers, scholars and saints of the past centuries in a very patriotic manner. Unfortunately, Dempster was so keen to demonstrate Scottish intellectual vigour that he recruited several distinctly non-Scottish figures to his cause, such as Alcuin of York. Nevertheless, he was justifiably convinced that Scotland had a scholarly and literary heritage worth celebrating.[40] The same theme was taken up in 1633 for the royal entry into Edinburgh of Charles I on his only return visit to his homeland. William Drummond of Hawthornden devised the scheme of pageantry to greet the king and George Jamesone painted a sequence of paintings to decorate 'stations' along the processional route. The most notable was a 'Parnassus' adorned with pictures representing the Muses and portraits of the 'Worthies' of Scottish culture, including Robert Henryson, William Elphinstone, Gavin Douglas, John Major, Hector Boece, David Lindsay and George Buchanan. The returning king was thus graphically reminded of the remarkable literary glories of his realm.[41]

8

TRIUMPH AND JOY

Renaissance Chivalry and Pageantry

The international cult of honour known as chivalry was so called because it formed a code of conduct for the mounted warrior or knight (*chevalier* in French). It had developed within the context of medieval warfare in the twelfth century and continued to shape the culture of the European nobility into the sixteenth century. It was widely believed that chivalry was an ancient code, devised by the great warriors of antiquity: Hector of Troy, Alexander the Great and Julius Caesar. This myth contributed greatly to the popularity of images of the Nine Worthies in the art of the period (see Chapters 3 and 4) and firmly associated chivalry with the spirit of the Renaissance. During the fifteenth century, chivalric culture gradually transformed from the practical, military purposes of medieval knighthood into the more ornamental and honorific interests of the Renaissance courtier: knights were expected to become more 'courtly' and 'civilised'. The medieval obsession with jousting persisted, but by the 1490s, weapons were blunted to minimise injuries, and there was a greater stress on pageantry and display than had once been the case. To be created (dubbed) a knight generally required noble birth and military service to a great lord or monarch. In the sixteenth century, it became possible for men of non-noble birth to obtain knighthoods through administrative or diplomatic service, but this was often regarded by the nobles as an inferior route. Kings and great magnates would dub knights on the battlefield or at the jousts and tournaments staged to celebrate special occasions, such as royal weddings, baptisms or coronations. The ideals of chivalric honour revolved around the concept of service. A virtuous knight was expected to serve his lord bravely in battle, to serve God piously as a defender of the Church and the faith (ideally, on crusade), and to serve society selflessly as a guardian of justice and protector of the weak, especially women and children. In many countries the notion of 'courtly love' was allied to chivalry, where a knight would offer a pristine, honourable devotion to a lady, with no expectation of reward. The 'courtly love' element of chivalric culture does not appear to have been very strongly expressed in Scotland, where military prowess seems to have been the dominant ethos for much of the period.[1]

The greatest expression of chivalric culture was the joust or tournament. Such events would often form part of the celebrations for great occasions and could also be staged seasonally: Shrovetide was a traditional time for jousting, and the spring and summer months were also possibilities. Typically, tournaments would be fought by teams of knights responding to a challenge. In the fifteenth century, the challenge was usually prompted simply by respect for an opponent's martial valour. By the sixteenth century, it was often framed within a fictitious scenario taken from Arthurian romance or something similar, so that costumes, props and disguises became part of the pageantry. The action would focus on a series of single-combats, where mounted knights tilting with lances would attempt to break their spears on their opponents' shields, or to unhorse their opponents completely. Fighting with swords or axes on foot at the barriers was common and there was sometimes a team combat called a *mêlée*. The idea of constructing a tournament around a theme taken from chivalric romance originated in the courts of the fifteenth-century Burgundian Low Countries, to which Scotland was connected by James II's marriage to Mary of Gueldres. For example, the celebrations for the marriage of Duke Charles to Margaret of York in Bruges in 1468 was marked by the *Pas d'Armes de l'Arbre d'Or* (Passage of Arms of the Tree of Gold), and the *Pas d'Armes de la Dame Sauvage* (Passage of Arms of the Wild Lady) was staged at Ghent in 1470. The notion of the 'passage of arms' was part of the scenario of the challenge: one team of knights would impede the passage of another until they agreed to fight for the honour of a lady. These events included the use of an artificial 'tree of esperance' or 'tree of honour', upon the branches of which the shields of arms of the competitors would be displayed. The role of the *dame sauvage* (or similar) would be taken by a lady of the court in elaborate costume.[2]

In the fifteenth century, there was an international brotherhood of knights errant who would tour the European courts, competing in chivalric combats to earn honour and glory. One such was Jacques de Lalaing, from the Low Countries, who was in the service of Philip the Good, duke of Burgundy. With two companions in arms, he visited the court of James II in February 1449 as part of the preparations for the king's marriage to Mary of Gueldres. De Lalaing issued a challenge to James Douglas, brother of the earl of Douglas, which was accepted, and lists were erected at Stirling so that the contest could be judged by the king. James II dubbed James Douglas and his two companions in the lists just before the combat started. The three Burgundians fought the three Scottish knights in a series of single-combats using lances, axes and daggers. According to the French and Burgundian chronicles, the Burgundians had the advantage when contest was stopped. Jacques de Lalaing then returned to Bruges where he won a tournament held to mark Mary of Gueldres' departure for Scotland. We do not know if any Scottish knights took part in the Bruges event, but the Stirling and Bruges tournaments were clearly both connected to the royal marriage.[3] Sadly, the Scottish sources give very little information about the event. The absence of the *Treasurer's Accounts* for the reigns of James I, II and III (apart from one year, 1473–4) is a major hindrance to the study of Scottish jousts and tournaments. Had these sources survived, they would probably have provided evidence of many more instances of fifteenth-century chivalric combats. As it is, before 1488, we know of only one tournament in the

reign of James I, held at Perth in October 1433, and the 1449 event at Stirling; there were surely many more.

The most famous Scottish tournaments were staged for James IV and are recorded in some detail in the *Treasurer's Accounts*, the poems of William Dunbar, and other sources. James was enthusiastic for all things chivalric and liked to joust in person. There were several small-scale jousts held in the 1490s, including one to celebrate the marriage of the king's cousin, Catherine Gordon, to the English pretender, Perkin Warbeck in 1496. Some lavish jousts were held to celebrate James's marriage to Margaret Tudor. A Scottish embassy had witnessed a sequence of jousts at the court of Henry VII in 1502 to celebrate the proxy marriage of James and Margaret, where knights were dubbed in honour of the new queen of Scots. James IV impressed the English visitors who accompanied his bride in 1503 with a similar sequence of jousts and tilts over three days in the main courtyard at Holyrood. The king created dozens of new knights and three new earls (Arran, Montrose and Glencairn) in honour of his queen. These men would have been expected to demonstrate special devotion to the service of their sovereign lady, and this is one of the few instances where the conventions of 'courtly love' can be identified operating in a Scottish context. James later held a midsummer joust in 1504, Shrove Tuesday jousts in 1505 and 1506, and another in July 1506 in honour of a visiting French knight, Antoine de la Bastie.[4]

The most elaborate tournaments staged by James IV were those of the Wild Knight and the Black Lady, held in June 1507 and again in May 1508. The event of 1507 may have been a celebration for the birth of a son (who died the next year)

and the spectacle was repeated in 1508 to mark the visit of Bernard Stewart, seigneur d'Aubigny. He was regarded as the flower of French chivalry and Dunbar wrote two poems in his honour (see Chapter 7). Stewart had served the French Crown with distinction in the Italian wars and had also been on crusade in Spain: he was present at the fall of Granada in 1492. His visit to Scotland in 1508 and his great renown possibly reinforced the king's interest in a pilgrimage or crusade to the Holy Land. James IV expressed a desire for such an expedition in conventional chivalric terms over several years but never actually undertook the journey. At the tournaments of 1507 and 1508, the king jousted in the role of the Wild Knight and invariably won the honours. The device of wild men or women was taken from chivalric romance and was common in Continental tournaments but had additional resonance in Scotland, where the Gaelic culture of the Highlands was often regarded as 'wild' by the Lowland Scots who dominated the court. Since James had forfeited the lordship of the Isles in the 1490s, his adoption of the persona of the Wild Knight might be interpreted as the king symbolically assuming command of the Highlands.[5] It seems likely that the Black Lady who presided over the tournaments was a real person, perhaps from Moorish Spain. Two (or possibly three) 'Moorish lassies' appear in the *Treasurer's Accounts* as ladies of the court at this time, and William Dunbar's poem 'Of a Black-Moor' states that 'My lady with the meikle lips' had landed in Scotland from 'the last ships'. He describes how the victors of the tournaments would be rewarded with a kiss from her lips. One of the portrait sketches in the *Recueil d'Arras* (see Chapter 4) depicts a rather exotic lady from the court of James IV, and it has been suggested that this might be a

l'egyptienne qui rendist santé part art de medecine
au Roy desroca tabandonmé des medecins

L'egiptienne qui rendit la santé au roi d'ecosse abandonné
des medecins

picture of the Black Lady. However, the sketch is not of a Moor but of a gypsy (or Egyptian) woman in a turban. The inscription in the portrait album states that she restored the health of the king when his doctors had given up hope (*L'egyptienne quy Rendist santé part art de medecine au Roy descoce abandonné des medecins*) but does not mention a chivalric role for her. At the tournaments of 1507 and 1508, the Black Lady was dressed in fine damasks, carried in a 'chair triumphal' and attended by two ladies in green and two squires in white (green and white were the Tudor livery colours). The tournament concluded with a banquet, at the end of which she seems to have been borne away into a theatrical 'cloud'. The pageantry also included a 'tree of esperance', a group of 'wild men' clad in goat skins, some timber and canvas models of winged creatures (perhaps dragons, which were Tudor heraldic beasts), a recreation of the Arthurian round table, and many colourful pavilions, banners and shields of arms.[6] These were clearly magnificent spectacles.

Jousting at the court of the adult James V does not seem to have been quite as theatrically staged as for his father, but there were many events noted in the financial accounts and James was clearly very keen on martial exploits. Lists were erected at Holyrood and Stirling on a seasonal pattern in the early years of the reign, as part of the celebrations for Easter, May Day and other festivals, and there were regular purchases of spears, swords and horse harness. On his visit to the court of Francis I, James seems to have spent most of the time between his betrothal (November 1536) and

his marriage (January 1537) jousting with the dauphin, who was obsessively chivalric. When the latter became King Henry II he continued to participate enthusiastically in tournaments, and his reign was brought to an abrupt end in 1559 when he was killed in a jousting accident. The dauphin even had a personal style of tournament armour and it is likely that this highly decorated armour is depicted on his portrait by Corneille de Lyon of c.1536 (Galleria Estense, Modena). James V returned from France with new sets of armour and harness of his own, one in the style of Francis I and one in the style of the dauphin, amongst others. At the Paris tournament held to celebrate the marriage of James V to Princess Madeleine, there was a stage at one end of the lists displaying a 'tree of honour' carrying the shields of arms of all the combatants, with two mannequins dressed as knights, carrying lances with banners in one hand and the shields of arms of Scotland and France in the other. James spent considerable sums on gilt-encrusted harness and feathered caparisons (decorative horse harness). The king of Scots, along with the earl of Lennox and the latter's brother, John, Lord Darnley (d.1563), were said to have excelled in the combats. Further entries appear in the royal accounts relating to lavish tournaments held in Scotland to celebrate James's second marriage to Mary of Guise at St Andrews in June 1538, and to mark the queen's coronation in February 1540 at Holyrood. James's jousting coats were made of brightly coloured velvets embroidered with gold crowns, thistles and other heraldic badges, and he clearly considered chival-

OPPOSITE. Jacques le Boucq, sketch of an 'Egyptian' (gypsy) lady from the *Recueil d'Arras*, 1560s.

ric honour to be an important aspect of his courtly culture.[7]

During her short personal reign, Mary, queen of Scots, maintained the martial aspects of chivalric culture at her court as far as she was able. As a woman, she could not joust in person and in any case, the death in the lists of her father-in-law, Henry II, had dampened the general enthusiasm for tournaments to an extent. Nevertheless, the less dangerous pastime of 'running at the ring' (where knights directed their lances at a target rather than a live opponent) was staged at her court and the competitors were often dressed in costumes and disguises. Elizabeth I of England demonstrated that a female monarch could utilise jousts and tournaments to bring honour and splendour to her court through her Accession Day tilts, which were inspired by Burgundian traditions and marked the anniversary of her ascent to the throne. However, the Elizabethan tilts did not reach their height until the 1580s and therefore could not have served as a model for Mary, queen of Scots, in the 1560s. The English practice did provide inspiration for the young James VI as he developed chivalric culture at his court in the 1580s and 1590s. James was a very active participant in 'running at the ring', and the tournament staged to celebrate the baptism of his eldest son in 1594 involved teams of knights representing Amazons, Turks, Moors (who failed to appear) and Knights of Malta. James himself jousted as a Knight of Malta, which provoked disapproving comments from some ministers of the Kirk. Smaller tournaments were arranged in 1599 and 1602 for the baptisms of Princess Margaret (where knights were dubbed and two marquesses were created) and of Prince Robert (where six knights were dubbed). After the royal court departed for England, knights continued to be dubbed (for example, at Charles I's coronation in 1633), but jousting was no longer practised in Scotland.[8]

Scottish chivalric culture was reinforced by considerable literary activity, which promoted and consolidated the knightly ethos of valour, honour and service. We have already considered the epic poems, Barbour's *The Bruce* and Harry's *The Wallace*, and some of Sir Gilbert Hay's tracts (see Chapter 7), and there were many other texts of a similar nature. Poems of chivalric romance included the anonymous *Golagros and Gawane* and *Sir Eglemor*, and manuals of knightly deportment included the *Porteous of Noblenes* (a translation from the French, *Bréviaire des Nobles*, by Alain Chartier, d.1430). The poems and the 'porteous' were all printed by Chepman and Myllar.[9] Many other chivalric books originated with the Scottish heralds. Heralds were the high priests of the cult of chivalry, who organised and policed tournaments and other public events, adjudicated disputes over precedence, genealogy and armorial bearings, announced royal proclamations, carried royal letters and messages, and accompanied foreign embassies as representatives of the Crown. For much of the period there were six Scottish heralds (Albany, Islay, Marchmont, Ross, Rothesay and Snowden), six pursuivants (Bute, Carrick, Dingwall, Kintyre, Ormond and Unicorn), with two extraordinary pursuivants created if necessary (Falkland and Stirling), about a dozen macers, and many messengers-at-arms. The entire 'office of arms' was under the authority of Lyon King of Arms, who was a senior officer of state. Lyon represented the person of the monarch, so he was crowned at his inauguration and to attack him was an act of treason.[10] Scottish heralds actively promoted chivalric culture. For example, Sir

William Cumming of Inverallochy, Marchmont
Herald, commissioned Adam Loutfut, Kintyre
Pursuivant, to translate a French heraldic treatise,
the *Deidis of Armorie*, into Scots in 1494. There
were several heraldic manuscripts produced in the
early sixteenth century, including those of John
Scrymgeour of Myres (the hereditary macer), Peter
Thomson (Bute Pursuivant and Islay Herald) and
John Meldrum (Marchmont Herald). Scrymgeour's
manuscript is largely a version of Adam Loutfut's
work: it includes instructions on how to run a
tournament and how to cry largesse (distribute
coins to the crowd), along with comments on the
offices of constable and marshal, the technicalities
of blazon and a chivalric code of conduct. Thomson's manuscript contains similar material with
information on the coronation of an emperor or
king, and an account of the jousting staged to celebrate the marriage of Katherine of Aragon to
Arthur, prince of Wales, in 1501. Meldrum's manuscript includes copies of two popular heraldic
treatises by the Italian Bartolus de Saxoferrato,
and the English writer Nicholas Upton.[11]

One of the most important types of heraldic
manuscript was the 'armorial', which recorded
the coats of arms of knightly families. Armorials
were usually intended to be definitive works of
reference, to be consulted in cases of dispute or
uncertainty, and the brightly painted manuscripts
are works of art in themselves. Some Scottish arms
are recorded in European armorials of the fourteenth and fifteenth centuries, but the earliest
known 'native' record of arms is the 'Scots Roll'
of 1455–8, which contains 114 coats of arms. In
1513 or shortly afterwards, the roll was in England where pictures of three 'Flodden Standards'
were added to the manuscript. In 1542, Sir David
Lindsay of the Mount, Lord Lyon, compiled a

Royal arms from Sir David Lindsay of the
Mount's armorial manuscript of c.1542.

much more comprehensive armorial manuscript to assist him in his duties. It contains the heraldic bearings of the Scottish royal family from the accession of the Stewarts, as well as the arms of 114 noble and over 300 lairdly families. At the beginning of the book are the arms of the mythical Prester John, the biblical Three Kings, the Nine Worthies of chivalric lore, and the European monarchs. Only one ecclesiastical coat of arms is included, that of Cardinal David Beaton. Thus Lindsay was placing the Scottish armigerous community in the company of the heroes of chivalric legend and the leading figures of contemporary chivalry. Lindsay's armorial was so highly regarded that in 1630 the Privy Council approved it as the official register of arms for the realm. It provided inspiration for many later manuscripts, such as Robert Forman's armorial of c.1562, the Slains Roll of c.1565 and the Hague Roll of c.1592. Heraldic registers were sometimes commissioned for individual lords or families, such as the Hamilton armorial of 1561, the Seton armorial of 1591 and Lord Crawford's armorial of 1601. The families concerned clearly wished to record the honour and status of their pedigrees and these books were often lavishly produced and highly decorated. One of the charming features of some manuscripts, such as those of Forman and Seton, is that the kings and queens of Scots are often shown in double portraits, with the king's arms on his surcoat or banner and the queen's on her skirt. A poignant double portrait in the Forman manuscript resolves a longstanding historical error. It depicts the two legitimate sons of King James V as small boys, a crown and coronet suspended over their heads because they did not live long enough to exercise any authority: both boys died as babies in April 1541. The elder prince was

A touching portrayal of the two legitimate sons of James V, who died as infants in 1541, from the armorial manuscript painted by Sir Robert Forman of Luthrie, Lyon King of Arms, for Mary, queen of Scots, in 1562. The boys were Queen Mary's older brothers.

called James, after his father, and, according to John Leslie, the name of the younger prince was Arthur. Following Leslie, this is the name that is usually given in most (but not all) modern histories. However, Leslie seems to have been confusing the baby with one of the short-lived sons of James IV, who in 1509 was certainly called Arthur. Robert Forman clearly names the prince of 1541 as Robert. Since Forman was appointed Ross Herald in 1540, he would have been present at the royal court, would have known the sad story of the deaths of the infant princes from personal experience, and would therefore have been unlikely to have been mistaken about the name of the younger boy. In 1562, when he wrote his armorial manuscript, Queen Mary was a childless widow and the Scottish succession was uncertain. Forman seems to have been expressing some regret as he records the fact that the elder prince would have become King James VI, had he survived.[12]

A characteristic feature of late-medieval and Renaissance chivalric culture was the foundation by sovereign princes of orders of chivalry. These were exclusive knightly brotherhoods (a few admitted ladies too), who would swear to obey the statutes of their order, wear distinctive insignia and robes, and were expected to maintain the highest standards of honourable deportment. The chivalric orders added lustre to the reputation of kings, who sought to present an image of knightly dignity and prowess. The orders also helped to bind nobles to their princes in ties of fellowship, loyalty and patriotism. Chivalric orders perpetuated the crusading ideal, and displayed a concern for piety through their veneration of patron saints and the provision of masses and prayers for the souls of departed brethren. It became customary for the princely heads of these fraternities to admit

one another into their orders on the clear understanding that such membership was intended as a mark of esteem, and that any oaths would be given to the head of an order only in that capacity, and not as a sovereign lord. The most prestigious knightly brotherhoods of the period were the English Order of the Garter (founded by Edward III in 1349), the Burgundian Order of the Golden Fleece (founded by Philip the Good in 1430), and the French Order of St Michael (founded by Louis XI in 1469), but there were many others. Although the Scottish kings from James III onwards frequently had their portraits, or coats of arms, depicted with a chivalric collar of thistles and a pendant of St Andrew, this seems to have been just a heraldic ornament rather than the insignia of a knightly order, and no actual thistle collars have been traced in the surviving wardrobe inventories. Contrary to popular belief, and rather surprisingly given the general enthusiasm for chivalric culture, there does not seem to have been a formally constituted Scottish chivalric order at this period. Evidence of statutes, robes, processions, chapter meetings, chapel services, membership invitations to fellow monarchs, or similar indications are lacking from the records. The Order of the Thistle was not founded until 1687 by James VII.[13]

Probably the most useful sources of information for royal membership of chivalric orders are the inventories of the royal wardrobe and jewel house, which list ceremonial robes and insignia. These records have not survived for the reigns of James I and II, and it is not clear to what, if any, orders these monarchs belonged. It is known that James I was knighted by Henry V of England in 1421, but it is usually stated that he was not admitted to the Order of the Garter. However, he was

knighted on St George's day (23 April) at Windsor, which is exactly when the annual chapter meetings of the Garter knights were held, so it would have been inconceivably perverse to knight the Scottish king at that time and not admit him to the order. James II was knighted by his father at his baptism in 1430. The wardrobe inventory taken on the death of James III in 1488 indicates that he was a member of the French Order of St Michael, since he owned a collar of golden cockleshells and a golden pendant of the archangel. He was actually one of the first knights of St Michael at the foundation of the order in 1469, and his brother, Alexander, duke of Albany, was also admitted to the order later. In addition, James III had a collar of the Danish Order of the Elephant and a golden collar with eight white swans set with pearls. It is not clear if this latter piece of jewellery was a chivalric collar, since it does not seem to correspond to the insignia of any known orders (the collar of the Order of the Swan of Brandenburg had only one image of a swan on the pendant, rather than eight on the chain, and did not admit foreign members). When James III knighted Anselm Adornes of Bruges in 1469, the king presented the new knight with a collar, misleadingly described as the 'order of the unicorn', which was probably a livery chain, i.e. a symbol of personal loyalty.[14]

The wardrobe inventories are missing for the reign of James IV and it is not known if he had membership of any chivalric orders. One might expect that he would have received the Order of the Elephant as a matter of course, since his mother, Queen Margaret, was a Danish princess, but there is no evidence of this in the records. James V was very proud of his membership of the most prestigious chivalric orders. He was admitted to the Order of the Golden Fleece in 1532 when Charles V was trying to tempt him into an imperial marriage; he became a knight of the Garter in 1535 following a peace treaty with his uncle, Henry VIII; and he was awarded the Order of St Michael in 1536 during the negotiations for his French marriage. The collars and robes of all three of these orders are recorded in the royal wardrobe inventories of 1539 and 1542, and the absence of any mention of corresponding regalia for a Scottish order suggests strongly that it did not exist at this time. However, when James had the arms and collars of his chivalric orders carved on the new gateway of Linlithgow Palace in the late 1530s, he did include a panel depicting a collar of the thistle and St Andrew, which gives the impression that there was a Scottish order of equal status to the others. This was probably an act of bravado, but, had the king lived longer, he might well have established an order of his own. After the death of James V, some chivalric impetus seems to have been lost, yet Queen Mary's former governor, the duke of Châtelherault, and her consort, Lord Darnley, were both admitted to the Order of St Michael, and James VI became a knight of the Garter in 1590.[15]

OPPOSITE. James V's chivalric panels on the outer gateway of Linlithgow Palace, originally carved in the 1530s and restored in the nineteenth century. From left to right the panels depict the English Order of the Garter (showing the English royal arms without the heraldry signifying a claim to the French throne), the Scottish Order of the Thistle, the Burgundian Order of the Golden Fleece (with the Spanish royal arms of Castile and Leon), and the French Order of St Michael.

Although not strictly orders of chivalry, it is possible to view the papal presents of sacred regalia to Scottish monarchs in a similar light, as part of an international culture of honour. The recipients certainly took pride in the highly symbolic gifts, which were used to strengthen diplomatic relations. For centuries, the popes have annually blessed a rose stem made of gold on the fourth Sunday of Lent (sometimes called Rose Sunday) and presented the precious artefact to specially favoured churches, shrines, or princes, as a mark of esteem, paternal affection, and recognition of loyalty to the Catholic Church. In 1486, James III received the golden rose at a time when he was establishing good relations with Innocent VIII. The same pope sent another golden rose to James IV in 1491, early in his reign. Mary received a golden rose from Pius IV in 1560, when she was queen of France. James IV also received a silver-gilt sceptre from Alexander VI in 1494 and a blessed cap and sword from Julius II in 1507. The blessed cap and sword, like the golden rose, were presented by the pontiffs annually (at Christmas, rather than Lent) as a mark of honour. The sword indicated that the recipient was regarded as a defender of the Church, and the cap, which was made of velvet embroidered with an image of a dove set with pearls, symbolised the power of the holy spirit. At Christmas 1536, Pope Paul III designated James V as the recipient of a papal cap and sword, to reward him for resisting Henry VIII's pleas to join in rejecting papal authority. James received the honours in a ceremonial high mass at Compiègne in February 1537. The golden roses, papal caps and sword of 1537 have not survived, but the papal sceptre and the sword of 1507 were incorporated into the coronation regalia of the Scottish monarchs and are today on display in Edinburgh Castle as part of the Honours of Scotland. Both the sword and the sceptre are elegant examples of Italian Renaissance design. The sceptre has a hexagonal shaft (extended in 1536) with incised grotesque decoration and an elaborate finial incorporating figures of the Virgin Mary, St James and St Andrew, topped by a polished rock crystal (said to have healing properties). The sword has a silver-gilt hilt, a scabbard covered in red velvet and silver gilt, and a silk belt with a silver-gilt buckle. Figures of Saints Peter and Paul are etched onto the heel of the blade, and the hilt, scabbard and belt are decorated with oak trees, leaves and acorns, which were motifs taken from the arms of Julius II. The graceful hilt has a double baluster shape with dolphin-shaped quillons (cross-pieces). Within the oak leaf roundel on the circular pommel there is a laurel wreath decoration, symbolic of victory.[16]

Alongside the sceptre and sword, the third and most important item in the coronation regalia, or Honours of Scotland, is the crown. The form of the fifteenth-century Scottish crown is uncertain because the images on coins, seals and paintings are inconsistent. Sometimes it is shown as an open circlet of *fleurs de lys*, sometimes crosses alternate with the *fleurs de lys*, and from the reign of James III onwards, it is sometimes (but not invariably) depicted as a 'closed' imperial crown, with arches across the top. The symbolism of the arched imperial crown was utilised in royal imagery from the 1480s onwards (see Chapter 1), but the first Scottish monarch who certainly possessed such a diadem was James V. The financial accounts of spring 1532 make it clear that at this time the crown was mended, enlarged and imperial arches were attached by Adam Leys, who was paid for 'making of the spryngis [arches]'. The new imperial crown was probably worn in public for the first

time at the inauguration of the College of Justice in Edinburgh on 27 May. The crown was adjusted again in January 1540 when John Mossman recast the circlet with additional gold and reattached the arches of 1532. Many of the gems on the crown are probably older than the remodelling work of 1532 and Mossman added 23 new stones in 1540. He also added the enamelled gold mound and cross, which sits at the point where the arches intersect, and the enamelled gold oak leaf decorations attached to the arches. These jewels, and the pearl and enamelled gold badges pinned to the bonnet between the arches, were purchased in Paris by Mossman in the autumn of 1539. A new purple velvet bonnet and case was also made. The new crown was worn by the king for the first time at the coronation of his second queen, Mary of Guise, at Holyrood on 22 February 1540. For this ceremony, Mossman also made a new crown and sceptre for the queen and the royal tailor produced two magnificent royal robes of purple velvet, the king's lined with ermine and the queen's with white taffeta. The king's robe used such large quantities of cloth that it probably had a train 50 feet long. At the coronation of Anna of Denmark in May 1590, her crown was an arched diadem: the circlet was set with 12 gemstones and 24 pearls, whilst the ball and cross on the top were set with many more pearls, a ruby and five diamonds. There seems to be no record of a new crown having been made for Anna, so an older crown may well have been reused: possibly Mary of Guise's crown from 1540, or perhaps a crown made for Mary, queen of Scots. Anna had a new coronation robe costing over £800, but there is no record of a new robe made for the king in 1590. At Anna's coronation, James VI wore a robe of purple velvet, lined with ermine, needing five earls to carry the train, which was almost certainly James V's garment reused. Neither the queen's regalia, nor the royal robes have survived but the monarch's crown is kept alongside the sword and sceptre in Edinburgh Castle to this day.[17]

The Honours of Scotland played a significant part in the pageantry surrounding the opening and closing of the parliaments of Scotland, known as the Riding of Parliament. It is thought that this ceremony originated in the 1520s, but it is first documented in the 1580s, and the most detailed descriptions are from the seventeenth and early eighteenth centuries. The Riding of Parliament was a parade on horseback which processed from the Palace of Holyroodhouse to the parliament chamber in the Edinburgh tolbooth, or to the parliament hall after it was built in the 1630s. The order of procession, the specific colours of the robes to be worn, and the number of servants allowed in a noble entourage were all carefully prescribed. The heralds and pursuivants took part in their armorial surcoats, and the sceptre, sword and crown would be carried in state to represent the authority of the monarch. The sceptre would also be used to touch Acts of Parliament as an indication of royal assent. The ceremony continued until the union of the Scottish and English parliaments in 1707, and has been revived in a modified form for the reconstituted Scottish parliament since 1999.[18]

The primary role for the Honours of Scotland was in the coronation ritual, which was the most solemn and sacred royal ceremony of the period. It marked the spiritual transformation of a prince into a sovereign, with divinely bestowed powers of majesty. Like the cult of chivalry, the coronation service had medieval roots. The inauguration ritual of the Gaelic kingdom of Dalriada involved

a blessing of the king by a cleric and the recitation of the royal genealogy, and these features persisted into the medieval ritual of the kings of Scots. Pictish kings were inaugurated on the Stone of Destiny at Scone, but this was not available for Scottish coronations after 1296 because Edward I of England had deposited the stone in Westminster Abbey. As part of the Scottish resistance to English claims of overlordship, Robert Bruce petitioned the papacy to grant him the rites of coronation and unction (anointing with holy oil), which were already practised by some other European monarchs, notably the kings of England and France and the Holy Roman Emperor. Pope John XXII granted the petition in a papal Bull just after Robert I's death in 1329. The new sacred ritual was used at the coronation of David II and Queen Joan in 1331 and at all subsequent Scottish coronations until the Reformation. The papal Bull authorised the bishop of St Andrews or the bishop of Glasgow to anoint Scottish kings with consecrated oil, to invest them with a crown and other regalia, and to receive from them an oath to eradicate heresy and to protect the Church. The ceremony would conclude with the assembled company giving oaths of fealty (loyalty) to the monarch. The most important part of the ritual was unction, which was akin to a sacrament, indicating that the king would be imbued with the holy spirit and would rule through divine grace. Perhaps the only significant modification of the ritual before the Reformation was the adoption of the arched 'imperial' crown, in place of an open circlet, with all its symbolic significance. After the Reformation, some changes were made to the ceremony: chiefly the eradication of any mention of papal authority, some modifications to the coronation oath, and a slight rearrangement of the order of proceedings. However, the essential elements of the ritual, including unction, were retained, and it seems clear that the band of revolutionaries who arranged the coronation service of James VI in July 1567 were so anxious about the dubious legality of their coup that they retained as much of the traditional ceremonial as possible, in an attempt to acquire a reassuring veneer of normality. At the coronation of Queen Anna in 1590 some ministers of the Kirk initially objected to the use of unction, but King James pointed out the biblical precedents and threatened to bring in a bishop to perform the ceremony, so Robert Bruce, minister of Edinburgh, agreed to perform the rite as a civil rather than an ecclesiastical act. Charles I was anointed at his Scottish coronation at Holyrood in 1633, but Charles II did not receive unction at Scone in 1651 because it was considered too 'papist'.[19]

All the Scottish monarchs from James II to James VI were crowned as minors in the midst of a crisis: James II after the assassination of his father, James III, IV, V and Mary following the sudden deaths of kings in or after a battle, and James VI only five days after the forced abdication of his mother. This meant that these coronations were organised rather hurriedly and did not display the full range of pomp and pageantry, since security was a much higher priority. The precise

OPPOSITE. The Honours of Scotland: the royal regalia consist of the imperial crown made for James V, and the sceptre and sword, both of which were papal gifts to James IV. They are kept in Edinburgh Castle.

details of the ceremonies are not fully recorded in any contemporary narrative accounts and the occasions were probably quite subdued: the coronation of James V in the aftermath of Flodden was traditionally known as 'the mourning coronation'. Consequently, the grandeur and spectacle of a Scottish coronation was most prominently expressed for the crowning of queens consort in happier times, and these elaborate ceremonies were calculated to enhance the honour of the king as much as the queen. Indeed, since it was understood that the queen was subordinate to her husband, he basked in her reflected glory. Joan Beaufort was already married to James I before he returned to his realm from English captivity, and so they were crowned together in a joint coronation at Scone in May 1424, but all the other queens consort had separate coronations at or shortly after their marriages. Mary of Gueldres and Margaret Tudor were crowned on their wedding days and the same was probably the case for Margaret of Denmark. James VI went to Oslo to marry his bride, so Anna's coronation was arranged some months later, after their return to Scotland. Mary of Guise's coronation was staged some 20 months after her wedding, when it was clear that she was expecting a child, who would become heir to the throne. There is no surviving record of the Scottish ritual for crowning a queen consort, but it has been established that the ladies were invested with a crown, sceptre and robe, and received unction and oaths of fealty. Before the Reformation, it is thought that queens did not have to give an oath because their marriage vows were sufficient to establish obedience to the king, but in 1590, Anna of Denmark gave an oath to support the Church and realm of Scotland.[20]

There is very little surviving documentary information on the weddings which preceded the consorts' coronations. For Joan Beaufort and James I, Margaret of Denmark and James III, and Mary of Guise and James V, we have little more than the date and place of the ceremonies: St Mary Overy, Southwark (now Southwark Cathedral), 2 February 1424; Holyrood Abbey, 13 July 1469; and St Andrews Cathedral, 18 June 1538 respectively. For the wedding of Mary of Gueldres and James II on 3 July 1449 at Holyrood, there is a French chronicle account which describes the lavish banquet following the ceremony: courses were brought to table in procession with a painted boar's head and banners displayed, a silver ship was used as a table decoration and there was a communal drinking bowl (mazer) which never ran dry. The celebrations are said to have lasted for five or six days and one might imagine that there was jousting and the creation of knights. An English herald recorded the wedding of Margaret Tudor and James IV on 8 August 1503. There was a lavish combined wedding and coronation service in Holyrood Abbey performed by the archbishop of Glasgow with many heralds and nobles in attendance. At the banquet, the king and queen presided in separate chambers, she under a golden cloth of estate. The heralds cried largesse, there was dancing and games, and bonfires were lit all over Edinburgh. Five days of jousting and feasting followed, and new knights and earls were created, as noted above.[21]

The most lavish Renaissance wedding celebrations were staged in Paris for the marriages of James V to Madeleine of France on 1 January 1537 and of Mary, queen of Scots, to Dauphin Francis on 24 April 1558. The later ceremony seems to have been modelled on the earlier one, since they were so similar in many respects. Both

couples processed along a raised walkway from the palace of the bishop of Paris to be married on a stage at the west door of the cathedral of Notre-Dame. Whilst the nuptial mass was celebrated in the cathedral, largesse was distributed to the crowd outside. After the ceremony, a dinner was held in the hall of the palace of the bishop of Paris, and in the evening there was a feast at the marble-topped table of the Palais de Justice, followed by dancing and masques. The banqueting halls were hung with rich cloths and tapestries, buffets displayed gold and silver plate, and musicians played throughout. The evening entertainment for James and Madeleine is not recorded in any detail, but for Mary and Francis there were figures dressed as the seven planetary deities, artificial horses 'ridden' around the hall and artificial ships 'sailed' around the floor by the princes. The symbolism was quite conventional: the seven planets were not only associated with astrological good fortune, but were also linked to the seven ages of man and the seven Virtues, whilst the 'ship of state' was another common device in royal imagery. The wedding of James VI and Anna of Denmark in Oslo on 23 November 1589 could not match the Paris ceremonies for splendour. Anna's fleet had attempted to sail to Scotland in September and had been driven back by storms, so James sailed to her rescue. Thus the wedding was conducted with as much grandeur as could be arranged at short notice and seems to have been rather modest. James and Anna then travelled to the Danish court at Kronborg for an extended honeymoon, where they were lavishly entertained until they set sail for Scotland on 21 April 1590.[22]

An example of Scottish Renaissance pageantry which is rather better documented than the coronations and weddings is the royal entry. This was a piece of civic ceremonial, organised (with assistance from the royal heralds) and paid for by the royal burghs, and with the full participation of the burgesses. It consisted of a formal procession through the streets, with speeches, spectacles and pageants presented at 'stations' along the route, to welcome a new king or queen on their first 'official' visit to a burgh. As it was the capital, entries into Edinburgh were more lavish and prestigious than entries into other towns. Since the Scottish monarchs came to their thrones as minors, royal entries were usually staged to mark the legal transition from childhood into adulthood in their fourteenth year. Royal entries were also staged for new queens consort, with the first one usually forming a prelude to the queen's coronation. There are no records of any fifteenth-century royal entries, but we may presume that some took place because the sixteenth-century events seem to have drawn on well-established traditions. The first to be documented was the Edinburgh entry of Margaret Tudor in 1503, which took place the day before her wedding and coronation at Holyrood, and Aberdeen staged an entry for her in 1511. It is possible that an Edinburgh entry was arranged for James V when he was 'erected' as king in 1524, but it has left no trace in the records. At the French court, on the orders of Francis I, James V was to be treated as if he were the dauphin, and he was therefore given a royal entry into Paris the day before his wedding to Princess Madeleine. An elaborate Edinburgh entry was planned for Madeleine's arrival in 1537, but the queen's ill health and untimely death prevented it. Mary of Guise received her first royal entry into St Andrews the day before her wedding in June 1538, and later had entries into Edinburgh (20 July 1538), Dundee (28 August 1539), Perth and Aberdeen

(both in the autumn of 1541). Mary, queen of Scots, received an Edinburgh entry on her return from France (2 September 1561), James VI was given an Edinburgh entry for his coming of age (19 October 1579) and another for his homecoming as king of the united realms of Scotland and England (16 May 1617). He also made official entries into Dundee, Aberdeen, St Andrews and Glasgow during 1580 and 1581. Anna of Denmark's Edinburgh entry in May 1590 was originally planned to precede her coronation, as was customary, but the ministers of the Kirk objected to such frivolity on a Sunday (coronations were traditionally held on Sundays), and so the entry was moved to the following Tuesday, 19 May. An Edinburgh entry was staged for Charles I on 15 June 1633 just before his coronation at Holyrood and this is the only Scottish royal entry for which there was an official printed account.[23]

The ceremonial entry provided an opportunity for the burgh to welcome and honour a new king or queen, and to celebrate the bright prospects of a new reign. It was customary for a delegation of burgesses to greet the monarch before the gates of the town, to present him or her with the keys of the burgh as a sign of loyalty, and to offer a 'propine' (formal gift) such as jewels or items of plate. The streets would have been hung with tapestries and banners, the townsfolk and courtiers would have worn their finest clothes, joyful music would have been played and sung, there would have been dancing and disguises (bands of men dressed as Moors or satyrs were common), and fountains would have run with wine. Within the carnival atmosphere there was also an opportunity for the burgh community to engage in a ritualised form of political dialogue with the crown. The plays, *tableaux* and scenery greeting the

monarch at stages along the processional route included the full range of Renaissance allegory and imagery, heavily laden with significant messages. Expressions of loyalty and devotion were accompanied by symbolic reminders of the responsibilities and duties of good rule. Thus there was a sense in which the royal entry was comparable to the 'advice to princes' literary genre (see Chapter 7). Biblical scenes such as the Judgement of Solomon could be used to remind a king that he should act with wisdom and justice; a scene of the Annunciation or the marriage of the Virgin would remind a queen that her first duty was to bear children. Classical deities often appeared: the Judgement of Paris could be used to compliment a queen, who could be compared to the three goddesses (Minerva, Juno and Venus) for beauty, nobility and grace, whilst the appearance of Bacchus and Ceres would express the hope that the new reign would bring fertility and prosperity; scenes of Apollo and the Muses would encourage the creation of a peaceful, rational and cultured society. Allegorical figures of the Virtues were commonly used to encourage the king or queen to cultivate such qualities in their rule: the three Spiritual Virtues (faith, hope and charity) or four Cardinal Virtues (prudence, justice, temperance, and fortitude) would sometimes be depicted trampling on corresponding vices. Other allegorical figures might include Peace, Plenty, Policy, or Liberality. Astrological pageants could be used to prophesy good fortune, the 'wheel of fortune' would indicate that fate could be fickle, and the genealogy of kings would remind a prince of the valour and virtue of his ancestors, which was to be emulated. The Renaissance entry bore some resemblance to the classical 'triumphs' staged for ancient Roman emperors and generals, a coincidence which encouraged the

erection of temporary structures akin to triumphal arches along the processional route and the use of antique motifs and decorations. The popularity of translations of Petrarch's *Trionfi* at the courts of the period would suggest that such parallels were well understood at the time.[24]

Before the Reformation, royal entries were undertaken in a spirit of common values and expectations, with the religious aspects quite prominent. In 1503, Queen Margaret was met by groups of clergy from Greyfriars and St Giles and offered crosses and relics to kiss. Many of the pageants (especially those with biblical themes) would have been similar to those presented for religious processions and festivals, such as the 'mystery' plays performed at Candlemas, Corpus Christi, or other festivals. The Corpus Christi procession also provided the model for the use of a portable canopy (or pall) of fine cloth, which in the religious festival was carried over the consecrated host, and in the royal entry was carried over the head of the monarch, symbolising that he or she reigned by divine grace. The keys of the town were often presented by a child dressed as an angel: in 1503, the angel handed them through the window of a tower, and at St Andrews in 1538 the angel descended in a theatrical 'cloud'. At the Reformation some tension and dissension was introduced into the spectacle. The Edinburgh entry of Mary, queen of Scots, in 1561 was that of a Catholic queen into a town dominated by a radical Protestant faction. There were still some expressions of loyalty and some compliments offered to the queen, but the didactic elements were much more strident than in any previous royal entry. The keys of the burgh were given to Mary not by an angel but by a smartly dressed boy descending from a mechanical globe, who also presented her with a Protes-

tant, English, Geneva Bible and psalter. Mary seems to have been surprised, even embarrassed, but was unable to refuse the gifts without causing public offence. Further along the route, a speech was made on the abolition of the mass. This had been enacted the previous year by a parliament which many, including Mary, regarded as having been convened illegally. The speech was followed by the burning of some kind of effigy. The accounts differ: it might have been some Old Testament figures representing false religion (Korah, Dathan and Abiram), or it might have been the effigy of a Catholic priest in the act of elevating the host. A little further on, another figure was burned, this time a dragon, representing the Antichrist (which for Protestants, meant the pope), and there was another speech about the abolition of the mass. This was taking the custom of 'advice to princes' to extremes; Mary was not so much instructed as insulted, and the public nature of the spectacle left her at a disadvantage. A few weeks later she took her revenge, dismissed the Provost and bailies, and installed a replacement burgh council of much more moderate Protestants. The Edinburgh entries of James VI in 1579 and of Anna in 1590 also included Protestant symbolism; such themes were prominent in 1579 and more muted in 1590. There were presentations of vernacular scriptures, antipapal imagery and prominent sermons, but the poise and dignity of the events were restored because both James and Anna were also Protestants (although Anna later converted to Catholicism).[25]

The most magnificent Scottish Renaissance triumphs were staged for the baptisms of the heirs to the throne in December 1566 and August 1594, both at Stirling Castle. The baptisms of royal children are very poorly documented before 1566:

dates, places and godparents are usually (but not always) recorded, purchases of candles and cloths sometimes appear in the financial accounts, and occasionally the creation of knights (including the baby princes) is noted. However, much more detailed accounts of the spectacles of 1566 and 1594 survive. Mary, queen of Scots, gave birth to Prince Charles James (the future James VI) on 19 June 1566 in Edinburgh Castle, and she clearly saw the arrival of a male heir as an opportunity to bring her fractious nobles together in a celebration of national reconciliation and hope for the future under the renewed Stewart dynasty. She sought to promote toleration and unity by becoming the patron of both Catholics and Protestants, urging them to live in harmony. She took as her model the Valois festivals staged at Bayonne in 1565 which stressed the role of Mary's brother-in-law, King Charles IX, as the great French peacemaker, following a bitter civil war. At Stirling, the baptismal party processed to the chapel royal with the baby under a canopy (symbolising divine grace) where he was baptised at the magnificent golden font sent by Queen Elizabeth, his godmother. The service was a Catholic ceremony, from which some Protestant nobles and guests absented themselves, but it was followed by an elaborate banquet in the great hall, which stressed the unity of the nation in front of foreign ambassadors. Presiding over the ceremonies were the 5th earl of Argyll (a Protestant and hereditary master of the royal household) and, the 5th Lord Seton (a Catholic and the

serving master of the household), both of whom carried white wands, symbolic of their offices, but also signs of reconciliation after a feud. Some years later, Seton had his portrait painted by Adrian Vanson in his magnificent scarlet and gold household robes (SNPG) and this picture gives some indication of the splendour of the attire worn at the baptism. The baby prince was knighted and formally invested as duke of Rothesay and Great Steward of Scotland. There followed three days of hunts, feasts, poetry, dance and theatre with many French and Italian influences. Men dressed as hobby-horses sang Italian songs, nymphs and satyrs appeared, celebratory Latin verses by George Buchanan were recited, and there was an Arthurian round table, which symbolically reminded the English ambassadors that Mary and her son had a claim to the English throne. The festival culminated in a mock siege of an artificial castle representing the monarchy, where an assault by costumed combatants including wild Highland men, Moors and devils, representing the forces of disorder, was repelled. There was then a firework display, which was possibly the first ever seen in Scotland. The imagery conflated the return of the classical golden age with the new Arthurian golden age of a united Britain forecast in Geoffrey of Monmouth's *Prophecies of Merlin*. Mary was compared to the goddesses Diana, Venus and Astraea, who brought harmony to a world of chaos. This remarkable Renaissance triumph promoted the idea of the Stewart dynasty as the only

OPPOSITE. Adrian Vanson, portrait of George, 5th Lord Seton, in his splendid robes as master of household to Mary, queen of Scots, painted c.1577. His wand of office is inscribed with Mary's cipher, and behind him is displayed his knightly armour.

guarantor of national peace, unity and prosperity. The spectacular collapse of Mary's regime only months later obscured the significance of the event but the essential message endured: James VI was able to take up similar themes a generation later.[26]

The festival staged for the baptism of Prince Henry Frederick in August 1594 was a similarly grand Renaissance spectacle. The name Henry was carefully chosen to appeal to the baby's godmother, Queen Elizabeth, by recalling her father and grandfather (the latter was an ancestor of the baby prince, from whom the Stewart claim to the English throne derived). The festivities were devised by Queen Anna's secretary and court poet, William Fowler, who was familiar with the customs of the English court and took them as a model. He also recorded the celebrations in a pageant book, which was published in both Edinburgh and London. The chapel royal was entirely rebuilt for the occasion to the proportions of Solomon's temple (see Chapter 2) and the divinity of kingship was stressed by comparing James to King David and Emperor Constantine as well as Solomon. On this occasion the baptismal service was a Protestant rite, so the English ambassadors were able to attend. Like his father, the baby was carried under a canopy, knighted, and invested as duke of Rothesay and Great Steward. There was a theatrical tournament which mimicked the Elizabethan Accession Day tilts, where teams of knights bore their own *imprese* (see Chapter 3). The king jousted as a Knight of Malta, presenting himself as a Protestant crusader willing to fight the infidel (for Turk, read Catholic). The Scottish custom was for the king

and queen to preside over segregated tables at feasts, but at the baptismal banquet ladies and gentlemen were seated next to each other in the English style. The spectacles at the banquet included a triumphant chariot drawn by a Moor containing the classical and allegorical goddesses, Ceres, Fecundity, Faith, Concord, Liberality and Perseverance. Originally, the chariot was to have been drawn by the king's tame lion, but it was thought that this might frighten the guests. The chariot was followed by a 'ship of state' crewed by Arion, Triton and Neptune, who distributed to the guests sugared confections shaped like fish. All the costumes and props used at the jousts and banquet were festooned with emblems and devices extolling the virtue and power of the Stewart dynasty.[27]

The most solemn Renaissance pageant was the royal or noble funeral. As with the royal weddings and early baptisms, fifteenth-century funerals are sparsely recorded. The dates and places of burials are usually documented, but few other details are noted. James I, Joan Beaufort and Margaret Tudor were buried at the Charterhouse of Perth, which the king had founded. James II, James V and Madeleine of France were buried at Holyrood Abbey, and Mary of Gueldres at her foundation of the church of the Holy Trinity in Edinburgh. Mary of Guise's body was sent back to France for burial in the convent of St Pierre, Rheims, and a memorial service was held for her at Notre-Dame, Paris, which was attended by her daughter. The tombs of James III and Margaret of Denmark are at Cambuskenneth Abbey, although the memorial visible today is a Victorian struc-

OPPOSITE. A Scottish royal funeral from the *Book of Hours of James IV and Margaret Tudor*, 1503. The picture shows a dolorous chapel and mourners in dule habits.

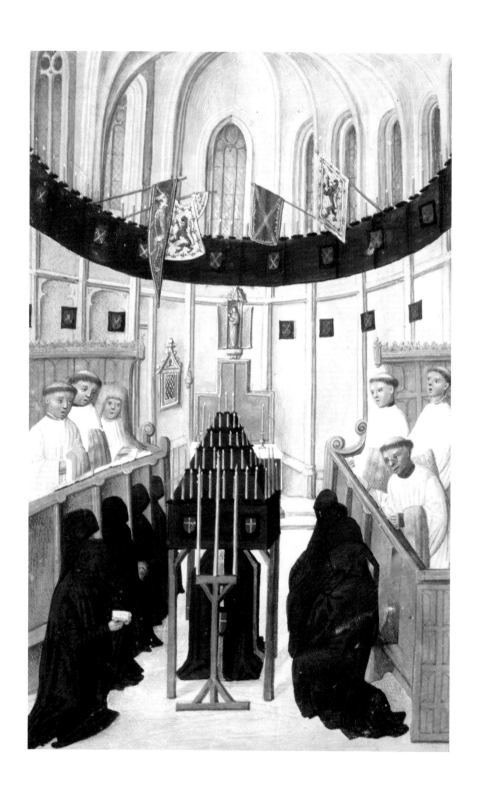

ture. The final resting place of James IV is uncertain. His body was taken from the battlefield at Flodden by the English forces and rested for a time at the Charterhouse of Sheen, Surrey. It was initially unburied because the king had died excommunicate. Henry VIII sought and obtained the pope's permission to give the Scottish king a Christian burial and suggested St Paul's Cathedral as a suitable location, but it is not clear exactly where, when, or if this took place. Mary, queen of Scots, was initially buried at Peterborough Cathedral, but was later moved to a splendid Renaissance tomb provided by her son at Westminster Abbey.[28]

The first Scottish Renaissance funeral for which we have much detail was that of Queen Madeleine at Holyrood in July 1537. The 16-year-old queen had lived only seven weeks in her Scottish realm and had not yet been crowned, but she was the eldest daughter of the king of France and therefore entitled to every possible mark of respect. The most notable feature of her obsequies was the use of mourning habits or 'dule' clothes (from the French, *deuil*, mourning). These were hooded black gowns resembling monks' habits, which were commonly worn for funerals at the Burgundian and French courts. According to George Buchanan, who was at the royal court in 1537, dule was worn for the first time in Scotland to honour Queen Madeleine. Considerable sums spent on such garments certainly appear in the financial accounts. Madeleine's coffin and bier were covered with purple and black velvet palls with white crosses, and the abbey church was hung with black draperies and 400 shields of arms. There was such a shortage of black cloth in Edinburgh that the merchants of Dundee were ordered to bring their stocks to the capital. As her coffin lay in state, a 'dolorous chapel' or *chapelle ardente* was placed over it. This was a raised wooden stand, decorated with black cloth, shields of arms and over 200 candles, where prayers for the repose of her soul would have been offered in a vigil which continued until the burial. Whilst her husband lived, the anniversary of Madeleine's death was marked annually with a ceremony known as her 'suffrage' or 'soul mass'. Hundreds of chaplains were assembled to say prayers for her soul in the abbey church, which was again decorated with arms, candles and black hangings.[29]

James V died at Falkland Palace on 14 December 1542 and was buried at Holyrood, in the same vault as Madeleine, on 8 January 1543. Sir David Lindsay of the Mount, Lord Lyon, was responsible for organising a grand heraldic funeral appropriate for a knight of the major chivalric orders, and the body was embalmed to allow time for the formal arrangements to be made. Nobles and lords were summoned to attend, and all the heralds and pursuivants were provided with dule habits. Many black velvet palls and hangings were used, alongside crimson and gold banners and shields of arms, and the coffin was again placed beneath a dolorous chapel. An effigy of the king was constructed and laid on a mattress, probably on top of the coffin. The effigy would have been a life-sized mannequin of the king in his prime, lying as if asleep but with his eyes open, dressed in royal robes and invested with replica regalia. It symbolised the enduring institution of the monarchy: the 'body natural' of the king was mortal, but the 'body politic' lived on. It is likely that heraldic 'achievements' were also used at the king's funeral, although crucial pages of the accounts have been lost, so we cannot be certain. These would have been symbols of his knightly status deposited at the tomb: replicas of his shield, helmet, crest,

gauntlets, banner and coat of arms. It was also common in heraldic funerals for a living knight to impersonate the deceased by wearing his armour, carrying his banner, and riding his caparisoned horse in the funeral cortège. It is likely that this was done for James V but it is not noted in the surviving accounts. An indication of how a royal heraldic funeral might have looked can be found in the *Book of Hours of James IV and Margaret Tudor*. The picture includes draperies, banners, shields of arms, a dolorous chapel, and mourners in dule habits. The saltire banners are given a red background rather than a blue one because the artist was Flemish, and in the Low Countries the cross of St Andrew was sometimes depicted in different colours. The king's household officers would have remained in post until the moment of burial, when they would have broken their wands of office and thrown them into the grave, having performed their last service for their lord and master. It was still possible to hold a heraldic funeral after the Reformation, and this seems to have occurred for the burial of the Regent Moray in February 1570. A civic procession was organised by the burgesses of Edinburgh to accompany the coffin from Holyrood to the funeral in St Giles' Kirk, and Sir James Kirkaldy of Grange, Provost of Edinburgh and Captain of the Castle, rode a black draped horse and carried the earl's standard to his tomb. An even more magnificent heraldic funeral was staged for the 1st marquess of Huntly in 1636, which involved a four-week procession from Dundee (where the marquess had died) to the burial in Elgin Cathedral. The pageantry included the processional display of banners, shields, pennants, caparisoned horses, and other heraldic symbols.[30]

Despite the deficiencies of the documentary sources, it is readily apparent that the chivalric culture of the Scottish court at this time was rich, diverse and in keeping with contemporary European practices. The elaborate pageantry of the jousts and tournaments, the observance of knightly conventions of honour, the obsession with heraldry, and the interest in armorial registers and chivalric orders indicated the strength of the Scottish Renaissance chivalric impulse. The honour and dignity of the kings and courtiers was made manifest in increasingly elaborate pageantry and ceremonial, which drew on Burgundian, French and English influences to a considerable extent. Royal weddings, entries, coronations, baptisms and funerals were designed to promote the image of the Stewart dynasty as equal in dignity to the grander princes of other realms. The status of the royal house was gradually enhanced by the adoption of the ideology and symbolism of imperial monarchy, and by the use of classical and allegorical imagery in public spectacle. The success of this programme may be indicated by a work of German Renaissance art. In 1515, Albrecht Dürer designed a magnificent *Ehrenpforte* (triumphal arch) in a Roman style for Emperor Maximilian I. The intricate scheme was published as a large-scale woodcut print involving 192 separate printing blocks, forming one of the largest prints ever produced. Among the many images and emblems decorating the arch is a sequence of busts of European monarchs, amongst whom a prominent position is allocated to the king of Scots.[31] The glory and honour of the Scottish realm and the Stewart dynasty was clearly acknowledged abroad as well as at home.

9

CONCLUSION

The Renaissance in Scotland

It should now be clear that the impact of the Renaissance in Scotland was much greater and more wide-ranging than has often been imagined. For a small and relatively poor kingdom, Scotland participated fully in most cultural developments of the period, and excelled in a few, presenting a vibrant, confident and impressive face to the outside world. The Scottish kingdom was very outward-looking and open to influences from the Low Countries, France, England, Germany, Scandinavia and Italy. The Church, the universities, the burgh communities, the nobility, and pre-eminently the royal court, provided numerous opportunities for fruitful, creative interaction and exchange. The various threads of Renaissance ideas and styles were woven into a rich and colourful cultural tapestry in Scotland. The adoption of classical ideas and the imitation of antique styles can be clearly identified, blended with a persistent attachment to late-Gothic embellishment. The imperial theme

was widely promoted, humanist intellectual values were applied actively in education and public life, and there was an enduring obsession with chivalry, heraldry and the castellated style of architecture.

Much of the impetus for Renaissance cultural development in Scotland originated in, or was connected to, the royal court. The Stewart monarchs from James I onwards adopted a coherent and consistent programme of cultural patronage, which aimed at supporting the dignity and honour of the Crown. The international status of the dynasty was enhanced by a sequence of prestigious royal marriages, and the presence of queens such as Mary of Gueldres, Margaret Tudor and Mary of Guise had a great impact. The cultural influences of the Burgundian Low Countries, and the English and French courts were considerably strengthened as a result, as was the confidence and exuberance of the Scottish court. The return of Mary, queen of Scots, with a thoroughly French

OPPOSITE. The magnificent *trompe l'oeil* cupola
from the ceiling of the gallery at Pinkie House, painted
for Alexander Seton, earl of Dunfermline, in 1613.

outlook, consolidated this process, albeit briefly. The adoption of the theory and imagery of imperial monarchy and the refashioning of the royal regalia were part of the same impulse, which was heavily reinforced by the sanctity of the coronation ritual. The claims of the Stewarts, as the heirs of Robert Bruce, to be the guardians of Scottish independence and nationhood, were pursued in the creation of a modern royal navy and extensive artillery, both of which reached a peak under James IV and James V, but declined thereafter. The construction of fine quadrangular palaces, designed for elegant and sophisticated living, at Linlithgow, Holyrood, Falkland, and the castles of Edinburgh and Stirling, provided the theatrical backdrop to the increasingly elaborate set-pieces of courtly pageantry and ceremonial. The tournaments of the Wild Knight and the Black Lady of 1507 and 1508 formed the high point of chivalric display, whilst the Stirling baptisms of 1566 and 1594 projected a very cosmopolitan image of the Scottish court.

In the visual arts, Scotland provided some of the earliest examples of Renaissance ideas and designs entering the British Isles. James III's silver coinage of the 1480s adopted Roman-style portraiture and imperial imagery. The corbels in the Great Hall of Edinburgh Castle represent Italianate sculptural styles and were carved by an Italian c.1511. The courtyard façades of Falkland Palace were created by French master masons in the 1530s in imitation of the Loire châteaux. The stained glass panels set into the windows of the Palace of Holyroodhouse in the 1530s were of antique designs imported from Flanders. The diamond-faceted façade of the 1580s at Crichton Castle is a remarkable survival, and the exuberant carvings of the Stirling Heads of c.1540 are some of the finest examples of a style which can be found in many locations across Europe at the time. Carved medallion heads within roundels became a very popular motif in Scottish design of the period. Some Renaissance pieces of the highest quality have a Scottish provenance. The *Trinity Altarpiece* is a masterpiece of Renaissance panel painting, and the *Book of Hours of James IV and Margaret Tudor* is one of the most exquisite illuminated manuscripts of the age. Archbishop Scheves' portrait medal, the Corneille portraits of James V and his two queens, and the Nuremberg gold cup are also of the finest Renaissance workmanship. The intellectual and artistic scheme of the painted ceiling of the gallery at Pinkie House is an extraordinarily learned and complex example of a genre which came to characterise Scottish art towards the end of the period. Alongside these outstanding pieces, Scottish Renaissance patrons commissioned a profusion of decorative and artistic works of lesser quality, but still of great interest. The sheer variety of visual decoration and imagery recorded in the inventories and financial accounts of the period gives a vivid impression of a lost world of colour, dignity and magnificence.

In areas other than the visual arts, the Scottish realm also nurtured some creative talents of European significance. Robert Carver's music is easily comparable to the compositions of his English and Continental contemporaries, and the chance survivals of fragments of other pieces of Scottish Renaissance music provide tantalising indications of a rich and inventive tradition. The loss of so much Scottish music at the Reformation was a terrible blow to the nation's cultural heritage. In literature, Gavin Douglas's *Eneados* was one of the finest achievements of the European Renaissance, reaching the highest standards in both translation and poetry. Similarly, Hector Boece and George

Buchanan were humanist scholars of international stature, greatly admired in many countries. Douglas, Boece and Buchanan sit at the pinnacle of a literary and intellectual culture, which is impressive in its depth and range. The works of Henryson, Dunbar, Lindsay, Scot, Montgomerie and other Scottish writers of the period are vibrant, versatile and engaging.

The Renaissance in Scotland formed one of the most creative, confident, and cosmopolitan episodes in the country's history. A small, relatively poor and marginal kingdom engaged fully with the international cultural trends and developments of the northern Renaissance. Scottish talent created a few extraordinary masterpieces amidst a rich profusion of lesser works. It is no longer possible to accept the myth that there was never a Renaissance in Scotland, or that the cultural developments of the period were weak and inferior to those of comparable states. The evidence of the surviving documents and artefacts is patchy, but what remains allows us to paint a fascinating picture of considerable creative power. The Renaissance architecture, decorative and applied arts, fine arts, military developments, music, literature, and pageantry of the two centuries between 1424 and 1625 successfully combined to project the glory and honour of the Scottish realm.

A corbel supporting the hammerbeam roof of the great hall at Edinburgh Castle, built for King James IV by about 1511. This is one of a series of corbels carved by an Italian mason in the Renaissance style. It carries an imperial crown and the king's cipher, I4R, for Jacobus 4 Rex, with the 4 at a rather jaunty angle. (See page 18.)

QVID·FACIAT·LETAS·SEGETES·
QVO·SIDERE·TERRAM·
ertere metenas ulmisq; adiungere uites
onueniat. que cura bou. qs cultus habendo
it pecoii. atz. apibus quanta experetia parcis
nc canere incipiam. Vos o clarissima mudi

NOTES

Chapter 1: Introduction

1 Andrea Thomas, 'The Renaissance' in T. M. Devine and Jenny Wormald (eds), *The Oxford Handbook of Modern Scottish History* (Oxford, 2012), 185–203.

2 Jane Stevenson and Peter Davidson, 'Ficino in Aberdeen: The Continuing Problem of the Scottish Renaissance', *Journal of the Northern Renaissance* 1, (2009), 64–8, at www.northernrenaissance.org.

3 Michelet's 17-volume *History of France* was published between 1833 and 1867. Volume 9 was entitled *La Renaissance*. Jacob Burckhardt, *The Civilization of the Renaissance in Italy: An Essay*, trans. S. G. C. Middlemore (Oxford and London, 1945). The German original was published in Basel in 1860.

4 Theodore E. Mommsen, 'Petrarch's Conception of the "Dark Ages"', *Speculum*, 17 (1942), 226–42.

5 A recent study of the Italian Renaissance is Marco Folin (ed.), *Courts and Courtly Arts in Renaissance Italy: Arts, Culture and Politics, 1395–1530* (Woodbridge, 2010).

6 For example, C. H. Haskins, *The Renaissance of the Twelfth Century* (Cambridge, MA, 1927).

7 Giorgio Vasari, *Lives of the Artists*, trans. J. C. and P. Bondanella (Oxford, 1991). The Italian original was published in Florence in 1550 and 1568.

8 For example, Ethan Matt Kavaler, *Renaissance Gothic: Architecture and the Arts in Northern Europe, 1470–1540* (New Haven, 2012).

9 A notable exception is Roderick J. Lyall, *Alexander Montgomerie: Poetry, Politics and Cultural Change in Jacobean Scotland* (Tempe, AZ, 2005), where Montgomerie's Mannerist aesthetic is taken seriously. Following English practice, the early Scottish Baroque of the 1630s has been described as 'the Scottish Jacobean style': Martin Kemp and Clare Farrow, 'Humanism in The Visual Arts, c.1530–c.1630' in John MacQueen (ed.), *Humanism in Renaissance Scotland* (Edinburgh, 1990), 32–47 at p.44.

10 Thomas DaCosta Kaufmann, 'The European Perspective' in Michael Andersen, Birgitte Bøggild Johannsen and Hugo Johannsen (eds), *Reframing the Danish Renaissance: Problems and Prospects in a European Perspective* (Copenhagen, 2011), 33–50.

11 David Ditchburn, *Scotland and Europe: The Medieval Kingdom and its Contacts with Christendom, 1214–1560, Volume 1: Religion, Culture and Commerce* (East Linton, 2001).

12 Ranald G. Nicholson, *Scotland: The Later Middle Ages* (Edinburgh, 1974), 281.

13 Michael Brown, *James I* (Edinburgh, 1994), especially 201–8; Brown, 'James I, 1406–1437' in Michael Brown and Roland Tanner (eds), *Scottish Kingship, 1306–1542: Essays in Honour of Norman Macdougall* (Edinburgh, 2008), 155–78.

14 Priscilla Bawcutt and Bridget Henisch, 'Scots Abroad in the Fifteenth Century: The Princesses Margaret, Isabella

OPPOSITE. An exquisite illumination from a manuscript of Virgil's *Georgics*, painted in Paris c.1460 by an Italian artist for a Scottish patron. The scenes depict: in the background, ploughing and sowing; in the foreground, harvesting and treading the grapes. Another scene from the same manuscript may be found on page viii.

and Eleanor' in Elizabeth Ewen and Maureen M. Meikle (eds), *Women in Scotland, c.1100–c.1750* (East Linton, 1999), 45–55.

15 Fiona Downie, 'Queenship in Late Medieval Scotland' and Roger Mason, 'Renaissance Monarchy? Stewart Kingship, 1469–1542' both in Brown and Tanner (eds), *Scottish Kingship*, 232–54 and 255–78.

16 Roger A. Mason, 'This Realm of Scotland is an Empire? Imperial Ideas and Iconography in Early Renaissance Scotland' in Barbara E. Crawford (ed.), *Church, Chronicle and Learning in Medieval and Early Renaissance Scotland* (Edinburgh, 1999), 73–91; Andrea Thomas, 'Crown Imperial: Coronation Ritual and Regalia in the Reign of James V' in Julian Goodare and Alasdair A. MacDonald (eds), *Sixteenth-Century Scotland: Essays in Honour of Michael Lynch* (Leiden, 2008), 43–67.

17 Charles G. Nauert Jr., *Humanism and the Culture of Renaissance Europe* (Cambridge, 1995); MacQueen (ed.), *Humanism in Renaissance Scotland*.

18 Katie Stevenson, *Chivalry and Knighthood in Scotland, 1424–1513* (Woodbridge, 2006).

Chapter 2: Palaces of Honour

1 Charles McKean, *The Scottish Château: The Country House of Renaissance Scotland* (Stroud, 2001), 39–58, 79–98.

2 Deborah Howard, *Scottish Architecture from the Reformation to the Restoration, 1560–1660* (Edinburgh, 1995), 116–29. See also *Tolbooths and Townhouses: Civic Architecture in Scotland to 1833*, Royal Commission on the Ancient and Historic Monuments of Scotland (Edinburgh, 1996), 82, 98–9. My thanks to Michael Lynch for alerting me to this reference.

3 George Hay, 'The Architecture of Scottish Collegiate Churches' in G. W. S. Barrow (ed.), *The Scottish Tradition: Essays in Honour of Ronald Gordon Cant* (Edinburgh, 1974), 56–70. See also Ian B. Cowan and David E. Easson, *Medieval Religious Houses in Scotland* (London, 1976).

4 Miles Glendinning and Aonghus MacKechnie, *Scottish Architecture* (London, 2004), 50.

5 Alan Macquarrie, 'Anselm Adornes of Bruges: Traveller in the East and Friend of James III' *Innes Review,* 33 (1982), 15–22.

6 Glendinning and MacKechnie, *Scottish Architecture*, 50; A. A. MacDonald, 'The Chapel of Restalrig: Royal Folly or Venerable Shrine?' in L. A. J. R. Houwen, A. A. MacDonald and S. L. Mapstone (eds), *A Palace in the Wild: Essays on Vernacular Culture and Humanism in Late-Medieval and Renaissance Scotland* (Leuven, 2000), 27–59.

7 *Accounts of the Lord High Treasurer of Scotland*, eds Thomas Dickson and Sir James Balfour Paul (12 vols, Edinburgh, 1877–1916), vi, 299; vii, 24; Audrey-Beth Fitch, 'Marian Devotion in Scotland and the Shrine of Loreto' in Edward J. Cowan and Lizanne Henderson (eds), *A History of Everyday Life in Medieval Scotland, 1000 to 1600* (Edinburgh, 2011), 274–88.

8 John G. Dunbar, *Scottish Royal Palaces* (East Linton, 1999), 5–10; Ian Campbell, 'A Romanesque Revival and the Early Renaissance in Scotland, c.1380–1513', *Journal of the Society of Architectural Historians*, 54 (1995), 302–25; Ian Campbell, 'Linlithgow's "Princely Palace" and its Influence on Europe', *Architectural Heritage*, 5 (1995), 1–20.

9 Campbell, 'Romanesque Revival', 302–4, 311–12.

10 The statues are named in an account of 1535, when they were repainted: *Accounts of the Masters of Works*, eds Henry M. Paton *et al.* (2 vols, Edinburgh, 1957 and 1982), i, 128.

11 Dunbar, *Scottish Royal Palaces*, 11–21.

12 Howard, *Scottish Architecture*, 40.

13 James VI stayed at Kronborg Castle from 21 January to early March 1590: David Stevenson, *Scotland's Last Royal Wedding: The Marriage of James VI and Anne of Denmark* (Edinburgh, 1997), 48.

14 St Mary's church was converted into an arsenal in the 1530s, demolished and replaced by barracks in the 1750s, which were in turn replaced by the Scottish National War Memorial in the 1920s. The western gunhouse was replaced by military offices in the eighteenth century.

15 Dunbar, *Scottish Royal Palaces*, 75–82.

16 Iain MacIvor, *Edinburgh Castle* (London, 1993), 72–7.

17 Howard, *Scottish Architecture*, 82, 90, 129–31, 134–8, 141, 145, 203.

18 Dunbar, *Scottish Royal Palaces*, 55–61.

19 The report by John Young, Somerset Herald, was later printed in John Leland, *De Rebus Britannicis Collectanea* (6 vols, London, 1770), iv, 258–300; Dunbar, *Scottish Royal Palaces*, 131–3.

20 Ibid., 61–5.

21 Andrea Thomas, *Princelie Majestie: The Court of James V of Scotland, 1528–1542* (Edinburgh, 2005), 7–9, 59–63.

22 Dunbar, *Scottish Royal Palaces*, 61–72; Thomas, *Princelie Majestie*, 63–6.

23 My thanks to Michael Lynch for drawing my attention to the Hollar print.

24 *Accounts of the Masters of Works*, i, 189–91.

25 Dunbar, *Scottish Royal Palaces*, 171; David McRoberts and Stephen Mark Holmes, *Lost Interiors: The Furnishings of Scottish Churches in the Later Middle Ages* (Edinburgh, 2012), 20–1. There are tiny fragments of glass surviving from elsewhere: J. M. Gray, 'Notes on Examples of Old Heraldic and other Glass', *Proceedings of the Society of Antiquaries of Scotland*, 26 (1891–2), 34–48.

26 Dunbar, *Scottish Royal Palaces*, 21–7; *Accounts of the Masters of Works*, i, 260.

27 Thomas, *Princelie Majestie*, 71–4; Dunbar, *Scottish Royal Palaces*, 27–37.

28 Marc Girouard, 'Falkland Palace, Fife I, *Country Life*, vol. 126, no. 3260 (Aug. 1959), 121.

29 D. Bentley-Cranch, 'An early Sixteenth-Century French Architectural source for the Palace of Falkland', *Review of Scottish Culture*, 2 (1986), 85–95; J. G. Dunbar, 'Some Sixteenth-Century French Parallels for the Palace of Falkland', ibid., 7 (1991), 3–8.

30 Norman MacDougall, *James IV* (Edinburgh, 2006), 217; Alasdair A. MacDonald, 'Princely Culture in Scotland under James III and James IV' in Martin Gosman, Alasdair MacDonald and Arjo Vanderjagt (eds), *Princes and Princely Culture, 1450–1650*, vol. 1 (Leiden, 2003), 150.

31 Dunbar, *Scottish Royal Palaces*, 40–1.

32 Richard Fawcett, *Stirling Castle* (London, 1995), 35–9.

33 Aonghus MacKechnie, 'Stirling's Triumphal Arch', *Welcome: News for Friends of Historic Scotland* (Sept. 1991), unpaginated.

34 Fawcett, *Stirling Castle*, 47–51; Dunbar, *Scottish Royal Palaces*, 39–49.

35 Richard Fawcett, 'The Architecture' and Michael Lynch, 'The Great Hall in the Reigns of Mary, Queen of Scots and James VI' both in Richard Fawcett (ed.), *Stirling Castle: The Restoration of the Great Hall* (York, 2001), 1–14, 15–22.

36 Jamie Cameron, *James V: The Personal Rule, 1528–1542* (East Linton, 1998), 288; Michael Lynch, 'The Reassertion of Princely Power in Scotland: The Reigns of Mary, Queen of Scots and King James VI' in Gosman, MacDonald and Vanderjagt (eds), *Princes and Princely Culture*, vol. 1, 224.

37 Jonathan Spangler, 'Aulic Spaces Transplanted: The Design and Layout of a Franco-Burgundian Court in a Scottish Palace', *The Court Historian*, 14 (June, 2009), 49–62.

38 Dunbar, *Scottish Royal Palaces*, 154–7

39 H. M. Shire, 'The King's House at Stirling: Its Carvings in Stone' in Janet Hadley Williams (ed.), *Stewart Style, 1513–1542: Essays on the Court of James V* (East Linton, 1996), 72–84.

40 Sally Rush, 'The Iconography of the External Sculpture' in conference proceedings on Stirling Castle Palace (forthcoming).

41 Fawcett, *Stirling Castle*, 55–61; Dunbar, *Scottish Royal Palaces*, 49–55; Thomas, *Princelie Majestie*, 74–77; McKean, *The Scottish Château*, 88–91.

42 Howard, *Scottish Architecture*, 30–5.

43 *Accounts of the Masters of Works*, ii, 239; Aonghus MacKechnie, 'James VI's architects and their architecture' in Julian Goodare and Michael Lynch (eds), *The Reign of James VI* (East Linton, 2000), 161–5; Ian Campbell and Aonghus MacKechnie, 'The "Great Temple of Solomon" at Stirling Castle', *Architectural History*, 54 (2011), 91–118. In this latter article, the authors suggest that the term 'pirament' might actually refer to a pediment rather than a pyramid: p95.

44 Dunbar, *Scottish Royal Palaces*, 87–94; Howard, *Scottish Architecture*, 26–30.

45 Howard, *Scottish Architecture*, 156.

46 Fawcett, *Stirling Castle*, 119–20; Howard, *Scottish Architecture*, 155–6.

47 Aonghus MacKechnie, 'Court and Courtier Architecture, 1424–1660' in Richard D. Oram and Geoffrey P. Stell (eds), *Lordship and Architecture in Medieval and Renaissance Scotland* (Edinburgh, 2005), 308–9; McKean, *The Scottish Château*, 94–8, 162–4.

48 Ibid., 39–58, 99–120.

49 Howard, *Scottish Architecture*, 84; McKean, *The Scottish Château*, 205–6.

50 Glendinning and MacKechnie, *Scottish Architecture*, 73; McKean, *The Scottish Château*, 213–18. See also Harry Gordon Slade, 'The Gordons and the North-East, 1452–1640' in Oram and Stell, *Lordship and Architecture*, 250–72, where it is suggested that the castellated style of the north-east was 'the autumnal flowering of the Middle Ages, not the spring flowering of the Renaissance', p.269. This would require an extremely late Middle Ages.

51 R. Maitland, *The Historie of the House of Seytoun*, ed. J. Fullarton (Bannatyne Club, 1829), 63.

52 Howard, *Scottish Architecture*, 106; McKean, *The Scottish Château*, 180–2.

53 Quoted in MacKechnie, 'Court and Courtier Architecture', 312.

54 Howard, *Scottish Architecture*, 100–4; McKean, *The Scottish Château*, 183–8.

55 Fawcett, *Stirling Castle*, 79–80.

56 Sir David Lynsday, *Selected Poems*, ed. Janet Hadley Williams (Glasgow, 2000), 79.

57 Howard, *Scottish Architecture*, 100–3; McKean, *The Scottish Château*, 77–8.

58 My thanks to Michael Lynch for explaining this to me in a private communication.

59 Charles McKean, 'The Scottish Renaissance Country Seat in its Setting', *Garden History: Journal of the Garden History Society*, 31 (2003), 148–9.

60 Howard, *Scottish Architecture*, 44–6, 104; A. R. Somerville, 'The Ancient Sundials of Scotland', *Proceedings of the Society of Antiquaries of Scotland*, 117 (1987), 233–64.

61 Richard Fawcett, 'Gothic or Classical? The Continuity of Medieval Forms in Scottish Church Architecture' in Rudolf Suntrup and Jan R. Veenstra (eds), *Konstruktion der Gegenwart und Zukunft, Shaping the Present and Future* (Frankfurt am Main, 2008), 93–120.

Chapter 3: Courtly Manner

1 Ian Campbell, 'Bishop Elphinstone's Tomb' in Jane Geddes (ed.), *King's College Chapel, Aberdeen, 1500–2000* (Leeds, 2000), 115–29.

2 Lorne Campbell, 'Scottish Patrons and Netherlandish Painters in the Fifteenth and Sixteenth Centuries' in Grant G. Simpson (ed.), *Scotland and the Low Countries, 1124–1994* (East Linton, 1996), 96; McRoberts and Holmes, *Lost Interiors*, 80–2, 126–7.

3 David McRoberts, 'The Manse of Stobo in 1542', *IR*, 22 (1971), 19–31, 101–9; John Warrack, *Domestic Life in Scotland, 1488–1688: A Sketch of the Development of Furniture and Household Usage* (London, 1920), 32–62; Ross MacKenzie, *A Scottish Renaissance Household: Sir William Hamilton and Newton Castle in 1559* (Darvel, 1990), 24–33.

4 Margaret H. B. Sanderson, *Cardinal of Scotland: David Beaton, c.1494-1546* (Edinburgh, 2001).

5 David H. Caldwell, 'The Beaton Panels – Scottish Carvings of the 1520s or 1530s' in John Higgit (ed.), *Medieval Art and Architecture in the Diocese of St Andrews* (London, 1994), 174–84.

6 Helena M. Shire, 'The Heraldic Ceiling of St Machar's Cathedral, Old Aberdeen, c.1520' in Hadley Williams, ed., *Stewart Style*, 63–72; McRoberts and Holmes, *Lost Interiors*, 15–16.

7 McRoberts and Holmes, *Lost Interiors*, 69–70; Sallyanne Simpson, 'The Choir Stalls and Rood Screen' and Richard Emerson, 'Bishop Stewart's Pulpit' both in Geddes (ed.), *King's College Chapel*, 74–97, 137–46

8 J. G. Dunbar, *The Stirling Heads* (Edinburgh, 1975); Helena. M. Shire, 'The King's House at Stirling: Its Carved Roundels in Wood' in Hadley Williams, ed., *Stewart Style*, 84–96. See also www.stirlingcastle.gov.uk/home/experience/highlights/stirlingheadsgallery

9 Michael Bath, *Renaissance Decorative Painting in Scotland* (Edinburgh, 2003), 185–90.

10 Kazimierz Kuczman, *Renesansowe Głowy Wawelskie* (Krakow, 2004), 199–208 has an English summary of the Polish text.

11 J. S. Richardson, 'Unrecorded Scottish Wood Carvings', *PSAS*, 60 (1925–6), 384–408.

12 www.stirlingcastle.gov.uk/home/experience/highlights/tapestries; *A Collection of Inventories and Other Records of the Royal Wardrobe and Jewelhouse; and of the Artillery and Munitioun in some of the Royal Castles, 1488-1606*, ed. T. Thomson (Edinburgh, 1815), 50, 126.

13 Much is listed in *Wardrobe Inventories*, ed. Thomson, and in *Inventaires de la royne descosse douairière de France*, ed. J. Robertson (Edinburgh, 1863), but the multiple volumes of the *Treasurer's Accounts* also record many purchases.

14 Amy L. Juhala, 'The Household and Court of King James VI of Scotland, 1567–1603' (University of Edinburgh unpublished Ph.D. thesis, 2000), 153–4.

15 Susan Groag Bell, *The Lost Tapestries of the City of Ladies: Christine de Pizan's Renaissance Legacy* (Berkeley, 2004).

16 Margaret H. Swain, *Historical Needlework: A Study of Influences in Scotland and Northern England* (London, 1970), 4, 25; Swain, 'The Lochleven and Linlithgow Hangings', *PSAS*, 124 (1994), 455–66.

17 Michael Bath, *Emblems for a Queen: The Needlework of Mary Queen of Scots* (London, 2008), 17–21, 147–57.

18 For example, 'The Inventory of the Chapel Royal at Stirling, 1505', ed. F. C. Eeles, *Transactions of the Scottish Ecclesiological Society*, 3 (1909–10), 310–25; *Wardrobe Inventories*, ed. Thomson, 51, 58, 112; 'King's College Inventory, 1542' in F. C. Eeles, *King's College Chapel* (Edinburgh, 1956), 4–69; McRoberts and Holmes, *Lost Interiors*, 142–9.

19 D. McRoberts, 'The Fetternear Banner', *IR*, 7 (1956), 69–86; McRoberts, 'Scottish Medieval Chalice Veils', *IR*, 15 (1964), 103–16; McRoberts and Holmes, *Lost Interiors*, 150–3.

20 Juhala, 'Household and Court of James VI', 170–1.

21 F. J. Shaw, 'Sumptuary Legislation in Scotland', *Juridical Review*, 24 (1979), 81–115.

22 In addition to the accounts and inventories already listed above, see also John Harrison, *The Wardrobe Inventories of James V*: http://sparc.scran.ac.uk/publications/level%20II/level2PublicationsMajor.html

23 Rosalind K. Marshall, '"To be the Kingis Grace ane Dowblett": The Costume of James V, King of Scots', *Costume: The Journal of the Costume Society*, 28 (1994), 14–21; Marshall, '"Hir Rob Ryall": The Costume of Mary of Guise', *Costume*, 12 (1978), 1–12; Juhala, 'Household and Court of James VI', 167–73; Jane Stevenson, 'Texts and Textiles: Self-Presentation among the Elite in Renaissance England', *Journal of the Northern Renaissance* 3.1 (Autumn 2011), 39–57: www.northernrenaissance.org

24 *Wardrobe Inventories*, ed. Thomson, 65; Rosalind K. Marshall, 'The Jewellery of James V, King of Scots', *Jewellery Studies*, 7 (1996), 79–86; Juhala, 'Household and Court of James VI', 155–67; Diana Scarisbrick, 'The Sixteenth Century' in R. K. Marshall and G. R. Dalgleish (eds), *The Art of Jewellery in Scotland* (Edinburgh, 1991), 12–23.

25 Juhala, 'Household and Court of James VI', 159–60; Scarisbrick, 'Sixteenth Century', 19.

26 John Leslie, *The History of Scotland from the Death of King James I in the Year 1436 to the Year 1561* (Edinburgh, 1830), 299.

27 Scarisbrick, 'Sixteenth Century', 14.

28 Diana Scarisbrick, 'The Aberdeen Jewel', *Burlington Magazine*, 130 (June 1988), 427–8.

29 Kirsten Aschengreen Piacenti and John Boardman, *Ancient and Modern Gems and Jewels in the Collection of Her Majesty the Queen* (London, 2008), 189.

30 Bath, *Renaissance Decorative Painting*, 129–31.

31 Piacenti and Boardman, *Ancient and Modern Gems and Jewels*, 183–5.

32 George Dalgleish and Henry Steuart Fothringham, *Silver Made in Scotland* (Edinburgh, 2008), 145, 151–2.

33 Ian Finlay, *Scottish Gold and Silver Work* (Stevenage, 1991), 75–83; McRoberts and Holmes, *Lost Interiors*, 23–4, 115–21; Dalgleish and Fothringham, *Silver Made in Scotland*, 142–4, 152.

34 Finlay, *Scottish Gold and Silver Work*, 61–73; Dalgleish and Fothringham, *Silver Made in Scotland*, 4–5, 33–5.

35 There is fragmentary and inconclusive evidence of possible medieval glass manufacture in Scotland: McRoberts and Holmes, *Lost Interiors*, 19. See also Jill Turnbull, *The Scottish Glass Industry, 1610–1750: 'To serve the whole nation with glass'* (Edinburgh, 2001).

36 I. H. Stewart, *The Scottish Coinage* (London, 1955), 67.

37 Ibid., 65–74; Donald Bateson, *Scottish Coins* (Aylesbury, 1987), 7–10.

38 D. H. Caldwell (ed.), *Angels, Nobles and Unicorns: Art and Patronage in Medieval Scotland* (Edinburgh, 1982), 101–2.

39 Stewart, *Scottish Coinage*, 75–6.

40 Ibid., 78

41 N. M. McQ. Holmes, *Scottish Coins in the National Museums of Scotland, Edinburgh, Part 1, 1526–1603* (Oxford, 2006), 3–10.

42 Bath, *Emblems for a Queen*, 38–42.

43 Holmes, *Scottish Coins*, 11–14.

Chapter 4: Bright Images

1 'Inventory of the Chapel Royal', ed. Eeles, 324.

2 *TA*, vi, 22; ibid., vii, 17, 19, 113, 132, 142, 161, 163, 177.

3 Warrack, *Domestic Life*, 50–1; MacKenzie, *Scottish Renaissance Household*, 30, 33. Some of Stobo's and Hamilton's books were probably printed, but clearly not all.

4 An inscription at the end of the manuscript (a colophon) reads: 'Florius infortunatus calamo parisius hunc librum exaravit. Deo gratias. Amen.' (The unfortunate Florio of Paris wrote this book with his quill. Thanks be to God. Amen.) It is not known why he considered himself unfortunate.

5 D'Arcy Jonathan Dacre Boulton, *The Knights of the Crown: The Monarchical Orders of Knighthood in Later Medieval Europe, 1325–1520* (Woodbridge, 2000), 428–31; Bawcutt and Henisch, 'Scots Abroad in the Fifteenth Century', 52.

6 Michael R. Apted and Susan Hannabuss, *Painters in Scotland, 1301–1700: A Biographical Dictionary* (Edinburgh, 1978), 40–1; Duncan Macmillan, *Scottish Art, 1460–2000* (Edinburgh, 2000), 31, 34–5.

7 Ibid., 28–9; David McRoberts, 'Catalogue of Scottish medieval Liturgical Books and Fragments', *IR*, 3 (1952), 49–63. The *Arbuthnott Missal* has been digitised: www.bl.uk/ttp2/hiddentreasures.html

8 *The Hours of the Virgin and St Ninian* has been digitised: www.ed.ac.uk/schools-departments/divinity/research/resources/late-medieval-scotland/scottish-book-hours/manuscript

9 David McRoberts, 'Dean Brown's Book of Hours', *IR*, 19 (1968), 144–67.

10 Leslie MacFarlane, 'The Book of Hours of James IV and Margaret Tudor', *IR*, 11 (1960), 3–21; Ishbel Barnes, 'The Book of Hours of James IV and Margaret Tudor, Austrian National Library, Vienna', *Forth Naturalist and Historian*, 25 (2002), 85–6; Macmillan, *Scottish Art*, 25–7.

11 David McRoberts, 'Notes on Scoto-Flemish Artistic Contacts', *IR*, 10 (1959), 91–2; McRoberts and Holmes, *Lost Interiors*, 35–6; 'Inventory of the Chapel Royal', ed. Eeles, 323; Apted and Hannabuss, *Painters in Scotland*, 68–9, 70–2; *TA*, vi, 250; *Wardrobe Inventories*, ed. Thomson, 104, 130.

12 C. Thompson and L. Campbell, *Hugo van der Goes and the Trinity Panels in Edinburgh* (Edinburgh, 1974); Macmillan, *Scottish Art*, 18–25.

13 G. Hay, 'A Scottish Altarpiece in Copenhagen', *IR*, 7 (1956), 5–10; McRoberts and Holmes, *Lost Interiors*, 39–40; Macmillan, *Scottish Art*, 24.

14 M. R. Apted and W. Norman Robertson, 'Late Fifteenth Century Church Paintings from Guthrie and Foulis Easter', *PSAS*, 95 (1961–2), 262–79.

15 D. McRoberts, 'A Sixteenth-Century Picture of Saint Bartholomew from Perth', *IR*, 10 (1959) 281–6; Macmillan, *Scottish Art*, 31–2; McRoberts and Holmes, *Lost Interiors*, 35–9, 108–9, 114–15.

16 Michael Bath, 'Andrew Bairhum, Giovanni Ferrerio and the "Lighter Style of Painting"', *Journal of the Northern Renaissance*, 2 (2010), 1–13: www.northernrenaissance.org

17 John Harrison, *The Wardrobe Inventories of James V*, 3, 48: http://sparc.scran.ac.uk/publications/level%20II/level2PublicationsMajor.html; Ron M. Brown, *The Art of Suicide* (London, 2001), 97–9, 102–8.

18 Kristin Eldyss Sorensen Zapalac, *'In His Image and Likeness': Political Iconography and Religious Change in Regensburg, 1500–1600* (Ithaca, NY, 1990), 225. John Harrison's surprise at the mention of the Lucretia panel in the warrant of 1543 is perhaps because it is listed alongside religious paintings, but this was clearly not unusual.

19 NRS, Liber Domicili, E.31/6, f. 97r.; Thomas, *Princelie Majestie*, 202.

20 David McRoberts, 'Material Destruction Caused by the Scottish Reformation', *IR*, 10 (1959), 126–72.

21 Apted and Hannabuss, *Painters in Scotland*, 68–9, 70–2; Campbell, 'Scottish Patrons', 90–1; Thomas, *Princelie Majestie*, 82–3.

22 *Visages d'antan: Le Recueil d'Arras, XIVe –XVIe s.*, ed. Albert Châtelet et Jacques Paviot (Lathuile, 2007), 190–214; Campbell, 'Scottish Patrons', 90–1.

23 *Visages d'antan*, ed. Châtelet and Paviot, 108–9, 118, 401, 409–10; Campbell, 'Scottish Patrons', 89–90. The inscription under Margaret's portrait identifies her as Louis' second wife, Charlotte of Savoy, but the style and likely dating of the portrait suggest that it probably depicts the Scottish dauphine.

24 Württembergische Landesbibliothek, Stuttgart, Diary of Jörg von Ehingen, Cod. hist. 4141, f.97.

25 Lorne Campbell and John Dick, 'The Portrait of Bishop Elphinstone' in Geddes (ed.), *King's College Chapel*, 102–3.

26 Robert Lindsay of Pitscottie, *The Historie and Cronicles of Scotland*, ed. Æ. J. G. MacKay (3 vols, Edinburgh, 1899–1911), i, 354.

27 Thomas, *Princelie Majestie*, 84–5; Dana Bentley-Cranch and Rosalind K. Marshall, 'Iconography and Literature in the Service of Diplomacy: The Franco-Scottish Alliance, James V and Scotland's two French Queens, Madeleine of France and Mary of Guise', in Hadley Williams (ed.), *Stewart Style*, 273–88; *Inventaires*, ed. Robertson, 16, 57; *Wardrobe Inventories*, ed. Thomson, 238.

28 Macmillan, *Scottish Art*, 40–7, 60.

29 Dana Bentley-Cranch, 'Effigy and Portrait in Sixteenth-Century Scotland', *ROSC*, 4 (1988), 9–23.

30 Macmillan, *Scottish Art*, 45–6, 58–63; Michael Lynch, 'Court Ceremony and Ritual', 76; Lynch, 'Reassertion of Princely Power', 220.

31 Bath, *Renaissance Decorative Painting*, 272–4; Bath, 'Lighter Style of Painting', 7–10.

32 A. Alciatus, *Emblemes de nouveau translatez en François* (Lyon, 1549).

33 Bath, *Renaissance Decorative Painting*, 239–41.

34 *Accounts of the Masters of Works*, ii, 256.

35 The Royal Commission on the Ancient and Historical Monuments of Scotland, *Stirlingshire: An Inventory of the Ancient Monuments* (2 vols, Edinburgh, 1963), i, 211–13 interprets the '6' as a 'C', but this is corrected in Campbell and MacKechnie, 'Great Temple of Solomon', 99.

36 Bath, *Renaissance Decorative Painting*. See also Bath, 'Literature, Art and Architecture' in Ian Brown, Thomas Owen Clancy, Murray Pittock, Susan Manning, Ksenija Horvat and Ashley Hales (eds), *The Edinburgh History of Scottish Literature, Volume 1: From Columba to the Union (until 1707)* (Edinburgh, 2007), 245–52.

37 Bath, *Renaissance Decorative Painting*, 104–21, 236–8.

38 Ibid., 185–90, 198–200, 217–20.

39 Maurice Lee Jr., 'King James's Popish Chancellor' in Ian B. Cowan and Duncan Shaw (eds), *The Renaissance and Reformation in Scotland: Essays in Honour of Gordon Donaldson* (Edinburgh, 1983), 170–82.

40 David Allan, *Philosophy and Politics in Later Stuart Scotland: Neo-Stoicism, Culture and Ideology in an Age of Crisis, 1540–1690* (East Linton, 2000).

41 Bath, *Renaissance Decorative Painting*, 79–103, 231–6.

Chapter 5: Mighty Foes

1 One study is David Eltis, *The Military Revolution in Sixteenth-Century Europe* (London, 1995). For the controversy over the concept of a 'military revolution' see Gervase Phillips, *The Anglo-Scots Wars, 1513–1550* (Woodbridge, 1999), 9–13.

2 *TA*, i, 65.

3 Angus Konstam, *Sovereigns of the Sea: The Quest to Build the Perfect Renaissance Battleship* (Hoboken, 2008), 25–31.

4 Michael Brown, *James I* (Edinburgh, 1994), 102–3, 117.

5 Steve Murdoch, *The Terror of the Seas? Scottish Maritime Warfare, 1513–1713* (Leiden, 2010), 79–110; W. Stanford Reid, *Skipper from Leith: The History of Robert Barton of Over Barnton* (Philadelphia, 1962), 33–110; Norman Macdougall, *James IV* (Edinburgh, 2006), 223–8, 238–42.

6 Ibid., 228–43.

7 Robert Lindsay of Pitscottie, *The Historie and Cronicles of Scotland*, ed. Æ. J. G. MacKay (3 vols, Edinburgh, 1899–1911), i, 251.

8 Norman Macdougall, 'The greattest scheip that ewer saillit in England or France': James IV's "Great Michael"' in Norman Macdougall (ed.), *Scotland and War AD 79–1918* (Edinburgh, 1991), 36–60; Macdougall, *James IV*, 266–9; Konstam, *Sovereigns of the Sea*, 83–122.

9 Murdoch, *Terror of the Seas*, 39–40.

10 Thomas, *Princelie Majestie*, 155–7; Cameron, *James V*, 235; Roger Mason, 'Renaissance and Reformation: The Sixteenth Century' in Jenny Wormald (ed.), *Scotland: A History* (Oxford, 2005), 107–42 at 119.

11 Thomas, *Princelie Majestie*, 157–60; *TA*, vii, 400, 438.

12 Thomas, *Princelie Majestie*, 160–2; Cameron, *James V*, 245–8.

13 Alexander Lindsay, 'The Navigation of King James V Round Scotland, the Orkney Isles and the Hebrides or Western Isles', ed. Nicholas d'Arfeville, trans. Robert Chapman, in *Miscellanea Scotica: A Collection of Tracts Relating to the History, Antiquities, Topography and Literature of Scotland* (3 vols, Glasgow, 1820), iii, 100–22; Thomas, *Princelie Majestie*, 162–3.

14 Murdoch, *Terror of the Seas*, 47–50.

15 Ibid., 57–60, 64.

16 Ibid., 127–34, 150–1; Julian Goodare, *State and Society in Early Modern Scotland* (Oxford, 1999), 165–6.

17 Macdougall, *James IV*, 227–8; Thomas, *Princelie Majestie*, 163–5; Phillips, *Anglo-Scots Wars*, 90–2.

18 Norman Macdougall, *James III* (Edinburgh, 2009), 44, 91; Geoffrey Stell, 'Late Medieval Defences in Scotland' in David H Caldwell (ed.) *Scottish Weapons and Fortifications, 1100–1800* (Edinburgh, 1981), 45.

19 Iain MacIvor, 'Artillery and Major Places of Strength in the Lothians and the East Border, 1513–1542' in Caldwell (ed.), *Scottish Weapons and Fortifications*, 105–19; Marcus Merriman, *The Rough Wooings: Mary Queen of Scots, 1542–1551* (East Linton, 2000), 329.

20 Cameron, *James V*, 209–18; McKean, *The Scottish Château*, 48–52, 84–93, 267–72; MacIvor, 'Artillery and Major Places', 124–32; Charles McKean, 'Sir James Hamilton of Finnart: A Renaissance Courtier-Architect', *Architectural History*, 42 (1999), 141–72.

21 Merriman, *Rough Wooings*, 248–55; Phillips, *Anglo-Scots Wars*, 178–81, 201–14; David H. Caldwell, *Scotland's Wars and Warriors: Winning Against the Odds* (Edinburgh, 1998), 64–7.

22 M. L. Bush, *The Government Policy of Protector Somerset* (London, 1975), 7–39.

23 Merriman, *Rough Wooings*, 257–8, 312–3.

24 Ibid., 321–30; Fawcett, *Stirling Castle*, 65–6; MacIvor, *Edinburgh Castle*, 56–8.

25 Ibid., 67–71; Howard, *Scottish Architecture*, 35.

26 Brown, *James I*, 115, 163.

27 C. Gaier, 'The Origins of Mons Meg', *Journal of the Arms and Armour Society*, 5 (1967), 425–31; Caldwell, *Scotland's Wars and Warriors*, 49–50; Fergus Cannan, *Scottish Arms and Armour* (Oxford, 2009), 58–9.

28 David H. Caldwell, 'Royal Patronage of Arms and Armour Making in Fifteenth and Sixteenth Century Scotland', in Caldwell (ed.), *Scottish Weapons and Fortifications*, 73–5; MacIvor, 'Artillery and Major Places', 97–9.

29 Thomas, *Princelie Majestie*, 170–7; Caldwell, *Scotland's Wars and Warriors*, 67–9; Cannan, *Scottish Arms and Armour*, 56–60; Caldwell, 'Royal Patronage of Arms', 76–8.

30 Cannan, *Scottish Arms and Armour*, 61–9.

31 Eltis, *Military Revolution*, 43–54; Goodare, *State and Society*, 136–50.

32 P. D. A. Harvey, *Maps in Tudor England* (London, 1993), 7–25.

33 Ibid., 27–41.

34 British Library, Cotton MS. Domitian Axviii, ff. 98v–99r; Harvey, *Maps in Tudor England*, 54–5.

35 Nigel Nicolson and Alasdair Hawkyard, *The Counties of Britain: A Tudor Atlas by John Speed* (1988), 265–8.

36 Jeffrey C. Stone, *The Pont Manuscript Maps of Scotland: Sixteenth-century Origins of a Blaeu Atlas* (Tring, 1989); Ian C. Cunningham (ed.), *The Nation Survey'd: Essays on Late Sixteenth-century Scotland as Depicted by Timothy Pont* (Edinburgh, 2006).

Chapter 6: Sounds Celestial

1 Jamie Reid-Baxter, 'Culture: Renaissance and Reformation (1460–1660): Music' and 'Music, Ecclesiastical' both in Michael Lynch (ed.), *The Oxford Companion to Scottish History* (Oxford, 2001), 130–3, 431–3. I am extremely grateful to Jamie Reid-Baxter for reading and commenting on this chapter, making many helpful suggestions, and sending me lots of additional references. My thanks go also to James Ross, who made some comments via Jamie Reid-Baxter.

2 John Harper, 'Music and Ceremonial, c.1500–1560' in Geddes (ed.) *King's College Chapel*, 28–34.

3 Gordon Munro, '"Sang Schwylls" and "Music Schools": Music Education in Scotland, 1560–1650' in Susan Forscher Weiss, Russell Murray and Cynthia J. Cyrus (eds), *Music Education in the Middle Ages and the Renaissance* (Bloomington, 2010), 65–83 at p. 65. See also Charles Rogers, *History of the Chapel Royal of Scotland* (Edinburgh, 1882).

4 John Durkan, 'Early Song Schools in Scotland' in Gordon Munro, Stuart Campbell, *et al.* (eds), *Notis Musycall: Essays on Music and Scottish Culture in Honour of Kenneth Elliott* (Glasgow, 2005), 125–7.

5 Isobel Woods Preece, *Our Awin Scottis Use: Music in the Scottish Church up to 1603* (Glasgow, 2000), 55–81.

6 The licence is printed in full in Woods Preece, *Our Awin Scottis Use*, 72. Spelling has been modernised here.

7 David McRoberts, 'The Medieval Scottish Liturgy Illustrated by Surviving Documents', *TSES* 15 (1957), 24–40; Alan Macquarrie, 'Scottish Saints' Legends in the *Aberdeen Breviary*', in Steve Boardman and Eila Williamson (eds), *The Cult of Saints and the Virgin Mary in Medieval Scotland* (Woodbridge, 2010), 143–57; Leslie J. Macfarlane, *William Elphinstone and the Kingdom of Scotland, 1431–1514: The Struggle for Order* (Aberdeen, 1995), 231–46.

8 Warwick Edwards, 'Polyphony in Thirteenth-Century Scotland' in Woods Preece, *Our Awin Scottis Use*, 225–71; Purser, *Scotland's Music*, 51–6. St Andrews Cathedral Priory was an Augustinian house rather than Dominican (and the Dominican friary of St Andrews was not founded until the fifteenth century), but there is a theory that the manuscript was copied by a Dominican called Simon Tailler who visited Paris in the 1250s: Kenneth Elliott and Frederick Rimmer, *A History of Scottish Music* (London, 1973), 8–9.

9 Walter Bower, *A History Book for Scots: Selections from Scotichronicon*, ed. D. E. R. Watt (Edinburgh, 1998), 285.

10 Macdougall, *James III*, 260–2; Purser, *Scotland's Music*, 81–92.

11 Woods Preece, *Our Awin Scottis Use*, 169–93; J. A. Tasioulas (ed.), *The Makars: The Poetry of Henryson, Dunbar and Douglas* (Edinburgh, 1999), 609. Spelling is modernised here.

12 Woods Preece, *Our Awin Scottis Use*, 150–68. Modern editions of Carver's works are published in the first volume of the 'Musica Scotica' series: *The Complete Works of Robert Carver and Two Anonymous Masses*, ed. Kenneth Elliot (Glasgow, 1996).

13 D. James Ross, 'Robert Carver, Canon of Scone: New Perspectives on the Scottish Renaissance Composer' in Munro, Campbell, *et al.* (eds), *Notis Musycall*, 95–114. I had previously accepted the identification of Robert Arnot of Stirling with Robert Carver of Scone: Thomas, *Princelie Majestie*, 105.

14 D. James Ross, *Musick Fyne: Robert Carver and the Art of Music in Sixteenth Century Scotland* (Edinburgh, 1993), 20–4, 27–8, 30–1, 34–9, 45–50; Purser, *Scotland's Music*, 83–91; Woods Preece, *Our Awin Scottis Use*, 150–68.

15 Alasdair A. MacDonald, 'A Note on Robert Carver's Motet *O Bone Jesu*' in Munro, Campbell, *et al.* (eds), *Notis Musycall*, 115–24; Purser, *Scotland's Music*, 84–91; Purser, 'Early Modern Music' in Bob Harris and Alan R. MacDonald (eds), *Scotland: The Making and Unmaking of the Nation*, *c.1100–1707* (5 vols, Dundee, 2006–7), ii, 212–24 at p. 214.

16 Ross, 'Robert Carver, Canon of Scone', 98–102; Ross, *Musick Fyne*, 51–4, 65–80.

17 Robertus Richardinus, *Commentary on the Rule of St Augustine*, ed. G. G. Coulton (Edinburgh, 1935), 78–80; Woods Preece, *Our Awin Scottis Use*, 89–96.

18 Ross, *Musick Fyne*, 29–31, 100, 124–5; Purser, *Scotland's Music*, 94.

19 Jamie Reid-Baxter, 'Thomas Wode, Christopher Goodman and the Curious Death of Scottish Music', *Scotlands*, 4 (1997), 1–20. I am indebted to Jamie Reid-Baxter for alerting me to this article.

20 Gordon J. Munro, 'The Scottish Reformation and its Consequences' in Woods Preece, *Our Awin Scottis Use*, 291–6; Purser, *Scotland's Music*, 95–100; Ross, *Musick Fyne*, 65–74.

21 Ross, *Musick Fyne*, 81–8; Munro, 'The Scottish Reformation and its Consequences', 273–7.

22 Jamie Reid-Baxter, 'Metrical Psalmody and the Bannatyne Manuscript: Robert Pont's Psalm 83', *Renaissance and Reformation*, 30 (2006-7), 41–62. I am indebted to Jamie Reid-Baxter for alerting me to this article.

23 Ross, *Musick Fyne*, 89–94; Munro, 'The Scottish Reformation and its Consequences', 277–94; Jamie Reid-Baxter, Michael Lynch and E. Patricia Dennison, *Jhone Angus: Monk of Dunfermline & Scottish Reformation Music* (Dunfermline, 2011).

24 Jamie Reid-Baxter, '"Judge and Revenge my Cause": The Earl of Morton, Andro Blackhall, Robert Sempill and the Fall of the House of Hamilton in 1579' in Sally Mapstone (ed.), *Older Scottish Literature* (Edinburgh, 2005), 467–92; Reid-Baxter, Lynch and Dennison, *Jhone Angus*, 38–9.

25 James Porter, 'Beatus ille qui misertus pauperis: The Historical Importance of Jean Servin's Settings of Buchanan's Psalm Paraphrases' in Philip Ford and Roger P. H. Green (eds), *George Buchanan, Poet and Dramatist* (Swansea, 2009), 113–35 at p.117.

26 Ross, *Musick Fyne*, 94–7, 101; Woods Preece, *Our Awin Scottis Use*, 195–8; Munro, 'The Scottish Reformation and its Consequences', 283–303; Philip Brett, 'English Music for the Scottish Progress of 1617' in Brett, *William Byrd and His Contemporaries: Essays and a Monograph* (London, 2007), 78–99. For the history of Scottish organs see Jim Inglis, *The Organ in Scotland before 1700* (Schagen, 1991) and McRoberts and Holmes, *Lost Interiors*, 82–5.

27 Warwick Edwards, 'The Musical Sources' in James Porter (ed.), *Defining Strains: The Musical Life of Scots in the Seventeenth Century* (Oxford, 2007), 47–71; John Purser, 'Greysteil' in Hadley Williams (ed.), *Stewart Style*, 142–52.

28 Robert Wedderburn, *The Complaynt of Scotland*, ed. A. M. Stewart (Edinburgh, 1979), 51–2; Thomas, *Princelie Majestie*, 99–100; Theo van Heijnsbergen, 'Amphibious Lyric: Literature, Music and Dry Land in Early-Modern Verse' in Munro, Campbell, *et al.* (eds), *Notis Musycall*, 165–80.

29 Ross, *Musick Fyne*, 120; Kenneth Elliott, '*Trip and Goe, Hey*: A Truly Scottish Song' in Hadley Williams (ed.), *Stewart Style*, 153–78.

30 Thomas, *Princelie Majestie*, 101–3; Ross, *Musick Fyne*, 122–8, 134–7; Helena Mennie Shire, *Song, Dance and Poetry of the Court of Scotland under King James VI* (Cambridge, 1969), 73–5.

31 Thomas, *Princelie Majestie*, 96–9; Mennie Shire, *Song, Dance and Poetry*, 73.

32 Keith Sanger and Alison Kinnaird, *Tree of Strings, Crann nan Teud: A History of the Harp in Scotland* (Edinburgh, 1992), 78–90; Ross, *Musick Fyne*, 128–32; Purser, *Scotland's Music*, 102–6.

33 John Purser, 'On the Trail of the Spies', *Scotlands*, 5 (1998), 23–44.

34 Ross, *Musick Fyne*, 133–9; Margaret M. McGowan, *Dance in the Renaissance: European Fashion, French Obsession* (New Haven, 2008), 1–3, 152; David J. Smith, 'Keyboard Music in Scotland: Genre, Gender, Context' in Porter (ed.), *Defining Strains*, 114–17; Purser, *Scotland's Music*, 106–11, 119–22; Michael Rossi, '"Musicall Humors": The Life and Music of Captain Tobias Hume, Gentleman' in Porter (ed.), *Defining Strains*, 155–80.

NOTES

Chapter 7: The Learned Muse

1 John Durkan, 'The Beginnings of Humanism in Scotland', *IR*, 4 (1953), 5–24, 119–22; Macdougall, *James III*, 245–82; Stevenson and Davidson, 'Ficino in Aberdeen', 76–7 at www.northernrenaissance.org

2 John Higgit (ed.), *Scottish Libraries: Corpus of British Medieval Library Catalogues, Volume 12* (London, 2006), 44–74, 155–66, 375–85. See also John Durkan and Anthony Ross, *Early Scottish Libraries* (Glasgow, 1961).

3 Macdougall, *James IV*, 214–15; Macfarlane, *William Elphinstone*, 231–46, 290–402.

4 J. Grant, *History of the Burgh Schools of Scotland* (Glasgow, 1876), 1–75; Janet P. Foggie, *Renaissance Religion in Urban Scotland: The Dominican Order, 1450–1560* (Leiden, 2003), 101–4.

5 John Durkan, 'Education in the Century of the Reformation', *IR*, 10 (1959), 67–90; Durkan, 'Schools and Schooling to 1696' in Lynch (ed.), *Oxford Companion to Scottish History*, 561–3. The posthumous publication of John Durkan, *Scottish Schools and Schoolmasters, 1560–1633*, ed. Jamie Reid-Baxter (Scottish History Society, forthcoming) is eagerly awaited.

6 *Acts of the Parliament of Scotland*, eds T. Thomson and C. Innes (12 vols, Edinburgh, 1814–75), ii, 238. Spelling has been modernised here.

7 Macfarlane, *William Elphinstone*, 290–402.

8 John Finlay, *Men of Law in Pre-Reformation Scotland* (East Linton, 2000), 53–71; A. M. Godfrey, *Civil Justice in Renaissance Scotland: The Origins of a Central Court* (Leiden, 2009), 94–160; Roger A. Mason, 'Laicisation and the Law: The Reception of Humanism in Early Renaissance Scotland' in Houwen, MacDonald and Mapstone (eds), *A Palace in the Wild*, 1–25.

9 Alec Ryrie, *The Origins of the Scottish Reformation* (Manchester, 2006), 98–103; W. J. Anderson, 'Some Documents of the Scottish Reformation', in David McRoberts (ed.), *Essays on the Scottish Reformation, 1513–1625* (Glasgow, 1962), 339–41. Hamilton's *Catechism* has been digitised: http://digital.nls.uk/scottish-printing-towns-1508-1800/pageturner.cfm?id=74616686

10 Durkan, 'Schools and Schooling', 561–3.

11 Alasdair A. MacDonald, 'Florentius Volusenus and Tranquillity of Mind: Some Applications of an Ancient Ideal' in Alasdair A. MacDonald, Zweder R. W. M. von Martels and Jan R. Veenstra (eds), *Christian Humanism: Essays in Honour of Arjo Vanderjagt* (Leiden, 2009), 119–38.

12 Macfarlane, *William Elphinstone*, 290–402; Stevenson and Davidson, 'Ficino in Aberdeen', 69–75 at www.northernrenaissance.org

13 John Durkan, 'Giovanni Ferrerio, Humanist: His Influence in Sixteenth-Century Scotland', in K. Robbins (ed.), *Religion and Humanism* (Oxford, 1981), 181–94; John Durkan, 'Education: The Laying of Fresh Foundations' in MacQueen (ed.), *Humanism*, 123–60.

14 Michael Lynch, 'The Origins of Edinburgh's "Toun College": A Revision Article', *IR*, 33 (1982), 3–14; Olaf D. Cuthbert, *A Flame in the Shadows: Robert Reid, Bishop of Orkney, 1541–1558* (Kirkwall, 1998); Steven J. Reid, *Humanism and Calvinism: Andrew Melville and the Universities of Scotland, 1560–1625* (Farnham, 2011), 15–48, 201–32. I am very grateful to Steven Reid for explaining his key findings to me prior to publication and for helping me to understand the significance of Ramism.

15 James Kirk, '"Melvillian" Reform in the Scottish Universities' in A. A. MacDonald, Michael Lynch and Ian B. Cowan (eds), *The Renaissance in Scotland: Studies in Literature, Religion, History and Culture Offered to John Durkan* (Leiden, 1994), 276–300; Ernest R. Holloway, *Andrew Melville and Humanism in Renaissance Scotland* (Leiden, 2011); Reid, *Humanism and Calvinism*.

16 Alastair J. Mann, *The Scottish Book Trade, 1500–1720: Print, Commerce and Print Control in Early Modern Scotland* (East Linton, 2000), 93, 223, 232; R. J. Lyall, 'Books and Book Owners in Fifteenth-Century Scotland' in Jeremy Griffiths and Derek Pearsall (eds), *Book Production and Publishing in Britain, 1375–1475* (Cambridge, 2007), 239–56.

17 Robert Dickson and John Philip Edmond, *Annals of Scottish Printing from the Introduction of the Art in 1507 to the Beginning of the Seventeenth Century* (Cambridge, 1890), 1–99; Antony Kamm, *Scottish Printed Books, 1508–2008* (2008), 8–13; Catherine van Buren 'The Chepman and Myllar Texts of Dunbar' in Sally Mapstone (ed.), *William Dunbar, 'The Nobill Poyet': Essays in Honour of Priscilla Bawcutt* (East Linton, 2001), 24–39. The Chepman and Myllar Prints and the *Aberdeen Breviary* have all been digitised by the National Library of Scotland: www.nls.uk/firstscottishbooks and http://digital.nls.uk/74487406 See also www.nls.uk/printing

18 Dickson and Edmond, *Annals of Scottish Printing*, 100–35; Mann, *Scottish Book Trade*, 1, 99, 115, 236; Thomas, *Princelie Majestie*, 150–1.

19 Dickson and Edmond, *Annals of Scottish Printing*, 273–376; Mann, *Scottish Book Trade*, 37–8, 91; Jane E. A. Dawson, *Scotland Reformed, 1488–1587* (Edinburgh, 2007), 228–9. See also Graham Tulloch, *A History of the Scots Bible with Selected Texts* (Aberdeen, 1989).

20 Colin Kidd and James Coleman, 'Mythical Scotland' in Devine and Wormald (eds), *Oxford Handbook*, 62–7; Roger A. Mason, '"Scotching the Brut": The Early History of Britain' in Jenny Wormald (ed.), *Scotland Revisited* (London, 1991), 49–60; Roger A. Mason, 'Chivalry and Citizenship: Aspects of National Identity in Renaissance Scotland' in Mason, *Kingship and the Commonweal: Political Thought in Renaissance and Reformation*

Scotland (East Linton, 1998), 78–103.

21 John Major, *A History of Greater Britain*, ed. and trans. Archibald Constable (Edinburgh, 1892), cxxxv.

22 Roger A. Mason, 'Kingship, Nobility and Anglo-Scottish Union: John Mair's *History of Greater Britain* (1521)', *IR*, 41 (1990), 182–222; Nicola Royan with Dauvit Broun, 'Versions of Scottish Nationhood, c.850–1707' in Ian Brown, Thomas Owen Clancy, Murray Pittock, Susan Manning, Ksenija Horvat and Ashley Hales (eds), *The Edinburgh History of Scottish Literature, Volume 1: From Columba to the Union (until 1707)* (Edinburgh, 2007), 177; Thomas, *Princelie Majestie*, 129–39.

23 Nicola Royan, 'The Relationship between the *Scotorum Historia* of Hector Boece and John Bellenden's *Chronicles of Scotland*' in Sally Mapstone and Juliette Wood (eds), *The Rose and the Thistle: Essays on the Culture of Late Medieval and Renaissance Scotland* (Edinburgh, 1998), 136–57; Royan with Broun, 'Versions of Scottish Nationhood', 177–83; John and Winifred MacQueen, 'Latin Prose Literature' in R. D. S. Jack (ed.), *The History of Scottish Literature, Volume 1: Origins to 1660* (Aberdeen, 1989), 235–7.

24 Royan with Broun, 'Versions of Scottish Nationhood', 180–1; Jack MacQueen, 'From Rome to Ruddiman: The Scoto-Latin Tradition' in Brown *et al.* (eds), *Edinburgh History of Scottish Literature*, i, 187–9; John and Winifred MacQueen, 'Latin Prose Literature', 237–9. See also I. D. Macfarlane, *Buchanan* (London, 1981).

25 The 1575 edition of Boece's *Scotorum Historia* with a parallel translation is available freely online from the Library of Humanistic Texts: www.philological.bham.ac.uk/library.html Other Scottish Renaissance texts available on the same site include works by George Buchanan and Florence Wilson and new texts are being added continually.

26 MacQueen, 'From Rome to Ruddiman', 189–203; Robert Crawford, *Scotland's Books: A History of Scottish Literature* (Oxford, 2009), 124–32, 185–9; James MacQueen, 'Scottish Latin Poetry' in Jack (ed.), *History of Scottish Literature*, i, 213–25; Philip Ford and Roger P. H. Green (eds), *George Buchanan: Poet and Dramatist* (Swansea, 2009); *Apollos of the North: Selected Poems of George Buchanan and Arthur Johnston*, ed. Robert Crawford (Edinburgh, 2006). See also the virtual exhibition of Buchanan's works at: specialcollections.st-and.ac.uk/virtualexhib.htm

27 John Barbour, *The Bruce*, ed. A. A. M. Duncan (Edinburgh, 2007); Blind Harry, *The Wallace*, ed. Anne McKim (Edinburgh, 2003).

28 Tasioulas (ed.), *The Makars*, 187–214; Crawford, *Scotland's Books*, 63–86; Nicola Royan, 'Medieval Literature' in Bob Harris and Alan R. MacDonald (eds), *Scotland: The Making and Unmaking of the Nation*,

c.1100–1707 (5 vols, Dundee, 2006–7), i, 201–17; John MacQueen, 'Poetry – James I to Henryson' in Jack (ed.), *History of Scottish Literature*, i, 55–71.

29 Tasioulas (ed.), *The Makars*, 13–186, 585–689; Sally Mapstone, 'Older Scots Literature and the Court' and Anthony J. Hasler, 'Robert Henryson' both in Brown *et al.* (eds), *Edinburgh History of Scottish Literature*, i, 273–85, 286–94; Gavin Douglas, *The Aeneid (1513)*, ed. Gordon Kendall (2 vols, London, 2011); Douglas Gray, 'Gavin Douglas' in Priscilla J. Bawcutt and Janet Hadley Williams (eds), *A Companion to Medieval Scottish Poetry* (Cambridge, 2006), 149–64. See also Priscilla J. Bawcutt, *Gavin Douglas: A Critical Study* (Edinburgh, 1976).

30 Tasioulas (ed.), *The Makars*, 265–581; Sir David Lyndsay, *Selected Poems*, ed. Janet Hadley Williams (Glasgow, 2000); Priscilla Bawcutt, *Dunbar the Makar* (Oxford, 1992); Carol Edington, *Court and Culture in Renaissance Scotland: Sir David Lindsay of the Mount* (East Linton, 1994).

31 Sir David Lindsay of the Mount, *Ane Satyre of the Thrie Estaitis*, ed. Roderick Lyall (Edinburgh, 1998); Thomas, *Princelie Majestie*, 140–4; Edington, *Court and Culture*, 115–41.

32 Sarah Carpenter, 'Early Scottish Drama' in Jack (ed.), *History of Scottish Literature*, i, 199–212; Bill Findlay, 'Performances and Plays' in Brown *et al.* (eds), *Edinburgh History of Scottish Literature*, i, 253–62; E. Patricia Dennison, 'Robin Hood in Scotland' in Julian Goodare and Alasdair A. MacDonald (eds), *Sixteenth-Century Scotland*, 169–88;

33 Jamie Reid-Baxter, '*Philotus*: The Transmission of a Delectable Treatise' in Theo van Heijnsbergen and Nicola Royan (eds), *Literature, Letters and the Canonical in Early Modern Scotland* (East Linton, 2002), 52–68; Jamie Reid-Baxter, 'Politics, Passion and Poetry in the Circle of James VI: John Burel and his surviving works' in Houwen, MacDonald and Mapstone (eds), *A Palace in the Wild*, 199–248.

34 *The Bannatyne Manuscript*, ed. W. Tod Ritchie (4 vols, Edinburgh, 1928–34); Theo van Heijnsbergen, 'Early Modern Literature' in Harris and MacDonald, (eds), *The Making and Unmaking of the Nation*, ii, 232–4; Gregory Kratzmann, 'Sixteenth-Century Secular Poetry' in Jack (ed.), *History of Scottish Literature*, i, 105–23; Theo van Heijnsbergen, 'Advice to a Princess: The Literary Articulation of a Religious, Political and Cultural Programme for Mary, Queen of Scots, 1562' in Julian Goodare and Alasdair A. MacDonald (eds), *Sixteenth Century Scotland*, 99–122.

35 Priscilla Bawcutt, 'James VI's Castalian Band: A Modern Myth', *Scottish Historical Review*, 80 (2001), 251–9; Roderick J. Lyall, 'James VI and the Sixteenth-Century Cultural Crisis' in Julian Goodare and Michael Lynch,

(eds), *The Reign of James VI*, 55–70; Roderick J. Lyall, *Alexander Montgomerie: Poetry, Politics and Cultural Change in Jacobean Scotland* (Tempe, 2005), 22–8, 344–7.

36 Roderick J. Lyall, 'The Marketing of James VI and I: Scotland, England and the Continental Book Trade', *Quaerendo*, 32 (2002), 204–17.

37 *Bittersweet within my Heart: The Collected Poems of Mary, Queen of Scots*, ed. Robin Bell (London, 1995); John Durkan, 'The Library of Mary, Queen of Scots', *IR*, 38 (1988), 71–101 at p.79.

38 Sarah M. Dunnigan, 'Scottish Women Writers c.1560–c.1650' in Douglas Gifford and Dorothy Macmillan (eds), *A History of Scottish Women's Writing* (Edinburgh, 1997), 15–43; Theo van Heijnsbergen, 'Masks of Revelation and "the 'female' tongues of men": Montgomerie, Christian Lyndsay, and the Writing Game at the Scottish Renaissance Court', in van Heijnsbergen and Royan (eds), *Literature, Letters and the Canonical*, 69–89.

39 Alasdair A. MacDonald, 'Allegorical (Dream-) Vision Poetry in Medieval and Early Modern Scotland', in Rudolf Suntrup and Jan. R. Veenstra (eds), *Himmel auf Erden, Heaven on Earth* (Frankfurt am Main, 2009), 167–76; *Poems of Elizabeth Melville, Lady Culross*, ed. Jamie Reid-Baxter (Edinburgh, 2010); *Elizabeth Melville, Lady Culross (c.1570–1640): Complete Writings*, ed. Jamie Reid-Baxter (forthcoming). I am very grateful to Jamie Reid-Baxter for sending me a copy of his 2010 edition, amongst many other helpful comments, suggestions, essays and articles.

40 Ulrike Moret, 'An Early Scottish National Biography: Thomas Dempster's *Historia Ecclesiastica Gentis Scotorum* (1627)' in Houwen, MacDonald and Mapstone (eds), *A Palace in the Wild*, 249–69.

41 Elizabeth McGrath, 'Local Heroes: The Scottish Humanist Parnassus for Charles I' in Edward Chaney and Peter Mack (eds), *England and the Continental Renaissance: Essays in Honour of J. B. Trapp* (Woodbridge, 1990), 257–70.

Chapter 8: Triumph and Joy

1 Stevenson, *Chivalry and Knighthood*, 2–12, 39–40, 189–92.

2 Richard Barber and Juliet Barker, *Tournaments: Jousts, Chivalry and Pageants in the Middle Ages* (Woodbridge, 2000), 107–37, 121–4. Louise Olga Fradenburg, *City, Marriage, Tournament: Arts of Rule in Late Medieval Scotland* (London, 1991), 192–224.

3 Christine McGladdery, *James II* (Edinburgh, 1990), 41–3; Stevenson, *Chivalry and Knighthood*, 52–3, 72–8, 179–82.

4 Leland, *Collectanea*, iv, 258–300; Stevenson, *Chivalry and Knighthood*, 83–94; Fradenburg, *City, Marriage, Tournament*, 91–122.

5 Macdougall, *James IV*, 198–207, 294–5; Stevenson, *Chivalry and Knighthood*, 94–8, 185–9.

6 *TA*, iii, pp. xlv–lii, 94, 113, 114, 257–61; ibid., iv, pp. lxxxiii–lxxxiv, 22, 119; Tasioulas (ed.), *The Makars*, 317–18; *Visages d'antan*, ed. Châtelet and Paviot, 192, 201; Macdougall, *James IV*, 294–5; Fradenburg, *City, Marriage, Tournament*, 225–64.

7 *TA*, vii, 13–14; Thomas, *Princelie Majestie*, 200–3.

8 John Guy, *My Heart is My Own: The Life of Mary, Queen of Scots* (London, 2004), 154; Susan Doran (ed.), *Elizabeth: The Exhibition at the National Maritime Museum* (London, 2003), 74–7, 91–7; Lynch, 'Court Ceremony and Ritual', 88–91; John Stuart, 3rd marquess of Bute, *Scottish Coronations* (Paisley, 1902), 74.

9 Stevenson, *Chivalry and Knighthood*, 133–69; Fradenburg, *City, Marriage, Tournament*, 172–91.

10 Katie Stevenson, 'Jurisdiction, Authority and Professionalisation: The Officers of Arms of Late Medieval Scotland' in Stevenson (ed.), *The Herald in Late Medieval Europe* (Woodbridge, 2009), 41–66; Stevenson, 'The Scottish King of Arms: Lyon's Place in the Hierarchy of the Late-Medieval Scottish Elite' in Torsten Hiltmann (ed.), *Les 'autres' rois: études sur la royauté comme notion hiérarchique dans la société au bas Moyen Age et au début de l'époque moderne* (Munich, 2010), 64–79. See also Charles J. Burnett and Mark D. Dennis, *Scotland's Heraldic Heritage: The Lion Rejoicing* (Edinburgh, 1997).

11 L. A. J. R. Houwen (ed.), *The Deidis of Armorie: A Heraldic Treatise and Bestiary* (2 vols, Edinburgh, 1994); NLS Adv. MSS, 31.5.2, 31.7.22, 31.6.5.

12 *The Scots Roll*, ed. Colin Campbell (Edinburgh, 1995); *Facsimile of an Ancient Heraldic Manuscript Emblazoned by Sir David Lyndsay of the Mount, Lyon King of Arms, 1542*, ed. W. D. Laing (Edinburgh 1822); *Lord Crawford's Armorial, Formerly Known as The Armorial of Sir David Lyndsay of the Mount Secundus*, ed. Alex Maxwell Findlater (Edinburgh, 2008); Bruce A. McAndrew, *Scotland's Historic Heraldry* (Woodbridge, 2006), 195, 272.

13 D'Arcy J. D. Boulton, *The Knights of the Crown: The Monarchical Orders of Knighthood in Later Medieval Europe, 1325–1520* (Woodbridge, 2000); Katie Stevenson, 'The Unicorn, St Andrew and the Thistle: Was there an Order of Chivalry in Late-Medieval Scotland?', *SHR*, 83 (2004), 3–22.

14 *Wardrobe Inventories*, ed. Thomson, 6, 10, 12; Stevenson, *Chivalry and Knighthood*, 47, 49–50, 81–2, 170, 172, 183, 185.

15 *Wardrobe Inventories*, ed. Thomson, 49, 76; Thomas, *Princelie Majestie*, 69, 206–10.

16 Charles Burns, 'Papal Gifts to Scottish Monarchs: The Golden Rose and the Blessed Sword', *IR*, 20 (1969), 150–94; Macdougall, *James III*, 294–7; Charles J. Burnett and Christopher J. Tabraham, *The Honours of Scotland:*

The Story of the Scottish Crown Jewels (Edinburgh, 1993), 16–23; Thomas, 'Crown Imperial', 55–9.

17 Burnett and Tabraham, *Honours of Scotland*, 24–7; Thomas, 'Crown Imperial', 59–67; Juhala, 'Household and Court of James VI', 203–10. I am very grateful to Amy Juhala for checking the accounts of 1590 for me.

18 A. J. Mann, 'The Scottish Parliament: The Role of Ritual and Procession in the Pre-1707 Parliament and the New Parliament of 1999', in E. Crewe and M. G. Müller (eds), *Rituals in Parliaments: Political, Anthropological and Historical Perspectives on Europe and the United States* (Frankfurt am Main, 2006), 135–58; A. J. Mann, 'Continuity and Change: The Culture of Ritual and Procession in the Parliaments of Scotland', *Parliaments, Estates and Representation*, 29 (2009), 143–58; Michael Lynch, 'The Emergence of a Capital City: Edinburgh, 1450–1603' in Suntrup and Veenstra (eds), *Shaping the Present and Future*, 221–43 at 238–9.

19 R. J. Lyall, 'The Medieval Scottish Coronation Service: Some Seventeenth-Century Evidence', *IR*, 28 (1977), 3–21; Thomas, 'Crown Imperial', 45–55; Maureen M. Meikle, 'Anna of Denmark's Coronation and Entry into Edinburgh, 1590: Cultural, Religious and Diplomatic Perspectives' in Julian Goodare and Alasdair A. MacDonald (eds), *Sixteenth-Century Scotland*, 277–94; Michael Lynch, 'Scotland's First Protestant Coronation: Revolutionaries, Sovereignty and the Cult of Nostalgia' in L. A. J. R. Houwen (ed.), *Literature and Religion in Late Medieval and Early Modern Scotland: Essays in Honour of Alasdair A. MacDonald* (Leuven, 2012), 177–208. I am very grateful to Michael Lynch for letting me read this essay prior to publication.

20 Downie, 'Queenship in Late Medieval Scotland', 232–54; Juhala, 'Household and Court of James VI', 203–10; Meikle, 'Anna of Denmark's Coronation', 277–94.

21 Mathieu D'Escouchy, *Chronique* (3 vols, Paris, 1863–4), i, 175–83; Leland, *Collectanea*, iv, 291–300; Rosalind K. Marshall, *Scottish Queens, 1034–1714* (East Linton, 2003), 49–87.

22 Thomas, *Princelie Majestie*, 187–8; Guy, *My Heart is My Own*, 85–9; *Ceremonial at the Marriage of Mary, Queen of Scots, with the Dauphin of France*, ed. W. Bentham (London, 1818); David Stevenson, *Scotland's Last Royal Wedding: The Marriage of James VI and Anne of Denmark* (Edinburgh, 1997), 34–9, 92–4.

23 Patrick Walker (ed.), *Documents Relative to the Reception at Edinburgh of the Kings and Queens of Scotland* (Edinburgh, 1822); Thomas, *Princelie Majestie*, 182–94; Lynch, 'Court Ceremony and Ritual', 74–9; William Drummond of Hawthornden, *The Entertainment of the High and Mighty Monarch Charles . . . into . . . Edinburgh, the Fifteenth of June, 1633* (Edinburgh, 1633).

24 Fradenburg, *City, Marriage, Tournament*, 91–122; Douglas Gray, 'The Royal Entry in Sixteenth-Century Scotland' in Mapstone and Wood (eds), *The Rose and the Thistle*, 10–37; Meikle, 'Anna of Denmark's Coronation', 287–94; John Burel, 'The Discription of the Queens Maiesties Maist Honorable Entry' in *James Watson's Choice Collection of Comic and Serious Scots Poems* ed. H. H. Wood (2 vols, Edinburgh, 1977–1991), vol. 1, part 2, pp. 1–15; McGrath, 'Local Heroes', 257–70; Ian Campbell, 'James IV and Edinburgh's First Triumphal Arches' in Deborah Mays (ed.), *The Architecture of Scottish Cities* (East Linton, 1997), 26–33.

25 A. A. MacDonald, 'Mary Stewart's Entry to Edinburgh: An Ambiguous Triumph', *IR*, 42 (1991), 101–10; P. Davidson, 'The Entry of Mary Stewart into Edinburgh, 1561, and Other Ambiguities', *Renaissance Studies*, 9 (1995), 416–29; A. R. MacDonald, 'The Triumph of Protestantism: The Burgh Council of Edinburgh and the Entry of Mary, Queen of Scots, 2 September 1561', *IR*, 48 (1997), 73–82; Lynch, 'Court Ceremony and Ritual', 74–88.

26 Michael Lynch, 'Queen Mary's Triumph: The Baptismal Celebrations at Stirling in December 1566', *SHR*, 69 (1990), 1–21; Lynch, 'The Great Hall', 15–22; Lynch, 'The Reassertion of Princely Power', 209–15.

27 Lynch, 'Court Ceremony and Ritual', 88–92; Lynch, 'The Great Hall', 19–22; Lynch, 'The Reassertion of Princely Power', 223–7; Juhala, 'Household and Court of James VI', 210–21; Clare McManus, 'Marriage and the Performance of the Romance Quest: Anne of Denmark and the Stirling Baptismal Celebrations for Prince Henry' in Houwen, MacDonald and Mapstone (eds), *A Palace in the Wild*, 175–98; Michael Bath, 'Literature, Art and Architecture', in Clancy and Pittock (eds), *Edinburgh History of Scottish Literature*, i, 245–52 at 251.

28 Macdougall, *James IV*, 300.

29 Thomas, *Princelie Majestie*, 210–11.

30 Ibid., 212–16; Juhala, 'Household and Court of James VI', 277–8; Thomas Innes of Learney, 'Processional Roll of a Scottish Armorial Funeral, Stated to Have Been Used for the Obsequies of George, 1st Marquess of Huntly, 1636', *PSAS*, 77 (1943), 154–73. I am indebted to Michael Lynch for drawing my attention to the Huntly funeral roll.

31 Alasdair A. MacDonald, 'Chivalry as a Catalyst of Cultural Change in Late-Medieval Scotland' in Rudolf Suntrup and Jan R. Veenstra (eds), *Tradition and Innovation in an Era of Change* (Frankfurt am Main, 2001), 151–76; Sven Lüken, 'Kaiser Maximilian I. und seine Ehrenpforte', *Zeitschrift für Kunstgeschichte*, 61 (1998), 50–3.

BIBLIOGRAPHY
AND RESOURCES

Selected Websites

Arbuthnott Missal: www.bl.uk/ttp2/hiddentreasures.html
Buchanan exhibition: specialcollections.st-
    and.ac.uk/virtualexhib.htm
Journal of the Northern Renaissance:
    www.northernrenaissance.org
Library of Humanistic Texts: www.philological.bham.ac.uk
Stirling Castle Palace Project: sparc.scran.ac.uk

CDs

Robert Carver, The Complete Sacred Choral Music, Cappella
    Nova/Alan Tavener (ASV Gaudeamus CD GAX 319, 3
    CDs)
Robert Carver: Master of the Scottish Renaissance, The
    Sixteen/Harry Christophers (Coro COR16051)
An Eternal Harmony, The Sixteen/Harry Christophers (Coro
    COR16010)
Robert Johnson: Laudes Deo and Other Motets, Cappella
    Nova/Alan Tavener (ASV Gaudeamus CD GAU154)
Kinloch His Fantassie: Scottish Keyboard Music, John Kitchen
    (harpsichord, virginal) (ASV Gaudeamus CD GAU134)
Lute Music from Scotland and France, Jakob Lindberg (lute)
    (BIS CD-201)
*Mary's Music: Songs and Dances from the Time of Mary
    Queen of Scots*, Scottish Early Music Consort/Warwick
    Edwards (Chandos CHAN 0529)
On the Banks of Helicon: Early Music of Scotland, The
    Baltimore Consort (Dorian DOR-90139)
Psalms for the Regents of Scotland (1567–1578), Edinburgh
    University Renaissance Singers/Noel O'Regan (EURS CD
    03)

Remember Me, My Deir, Coronach/D. James Ross (CMF CD
    CO3)
Sacred Music for Mary, Queen of Scots, Cappella Nova/Alan
    Tavener (ASV Gaudeamus CD GAU136)
A Scots Tune, Coronach/D. James Ross (CMF CD CO2)
*A Scottish Mass of 1546 – Choral and Instrumental Music
    from Renaissance Scotland*, Musick Fyne & Coronach/D.
    James Ross (CMF CD 004)
*Taverner, Browne, Carver: Masterworks from Late-medieval
    England and Scotland*, Taverner Choir/Andrew Parrott
    (EMI Reflexe CDC 7496612)
The Thistle and the Rose: Music from The Carver Choirbook,
    Cappella Nova/Alan Tavener (ASV Gaudeamus CD
    GAU342)
*Thus Spak Apollo Myne: The Songs of Alexander
    Montgomerie*, Paul Rendall (tenor), Rob MacKillop (lute)
    (ASV Gaudeamus CD GAU249)
Whip my Towdie, Coronach/D. James Ross (CMF CD CO1)
The Wode Collection, Dunedin Consort, Fretwork, David
    Miller (lute) (Linn CKD 388)

Books and Articles

Accounts of the Lord High Treasurer of Scotland, eds Thomas
    Dickson, James Balfour Paul and C. T. McInnes (13 vols,
    Edinburgh, 1877–1978)
Accounts of the Masters of Works, eds Henry M. Paton, John
    Imrie and John G. Dunbar (2 vols, Edinburgh, 1957 and
    1982)
Acts of the Parliament of Scotland, eds T. Thomson and C.
    Innes (12 vols, Edinburgh, 1814–75)
Alciatus, A. *Emblemes de nouveau translatez en François*
    (Lyon, 1549)

Allan, David, *Philosophy and Politics in Later Stuart Scotland: Neo-Stoicism, Culture and Ideology in an Age of Crisis, 1540–1690* (East Linton, 2000)

Andersen, Michael, Bøggild Johannsen, Birgitte, Johannsen, Hugo (eds), *Reframing the Danish Renaissance: Problems and Prospects in a European Perspective* (Copenhagen, 2011)

Apted, Michael R. and Hannabuss, Susan, *Painters in Scotland, 1301–1700: A Biographical Dictionary* (Edinburgh, 1978)

Apted, M. R. and Robertson, W. Norman, 'Late Fifteenth Century Church Paintings from Guthrie and Foulis Easter', *PSAS*, 95 (1961–2), 262–79

Aschengreen Piacenti, Kirsten and Boardman, John, *Ancient and Modern Gems and Jewels in the Collection of Her Majesty the Queen* (London, 2008)

Bannatyne Manuscript, The, ed. W. Tod Ritchie (4 vols, Edinburgh, 1928–34)

Barber, Richard and Barker, Juliet, *Tournaments: Jousts, Chivalry and Pageants in the Middle Ages* (Woodbridge, 2000)

Barbour, John, *The Bruce*, ed. A. A. M. Duncan (Edinburgh, 2007)

Barnes, Ishbel, 'The Book of Hours of James IV and Margaret Tudor, Austrian National Library, Vienna', *Forth Naturalist and Historian*, 25 (2002), 85–6

Barrow, G. W. S (ed.), *The Scottish Tradition: Essays in Honour of Ronald Gordon Cant* (Edinburgh, 1974)

Bateson, Donald, *Scottish Coins* (Aylesbury, 1987)

Bath, Michael, 'Andrew Bairhum, Giovanni Ferrerio and the "Lighter Style of Painting"', *Journal of the Northern Renaissance*, 2 (2010), 1–13

Bath, Michael, *Emblems for a Queen: The Needlework of Mary Queen of Scots* (London, 2008)

Bath, Michael, *Renaissance Decorative Painting in Scotland* (Edinburgh, 2003)

Bawcutt, Priscilla J. and Hadley Williams, Janet (eds), *A Companion to Medieval Scottish Poetry* (Cambridge, 2006)

Bawcutt, Priscilla, *Dunbar the Makar* (Oxford, 1992)

Bawcutt, Priscilla J., *Gavin Douglas: A Critical Study* (Edinburgh, 1976)

Bawcutt, Priscilla, 'James VI's Castalian Band: A Modern Myth', *SHR*, 80 (2001), 251–9

Bentley-Cranch, Dana, 'Effigy and Portrait in Sixteenth-Century Scotland', *ROSC*, 4 (1988), 9–23

Bentley-Cranch, D., 'An Early Sixteenth-Century French Architectural Source for the Palace of Falkland', *ROSC*, 2 (1986), 85–95

Boardman, Steve and Williamson, Eila (eds), *The Cult of Saints and the Virgin Mary in Medieval Scotland* (Woodbridge, 2010)

Boulton, D'Arcy Jonathan Dacre, *The Knights of the Crown: The Monarchical Orders of Knighthood in Later Medieval Europe, 1325–1520* (Woodbridge, 2000)

Bower, Walter, *A History Book for Scots: Selections from Scotichronicon*, ed. D. E. R. Watt (Edinburgh, 1998)

Brett, Philip, *William Byrd and His Contemporaries: Essays and a Monograph* (London, 2007)

Brown, Ian, Clancy, Thomas Owen, Pittock, Murray, Manning, Susan, Horvat, Ksenija, and Hales, Ashley (eds), *The Edinburgh History of Scottish Literature, Volume 1: From Columba to the Union (until 1707)* (Edinburgh, 2007)

Brown, Michael, *James I* (Edinburgh, 1994)

Brown, Michael and Tanner, Roland (eds), *Scottish Kingship, 1306–1542: Essays in Honour of Norman Macdougall* (Edinburgh, 2008)

Brown, Ron M., *The Art of Suicide* (London, 2001)

Buchanan, George and Johnston, Arthur, *Apollos of the North: Selected Poems of George Buchanan and Arthur Johnston*, ed. Robert Crawford (Edinburgh, 2006)

Burckhardt, Jacob, *The Civilization of the Renaissance in Italy: An Essay*, trans. S. G. C. Middlemore (Oxford and London, 1945)

Burnett, Charles J. and Tabraham, Christopher J., *The Honours of Scotland: The Story of the Scottish Crown Jewels* (Edinburgh, 1993)

Burnett, Charles J. and Dennis, Mark D., *Scotland's Heraldic Heritage: The Lion Rejoicing* (Edinburgh, 1997)

Burns, Charles, 'Papal Gifts to Scottish Monarchs: The Golden Rose and the Blessed Sword', *IR*, 20 (1969), 150–94

Bush, M. L., *The Government Policy of Protector Somerset* (London, 1975)

Caldwell, D. H. (ed.), *Angels, Nobles and Unicorns: Art and Patronage in Medieval Scotland* (Edinburgh, 1982)

Caldwell, David H., *Scotland's Wars and Warriors: Winning Against the Odds* (Edinburgh, 1998)

Caldwell, David H. (ed.), *Scottish Weapons and Fortifications, 1100–1800* (Edinburgh, 1981)

Cameron, Jamie, *James V: The Personal Rule, 1528–1542* (East Linton, 1998)

Campbell, Ian, 'Linlithgow's "Princely Palace" and its Influence on Europe', *Architectural Heritage*, 5 (1995), 1–20

Campbell, Ian, 'A Romanesque Revival and the Early Renaissance in Scotland, c.1380–1513', *Journal of the Society of Architectural Historians*, 54 (1995), 302–25

Campbell, Ian and MacKechnie, Aonghus, 'The "Great Temple of Solomon" at Stirling Castle', *Architectural History*, 54 (2011), 91–118

Cannan, Fergus, *Scottish Arms and Armour* (Oxford, 2009)

Carver, Robert, *The Complete Works of Robert Carver and Two Anonymous Masses*, ed. Kenneth Elliott (Glasgow, 1996)

Ceremonial at the Marriage of Mary, Queen of Scots, with the Dauphin of France, ed. W. Bentham (London, 1818)

Chaney, Edward and Mack, Peter (eds), *England and the Continental Renaissance: Essays in Honour of J. B. Trapp* (Woodbridge, 1990)

A Collection of Inventories and Other Records of the Royal Wardrobe and Jewelhouse; and of the Artillery and Munitioun in some of the Royal Castles, 1488–1606, ed. T. Thomson (Edinburgh, 1815)

Cowan, Edward J. and Henderson, Lizanne (eds), *A History of Everyday Life in Medieval Scotland, 1000 to 1600* (Edinburgh, 2011)

Cowan, Ian B. and Easson, David E., *Medieval Religious Houses in Scotland* (London, 1976)

Cowan, Ian B. and Shaw, Duncan (eds), *The Renaissance and Reformation in Scotland: Essays in Honour of Gordon Donaldson* (Edinburgh, 1983)

Crawford, Barbara E. (ed.), *Church, Chronicle and Learning in Medieval and Early Renaissance Scotland* (Edinburgh, 1999)

Crawford, Robert, *Scotland's Books: A History of Scottish Literature* (Oxford, 2009)

Crewe, E. and Müller, M. G. (eds), *Rituals in Parliaments: Political, Anthropological and Historical Perspectives on Europe and the United States* (Frankfurt am Main, 2006),

Cunningham, Ian C. (ed.), *The Nation Survey'd: Essays on Late Sixteenth-century Scotland as Depicted by Timothy Pont* (Edinburgh, 2006)

Cuthbert, Olaf D., *A Flame in the Shadows: Robert Reid, Bishop of Orkney, 1541–1558* (Kirkwall, 1998)

Dalgleish, George and Steuart Fothringham, Henry, *Silver Made in Scotland* (Edinburgh, 2008)

Davidson, P., 'The Entry of Mary Stewart into Edinburgh, 1561, and Other Ambiguities', *Renaissance Studies*, 9 (1995), 416–29

Dawson, Jane E. A., *Scotland Reformed, 1488–1587* (Edinburgh, 2007)

Devine, T. M. and Wormald, Jenny (eds), *The Oxford Handbook of Modern Scottish History* (Oxford, 2012)

Dickson, Robert and Edmond, John Philip, *Annals of Scottish Printing from the Introduction of the Art in 1507 to the Beginning of the Seventeenth Century* (Cambridge, 1890)

Ditchburn, David, *Scotland and Europe: The Medieval Kingdom and its Contacts with Christendom, 1214–1560, Volume 1: Religion, Culture and Commerce* (East Linton, 2001)

Doran, Susan (ed.), *Elizabeth: The Exhibition at the National Maritime Museum* (London, 2003)

Douglas, Gavin, *The Aeneid (1513)*, ed. Gordon Kendall (2 vols, London, 2011)

Drummond, William, of Hawthornden, *The Entertainment of the High and Mighty Monarch Charles . . . into . . . Edinburgh, the Fifteenth of June, 1633* (Edinburgh, 1633)

Dunbar, J. G., *The Stirling Heads* (Edinburgh, 1975)

Dunbar, John G., *Scottish Royal Palaces: The Architecture of the Royal Residences during the Late Medieval and Early Renaissance Periods* (East Linton, 1999)

Dunbar, J. G., 'Some Sixteenth-Century French Parallels for the Palace of Falkland', *ROSC*, 7 (1991), 3–8

Durkan, John, 'The Beginnings of Humanism in Scotland', *IR*, 4 (1953), 5–24, 119–22

Durkan, John and Ross, Anthony, *Early Scottish Libraries* (Glasgow, 1961)

Durkan, John, 'Education in the Century of the Reformation', *IR*, 10 (1959), 67–90

Durkan, John, 'The Library of Mary, Queen of Scots', *IR*, 38 (1988), 71–101

Durkan, John, *Scottish Schools and Schoolmasters, 1560–1633*, ed. Jamie Reid-Baxter (Edinburgh, forthcoming)

Edington, Carol, *Court and Culture in Renaissance Scotland: Sir David Lindsay of the Mount* (East Linton, 1995)

Eeles, F. C., *King's College Chapel* (Edinburgh, 1956)

Elliott, Kenneth and Rimmer, Frederick, *A History of Scottish Music* (London, 1973)

Eltis, David, *The Military Revolution in Sixteenth-Century Europe* (London, 1995)

Escouchy, Mathieu D', *Chronique* (3 vols, Paris, 1863–4)

Ewen, Elizabeth and Meikle, Maureen (eds), *Women in Scotland, c.1100–c.1750* (East Linton, 1999)

Fawcett, Richard, *Stirling Castle* (London, 1995)

Fawcett, Richard (ed.), *Stirling Castle: The Restoration of the Great Hall* (York, 2001)

Finlay, Ian, *Scottish Gold and Silver Work* (Stevenage, 1991)

Finlay, John, *Men of Law in Pre-Reformation Scotland* (East Linton, 2000)

Foggie, Janet P., *Renaissance Religion in Urban Scotland: The Dominican Order, 1450–1560* (Leiden, 2003)

Folin, Marco (ed.), *Courts and Courtly Arts in Renaissance Italy: Arts, Culture and Politics, 1395–1530* (Woodbridge, 2010)

Ford, Philip and Green, Roger P. H. (eds), *George Buchanan, Poet and Dramatist* (Swansea, 2009)

Fradenburg, Louise Olga, *City, Marriage, Tournament: Arts of Rule in Late Medieval Scotland* (London, 1991)

Gaier, C., 'The Origins of Mons Meg', *Journal of the Arms and Armour Society*, 5 (1967), 425–31

Geddes, Jane (ed.), *King's College Chapel, Aberdeen, 1500–2000* (Leeds, 2000)

Gifford, Douglas and McMillan, Dorothy (eds), *A History of Scottish Women's Writing* (Edinburgh, 1997)

Girouard, Marc, 'Falkland Palace, Fife, I', *Country Life*, 126 (1959), 118–21

Glendinning, Miles and MacKechnie, Aonghus, *Scottish Architecture* (London, 2004)

Godfrey, A. M., *Civil Justice in Renaissance Scotland: The Origins of a Central Court* (Leiden, 2009)

Goodare, Julian and Lynch, Michael (eds), *The Reign of James VI* (East Linton, 2000)

Goodare, Julian and MacDonald, Alasdair A. (eds), *Sixteenth-Century Scotland: Essays in Honour of Michael Lynch* (Leiden, 2008)

Goodare, Julian, *State and Society in Early Modern Scotland* (Oxford, 1999)

Gosman, Martin, MacDonald, Alasdair and Vanderjagt, Arjo (eds), *Princes and Princely Culture, 1450–1650, Volume 1* (Leiden, 2003)

Grant, J., *History of the Burgh Schools of Scotland* (Glasgow, 1876)

Gray, J. M., 'Notes on Examples of Old Heraldic and other Glass', *PSAS*, 26 (1891–2), 34–48

Griffiths, Jeremy and Pearsall, Derek (eds), *Book Production and Publishing in Britain, 1375–1475* (Cambridge, 2007)

Groag Bell, Susan, *The Lost Tapestries of the City of Ladies: Christine de Pizan's Renaissance Legacy* (Berkeley, 2004)

Guy, John, *My Heart is My Own: The Life of Mary, Queen of Scots* (London, 2004)

Hadley Williams, Janet (ed.), *Stewart Style, 1513–1542: Essays on the Court of James V* (East Linton, 1996)

Harris, Bob and MacDonald, Alan R. (eds), *Scotland: The Making and Unmaking of the Nation, c.1100–1707* (5 vols, Dundee, 2006–7)

Harrison, John G., *Rebirth of a Palace: The Royal Court at Stirling Castle* (Historic Scotland, 2011)

Harvey, P. D. A., *Maps in Tudor England* (London, 1993)

Harry, Blind, *The Wallace*, ed. Anne McKim (Edinburgh, 2003)

Haskins, C. H., *The Renaissance of the Twelfth Century* (Cambridge, MA, 1927)

Hay, G., 'A Scottish Altarpiece in Copenhagen', *IR*, 7 (1956), 5–10

Heijnsbergen, Theo van and Royan, Nicola (eds), *Literature, Letters and the Canonical in Early Modern Scotland* (East Linton, 2002)

Higgit, John (ed.), *Medieval Art and Architecture in the Diocese of St Andrews* (London, 1994)

Higgit, John (ed.), *Scottish Libraries: Corpus of British Medieval Library Catalogues, Volume 12* (London, 2006)

Hiltmann, Torsten (ed.), *Les 'autres' rois: études sur la royauté comme notion hiérarchique dans la societé au bas Moyen Age et au début de l'époque moderne* (Munich, 2010)

Holloway, Ernest R., *Andrew Melville and Humanism in Renaissance Scotland* (Leiden, 2011)

Holmes, N. M. McQ., *Scottish Coins in the National Museums of Scotland, Edinburgh, Part 1, 1526–1603* (Oxford, 2006)

Houwen, L. A. J. R. (ed.), *The Deidis of Armorie: A Heraldic Treatise and Bestiary* (2 vols, Edinburgh, 1994)

Houwen, L. A. J. R. (ed.), *Literature and Religion in Late Medieval and Early Modern Scotland: Essays in Honour of Alasdair A. MacDonald* (Leuven, 2012)

Houwen, L. A. J. R., MacDonald, A. A. and Mapstone, S. L. (eds), *A Palace in the Wild: Essays on Vernacular Culture and Humanism in Late-Medieval and Renaissance Scotland* (Leuven, 2000)

Howard, Deborah, *Scottish Architecture from the Reformation to the Restoration, 1560–1660* (Edinburgh, 1995)

Inglis, Jim, *The Organ in Scotland before 1700* (Schagen, 1991)

Innes, Thomas, of Learney, 'Processional Roll of a Scottish Armorial Funeral, Stated to Have Been Used for the Obsequies of George, 1st Marquess of Huntly, 1636', *PSAS*, 77 (1943), 154–73

Inventaires de la royne descosse douairière de France, ed. J. Robertson (Edinburgh, 1863)

'The Inventory of the Chapel Royal at Stirling, 1505', ed. F. C. Eeles, *TSES*, 3 (1909-10), 310–25

Jack, R. D. S. (ed.), *The History of Scottish Literature, Volume 1: Origins to 1660* (Aberdeen, 1989)

Juhala, Amy L., 'The Household and Court of King James VI of Scotland, 1567–1603' (University of Edinburgh unpublished Ph.D. thesis, 2000)

Kamm, Antony, *Scottish Printed Books, 1508–2008* (Edinburgh, 2008)

Kavaler, Ethan Matt, *Renaissance Gothic: Architecture and the Arts in Northern Europe, 1470–1540* (New Haven, 2012)

Konstam, Angus, *Sovereigns of the Sea: The Quest to Build the Perfect Renaissance Battleship* (Hoboken, 2008)

Kuczman, Kazimierz, *Renesansowe Głowy Wawelskie* (Krakow, 2004)

Leland, John, *De Rebus Britannicis Collectanea* (6 vols, London, 1770)

Leslie, John, *The History of Scotland from the Death of King James I in the Year 1436 to the Year 1561* (Edinburgh, 1830)

Lindsay, Alexander, 'The Navigation of King James V Round Scotland, the Orkney Isles and the Hebrides or Western Isles', ed. Nicholas d'Arfeville, trans. Robert Chapman, in *Miscellanea Scotica: A Collection of Tracts Relating to the History, Antiquities, Topography and Literature of Scotland* (3 vols, Glasgow, 1820), iii, 100–22

Lindsay, Sir David of the Mount, *Ane Satyre of the Thrie Estaitis*, ed. Roderick Lyall (Edinburgh, 1998)

Lord Crawford's Armorial, Formerly Known as The Armorial of Sir David Lyndsay of the Mount Secundus, ed. Alex Maxwell Findlater (Edinburgh, 2008)

Lüken, Sven, 'Kaiser Maximilian I. und seine Ehrenpforte', *Zeitschrift für Kunstgeschichte*, 61 (1998), 449–90

Lyall, Roderick J. *Alexander Montgomerie: Poetry, Politics and Cultural Change in Jacobean Scotland* (Tempe, AZ, 2005)

Lyall, Roderick J., 'The Marketing of James VI and I: Scotland, England and the Continental Book Trade', *Quaerendo*, 32 (2002), 204–17

Lyall, R. J., 'The Medieval Scottish Coronation Service: Some Seventeenth-Century Evidence', *IR*, 28 (1977), 3–21

Lynch, Michael, 'The Origins of Edinburgh's "Toun College": A Revision Article', *IR*, 33 (1982), 3–14

Lynch, Michael (ed.), *The Oxford Companion to Scottish History* (Oxford, 2001)

Lynch, Michael, 'Queen Mary's Triumph: The Baptismal Celebrations at Stirling in December 1566', *SHR*, 69 (1990), 1–21

Lyndsay, Sir David, *Facsimile of an Ancient Heraldic Manuscript Emblazoned by Sir David Lyndsay of the Mount, Lyon King of Arms, 1542*, ed. W. D. Laing (Edinburgh, 1822)

Lyndsay, Sir David, *Selected Poems*, ed. Janet Hadley Williams (Glasgow, 2000)

McAndrew, Bruce A., *Scotland's Historic Heraldry* (Woodbridge, 2006)

MacDonald, Alasdair A., von Martels, Zweder R. W. M. and Veenstra, Jan R. (eds), *Christian Humanism: Essays in Honour of Arjo Vanderjagt* (Leiden, 2009)

MacDonald, A. A., 'Mary Stewart's Entry to Edinburgh: An Ambiguous Triumph', *IR*, 42 (1991), 101–10

MacDonald, A. A., Lynch, Michael and Cowan, Ian B. (eds), *The Renaissance in Scotland: Studies in Literature, Religion, History and Culture Offered to John Durkan* (Leiden, 1994)

MacDonald, A. R., 'The Triumph of Protestantism: The Burgh Council of Edinburgh and the Entry of Mary, Queen of Scots, 2 September 1561', *IR*, 48 (1997), 73–82

Macdougall, Norman, *James III* (Edinburgh, 2009)

Macdougall, Norman, *James IV* (Edinburgh, 2006)

Macdougall, Norman (ed.), *Scotland and War AD 79–1918* (Edinburgh, 1991)

Macfarlane, I. D., *Buchanan* (London, 1981)

Macfarlane, Leslie, 'The Book of Hours of James IV and Margaret Tudor', *IR*, 11 (1960), 3–21

Macfarlane, Leslie J., *William Elphinstone and the Kingdom of Scotland, 1431–1514: The Struggle for Order* (Aberdeen, 1995)

McGladdery, Christine, *James II* (Edinburgh, 1990)

McGowan, Margaret M., *Dance in the Renaissance: European Fashion, French Obsession* (New Haven, 2008)

MacIvor, Iain, *Edinburgh Castle* (London, 1993)

McKean, Charles, *The Scottish Château: The Country House in Renaissance Scotland* (Stroud, 2001)

McKean, Charles, 'The Scottish Renaissance Country Seat in its Setting', *Garden History: Journal of the Garden History Society*, 31 (2003), 141–62

McKean, Charles, 'Sir James Hamilton of Finnart: A Renaissance Courtier-Architect', *Architectural History*, 42 (1999), 141–72

MacKechnie, Aonghus, 'Stirling's Triumphal Arch', *Welcome: News for Friends of Historic Scotland* (1991), unpaginated

MacKenzie, Ross, *A Scottish Renaissance Household: Sir William Hamilton and Newton Castle in 1559* (Darvel, 1990)

Macmillan, Duncan, *Scottish Art, 1460–2000* (Edinburgh, 2000)

Macquarrie, Alan, 'Anselm Adornes of Bruges: Traveller in the East and Friend of James III', *IR*, 33 (1982), 15–22

MacQueen, John (ed.), *Humanism in Renaissance Scotland* (Edinburgh, 1990)

McRoberts, David, 'Catalogue of Scottish Medieval Liturgical Books and Fragments', *IR*, 3 (1952), 49–63

McRoberts, David, 'Dean Brown's Book of Hours', *IR*, 19 (1968), 144–67

McRoberts, David (ed.), *Essays on the Scottish Reformation, 1513–1625* (Glasgow, 1962)

McRoberts, David, 'The Fetternear Banner', *IR*, 7 (1956), 69–86

McRoberts, David and Holmes, Stephen Mark, *Lost Interiors: The Furnishings of Scottish Churches in the Later Middle Ages* (Edinburgh, 2012)

McRoberts, David, 'The Manse of Stobo in 1542', *IR*, 22 (1971), 19–31, 101–9

McRoberts, David, 'Material Destruction Caused by the Scottish Reformation', *IR*, 10 (1959), 126–72

McRoberts, David, 'The Medieval Scottish Liturgy Illustrated by Surviving Documents', *TSES*, 15 (1957), 24–40

McRoberts, David, 'Notes on Scoto-Flemish Artistic Contacts', *IR*, 10 (1959), 91–6

McRoberts, David, 'Scottish Medieval Chalice Veils', *IR*, 15 (1964), 103–16

McRoberts, David, 'A Sixteenth-Century Picture of Saint Bartholomew from Perth', *IR*, 10 (1959), 281–6

Maitland, R., *The Historie of the House of Seytoun*, ed. J. Fullarton (Edinburgh, 1829)

Major, John, *A History of Greater Britain*, ed. and trans. Archibald Constable (Edinburgh, 1892)

Mann, A. J., 'Continuity and Change: The Culture of Ritual and Procession in the Parliaments of Scotland', *Parliaments, Estates and Representation*, 29 (2009), 143–58

Mann, Alastair J., *The Scottish Book Trade, 1500–1720: Print, Commerce and Print Control in Early Modern Scotland* (East Linton, 2000)

Mapstone, Sally (ed.), *Older Scots Literature* (Edinburgh, 2005)

Mapstone, Sally and Wood, Juliette (eds), *The Rose and the Thistle: Essays on the Culture of Late Medieval and Renaissance Scotland* (Edinburgh, 1998)

Mapstone, Sally (ed.), *William Dunbar, 'The Nobill Poyet': Essays in Honour of Priscilla Bawcutt* (East Linton, 2001)

Marshall, R. K. and Dalgleish, G. R. (eds), *The Art of Jewellery in Scotland* (Edinburgh, 1991)

Marshall, Rosalind K., '"Hir Rob Ryall": The Costume of Mary of Guise', *Costume: The Journal of the Costume Society*, 12 (1978), 1–12

Marshall, Rosalind K., 'The Jewellery of James V, King of Scots', *Jewellery Studies*, 7 (1996), 79–86

Marshall, Rosalind K., *Scottish Queens, 1034–1714* (East Linton, 2003)

Marshall, Rosalind K., '"To be the Kingis Grace ane Dowblett": The Costume of James V, King of Scots', *Costume: The Journal of the Costume Society*, 28 (1994), 14–21

Mary, queen of Scots, *Bittersweet within my Heart: The Collected Poems of Mary, Queen of Scots*, ed. Robin Bell (London, 1995)

Mason, Roger A., *Kingship and Commonweal: Political Thought in Renaissance and Reformation Scotland* (East Linton, 1998)

Mason, Roger A., 'Kingship, Nobility and Anglo-Scottish Union: John Mair's *History of Greater Britain* (1521)', *IR*, 41 (1990), 182–222

Mays, Deborah (ed.), *The Architecture of Scottish Cities* (East Linton, 1977)

Melville, Elizabeth, *Elizabeth Melville, Lady Culross (c.1570–1640): Complete Writings*, ed. Jamie Reid-Baxter (Edinburgh, forthcoming)

Melville, Elizabeth, *Poems of Elizabeth Melville, Lady Culross*, ed. Jamie Reid-Baxter (Edinburgh, 2010)

Merriman, Marcus, *The Rough Wooings: Mary Queen of Scots, 1542–1551* (East Linton, 2000)

Michelet, Jules, *Histoire de France* (17 vols, Paris, 1833–67)

Mommsen, Theodore, 'Petrarch's Conception of the "Dark Ages"', *Speculum*, 17 (1942), 226–42

Munro, Gordon, Campbell, Stuart, Hair, Greta-Mary, Mackay, Margaret A., Moohan, Elaine and Hair, Graham (eds), *Notis Musycall: Essays on Music and Scottish Culture in Honour of Kenneth Elliott* (Glasgow, 2005)

Murdoch, Steve, *The Terror of the Seas? Scottish Maritime Warfare, 1513–1713* (Leiden, 2010)

Nauert Jr., Charles G, *Humanism and the Culture of Renaissance Europe* (Cambridge, 1995)

Nicholson, Ranald G., *Scotland: The Later Middle Ages* (Edinburgh, 1974)

Nicolson, Nigel and Hawkyard, Alasdair, *The Counties of Britain: A Tudor Atlas by John Speed* (London, 1988)

Oram, Richard D. and Stell, Geoffrey P. (eds), *Lordship and Architecture in Medieval and Renaissance Scotland* (Edinburgh, 2005)

Phillips, Gervase, *The Anglo-Scots Wars, 1513–1550* (Woodbridge, 1999)

Pitscottie, Robert Lindsay of, *The Historie and Cronicles of Scotland*, ed. Æ. J. G. MacKay (3 vols, Edinburgh, 1899–1911)

Porter, James (ed.), *Defining Strains: The Musical Life of Scots in the Seventeenth Century* (Oxford, 2007)

Purser, John, 'On the Trail of Spies', *Scotlands*, 5 (1998), 23–44

Purser, John, *Scotland's Music: A History of the Traditional and Classical Music of Scotland from the Earliest Times to the Present Day* (Edinburgh, 1992)

Reid, Steven J., *Humanism and Calvinism: Andrew Melville and the Universities of Scotland, 1560–1625* (Farnham, 2011)

Reid, W. Stanford, *Skipper from Leith: The History of Robert Barton of Over Barnton* (Philadelphia, 1962)

Reid-Baxter, Jamie, Lynch, Michael and Dennison, E. Patricia, *Jhone Angus: Monk of Dunfermline & Scottish Reformation Music* (Dunfermline, 2011)

Reid-Baxter, Jamie, 'Metrical Psalmody and the Bannatyne Manuscript: Robert Pont's Psalm 83', *Renaissance and Reformation*, 30 (2006–7), 41–62

Reid-Baxter, Jamie, 'Thomas Wode, Christopher Goodman and the Curious Death of Scottish Music', *Scotlands*, 4 (1997), 1–20

Richardinus, Robertus, *Commentary on the Rule of St Augustine*, ed. G. G. Coulton (Edinburgh, 1935)

Richardson, J. S., 'Unrecorded Scottish Wood Carvings', *PSAS*, 60 (1925–26), 384–408

Robbins, K. (ed.), *Religion and Humanism* (Oxford, 1981)

Rogers, Charles, *History of the Chapel Royal of Scotland* (Edinburgh, 1882)

Ross, James D., *Musick Fyne: Robert Carver and the Art of Music in Sixteenth Century Scotland* (Edinburgh, 1993)

Royal Commission on the Ancient and Historic Monuments of Scotland, *Tolbooths and Townhouses: Civic Architecture in Scotland to 1833* (Edinburgh, 1996)

Royal Commission on the Ancient and Historic Monuments of Scotland, *Stirlingshire: An Inventory of the Ancient Monuments* (2 vols, Edinburgh, 1963)

Ryrie, Alec, *The Origins of the Scottish Reformation* (Manchester, 2006)

Sanderson, Margaret H. B., *Cardinal of Scotland: David Beaton, c.1494–1546* (Edinburgh, 2001)

Sanger, Keith and Kinnaird, Alison, *Tree of Strings, Crann nan Teud: A History of the Harp in Scotland* (Edinburgh, 1992)

Scarisbrick, Diana, 'The Aberdeen Jewel', *Burlington Magazine*, 130 (June 1988), 427–8

Scots Roll, The, ed. Colin Campbell (Edinburgh, 1995)

Shaw, F. J., 'Sumptuary Legislation in Scotland', *Juridical Review*, 24 (1979), 81–115

Shire, Helena Mennie, *Song, Dance and Poetry of the Court of Scotland under King James VI* (Cambridge, 1969)

Simpson, Grant G. (ed.), *Scotland and the Low Countries, 1124–1994* (East Linton, 1996)

Somerville, A. R., 'The Ancient Sundials of Scotland', *PSAS*, 117 (1987), 233–64

Spangler, Jonathan, 'Aulic Spaces Transplanted: The Design and Layout of a Franco-Burgundian Court in a Scottish Palace', *The Court Historian*, 14 (2009), 49–62

Stevenson, David, *Scotland's Last Royal Wedding: The Marriage of James VI and Anne of Denmark* (Edinburgh, 1997)

Stevenson, Jane and Davidson, Peter, 'Ficino in Aberdeen: The Continuing Problem of the Scottish Renaissance', *Journal of the Northern Renaissance*, 1 (2009), 64–87

Stevenson, Jane, 'Texts and Textiles: Self-Presentation among the Elite in Renaissance England', *Journal of the Northern Renaissance*, 3 (2011), 39–57

Stevenson, Katie, *Chivalry and Knighthood in Scotland, 1424–1513* (Woodbridge, 2006)

Stevenson, Katie (ed.), *The Herald in Late Medieval Europe* (Woodbridge, 2009)

Stevenson, Katie, 'The Unicorn, St Andrew and the Thistle: Was there an Order of Chivalry in Late-Medieval Scotland?', *SHR*, 83 (2004), 3–22

Stewart, I. H., *The Scottish Coinage* (London, 1955)

Stone, Jeffrey C., *The Pont Manuscript Maps of Scotland: Sixteenth-century Origins of a Blaeu Atlas* (Tring, 1989)

Stuart, John, 3rd marquess of Bute, *Scottish Coronations* (Paisley, 1902)

Suntrup, Rudolf and Veenstra, Jan R. (eds), *Himmel auf Erden, Heaven on Earth* (Frankfurt am Main, 2009)

Suntrup, Rudolf and Veenstra, Jan R. (eds), *Konstruktion der Gegenwart und Zukunft, Shaping the Present and Future* (Frankfurt am Main, 2008)

Suntrup, Rudolf and Veenstra, Jan R. (eds), *Tradition and Innovation in an Era of Change* (Frankfurt am Main, 2001)

Swain, Margaret H., *Historical Needlework: A Study of Influences in Scotland and Northern England* (London, 1970)

Swain, Margaret H., 'The Lochleven and Linlithgow Hangings', *PSAS*, 124 (1994), 455–66

Tasioulas, J. A. (ed.), *The Makars: The Poetry of Henryson, Dunbar and Douglas* (Edinburgh, 1999)

Thomas, Andrea, *Princelie Majestie: The Court of James V of Scotland, 1528–1542* (Edinburgh, 2005)

Thompson, C. and Campbell, L., *Hugo van der Goes and the Trinity Panels in Edinburgh* (Edinburgh, 1974)

Tulloch, Graham, *A History of the Scots Bible with Selected Texts* (Aberdeen, 1989)

Turnbull, Jill, *The Scottish Glass Industry, 1610–1750: 'To serve the whole nation with glass'* (Edinburgh, 2001)

Vasari, Giorgio, *Lives of the Artists*, trans. J. C. and P. Bondanella (Oxford, 1991)

Visages d'antan: Le Recueil d'Arras, XIVe–XVIe s., ed. Albert Châtelet et Jacques Paviot (Lathuile, 2007)

Walker, Patrick (ed.), *Documents Relative to the Reception at Edinburgh of the Kings and Queens of Scotland* (Edinburgh, 1822)

Warrack, John, *Domestic Life in Scotland, 1488–1688: A Sketch of the Development of Furniture and Household Usage* (London, 1920)

Watson, James, *James Watson's Choice Collection of Comic and Serious Scots Poems*, ed. H. H. Wood (2 vols, Edinburgh, 1977 and 1991)

Wedderburn, Robert, *The Complaynt of Scotland*, ed. A. M. Stewart (Edinburgh, 1979)

Weiss, Susan Forscher, Murray, Russell and Cyrus, Cynthia J. (eds), *Music Education in the Middle Ages and the Renaissance* (Bloomington, 2010)

Woods Preece, Isobel, *Our Awin Scottis Use: Music in the Scottish Church up to 1603* (Glasgow, 2000)

Wormald, Jenny, *Court, Kirk and Community: Scotland, 1470–1625* (Edinburgh, 1981)

Wormald, Jenny (ed.), *Scotland: A History* (Oxford, 2005)

Wormald, Jenny (ed.), *Scotland Revisited* (London, 1991)

Zapalac, Kristin Eldyss Sorensen, *'In His Image and Likeness': Political Iconography and Religious Change in Regensburg, 1500–1600* (Ithaca, NY, 1990)

PICTURE CREDITS

OPPOSITE. An allegorical figure representing Sight from a ceiling depicting the five senses painted in the early seventeenth century, originally at Dean House, Edinburgh. The skyline of Edinburgh is shown in the background. (See page 107.)

INDEX